RHETORIC Versus REALITY

What We Know and What We Need to Know About Vouchers and Charter Schools

Brian P. Gill
P. Michael Timpane
Karen E. Ross
Dominic J. Brewer

RAND
EDUCATION

Supported by the Gund Foundation, Spencer Foundation, Annie E. Casey Foundation and Carnegie Corporation of New York

The research described in this report was supported by the Gund Foundation, Spencer Foundation, Annie E. Casey Foundation and Carnegie Corporation of New York.

Library of Congress Cataloging-in-Publication Data

Rhetoric versus reality : what we know and what we need to know about vouchers and charter schools / Brian P. Gill ... [et al.].
    p. cm.
    "MR-1118."
    Includes bibliographical references.
    ISBN 0-8330-2765-4
    1. Educational vouchers. 2. Charter schools. 3. School choice. 4. Educational vouchers—United States. 5. Charter schools—United States. 6. School choice—United States. I. Gill, Brian P., 1968–

LB2828.7 .R44 2001
379.1'11—dc21

2001048903

RAND is a nonprofit institution that helps improve policy and decisionmaking through research and analysis. RAND® is a registered trademark. RAND's publications do not necessarily reflect the opinions or policies of its research sponsors.

Cover design by Eileen Delson La Russo

Published 2001 by RAND
1700 Main Street, P.O. Box 2138, Santa Monica, CA 90407-2138
1200 South Hayes Street, Arlington, VA 22202-5050
201 North Craig Street, Suite 102, Pittsburgh, PA 15213
RAND URL: http://www.rand.org/
To order RAND documents or to obtain additional information, contact Distribution Services: Telephone: (310) 451-7002;
Fax: (310) 451-6915; Email: order@rand.org

Education vouchers and charter schools are two of the most prominent and far-reaching forms of family choice policies currently in evidence in the nation's elementary and secondary schools. As such, they present important challenges to the traditional provision of public education in schools that are created, governed, funded, and operated by state and local authorities.

This book reviews the theoretical foundations for vouchers and charter schools and the empirical evidence of their effectiveness as set forth in hundreds of recent reports and studies. The literature analyzed includes studies that directly examine voucher and charter schools, in the United States and abroad, and, where relevant, comparisons between existing public and private schools. This book also examines the ways in which multiple dimensions of policy design—such as targeting, funding levels and limitations, admissions policies, academic standards and assessments, and accountability—will determine the nature and extent of any specific program's impact. The findings will be of interest to policymakers, researchers, and educators at every level of the education system who must assess numerous proposals for vouchers, charter schools, and other forms of family choice in education.

The research and analysis reported here is part of a larger body of research conducted by RAND Education on school reform, assessment and accountability, and teachers and teaching. The debate over vouchers and charter schools lends itself well to RAND Education's mission—to bring accurate data and careful objective analysis to the national debate on education policy. RAND Education identifies new trends, problems, and opportunities and strives to give the policy community and the American public a clear picture of the choices they face in educating America's citizens.

CONTENTS

In today's context of widespread dissatisfaction with America's public education system, a variety of reforms have been proposed to improve educational outcomes. One of the most controversial proposals is to provide parents with a financial grant, or "voucher," for use at any public or private school. Proponents argue that students using vouchers would be able to attend more-effective and more-efficient schools; that the diversity of choices available would promote parental liberty and, if properly designed, benefit poor and minority youth; and that the competitive threat vouchers pose would induce public schools to improve. Everyone would then be better off. In what has become a fiercely contentious and highly political debate, opponents claim that vouchers would destroy public schools, exacerbate inequities in student outcomes, increase school segregation, breach the constitutional wall between church and state, and undermine the fabric of democracy by promoting narrow, particularistic forms of schooling.

Another proposal for education reform, less controversial among policymakers and the public, is to establish "charter" schools—i.e., schools of choice that are funded by public money but are self-governing, operating outside the traditional system of public-school governance under a quasi contract, or "charter," issued by a governmental agency such as a school district or a state education authority. A few voices have been raised in opposition to charter schools, expressing concerns about their possibly leading to stratification in student placement and balkanization in curriculum. For the most part, however, charter schools have achieved considerable popularity across the political spectrum, with policy arguments centering on the terms and conditions of public oversight—collective bargaining provisions, applicability of assessment and accountability programs, admissions policies, etc. Advocates argue that charter schools will serve as laboratories for pedagogical innovation, provide havens for students who have been poorly served by traditional public schools, promote parental involvement and satisfaction, improve academic achievement, and save public education.

Conceptually and structurally, vouchers and charters challenge the "common school" model that has been the basis for the American public-education system for most of the nation's history. Opponents fear that privatizing the governance and operation of schools will undermine their public purposes; supporters believe that autonomously operated voucher and charter schools can serve the public purposes of the educational system even though they are not owned and operated by government. Policymakers need empirical information on the effects of vouchers and charters if they are to assess their merits and resolve this dispute.

This book has four aims. First, we identify and articulate the range of empirical questions that ought to be answered to fully assess the wisdom of policies promoting vouchers or charter schools, thereby establishing a theoretical framework that accounts for the multiple purposes of public education. Second, we examine the existing empirical evidence on these questions, providing a broad assessment of what is currently known about the effects of vouchers and charters in terms of academic achievement and otherwise. Third, we discuss the important empirical questions that are as yet unresolved and consider the prospects for answering them in the future. Fourth, we explore the design details of voucher and charter policies, concluding with recommendations for policymakers considering their enactment.

The empirical evidence discussed in this report is derived from an exhaustive review of the existing literature on vouchers and charter schools, from studies of other forms of school choice in the United States and abroad, and from comparative studies of public and private schools.

DEFINING THE RELEVANT EMPIRICAL ISSUES

This book seeks to define the full range of questions that policymakers should ask about the empirical effects of school choice. Deriving those questions and assessing the wisdom of a voucher or charter law require a full understanding of the varied goals that a system of schooling should promote. We divide the major goals and empirical questions into five broad outcome dimensions constructed to reflect the explicit and implicit goals present in the arguments of both the supporters and the opponents of educational choice and in the philosophical positions of those who have supported a public role in education over the last two centuries:

- *Academic achievement*: Will vouchers/charters promote the academic skills, knowledge, and attainment of their students? How will they affect the achievement of those who remain in assigned public schools?

- *Choice*: What is the parental demand for vouchers/charters? Will they induce a supply response that makes a variety of desirable school options available? What do voucher/charter parents think of their children's schools?

- *Access*: Will voucher/charter programs be available to those who presently lack such options, notably low-income (frequently nonwhite) residents of inner cities? Will they provide any options for students with special needs?

- *Integration:* Will vouchers/charters increase or reduce the integration of students across and within schools and communities by race/ethnicity and socioeconomic status?

- *Civic socialization*: Will vouchers/charters contribute to the socialization of responsible, tolerant, democratically active citizens, or will they promote intolerance and balkanization?

WHAT IS KNOWN FROM THE EXISTING EMPIRICAL EVIDENCE

Our evaluation of the existing evidence indicates that many of the important empirical questions about vouchers and charters have not yet been answered. Indeed, it would be fair to say that none of the important empirical questions has been answered definitively. Even the strongest evidence is based on programs that have been operating for only a short period of time with a small number of participants, so serious questions about generalizability remain. Nevertheless, the evidence is converging in some areas. In particular:

Academic Achievement

- Small-scale, experimental privately funded voucher programs targeted to low-income students suggest a possible (but as yet uncertain) modest achievement benefit for African-American students after one to two years in voucher schools (as compared with local public schools).

- For children of other racial/ethnic groups, attendance at voucher schools has not provided consistent evidence of either benefit or harm in academic achievement.

- Achievement results in charter schools are mixed, but they suggest that charter-school performance improves after the first year of operation. None of the studies suggests that charter-school achievement outcomes are dramatically better or worse on average than those of conventional public schools.

Choice

- Parental satisfaction levels are high in virtually all voucher and charter programs studied, indicating that parents are happy with the school choices made available by the programs. In the experimental voucher programs that have been studied for two successive years, levels of parental satisfaction declined slightly in the second year but remained substantially higher than those of public-school comparison groups.

Access

- Programs explicitly designed with income qualifications have succeeded in placing low-income, low-achieving, and minority students in voucher schools.

- In most choice programs (whether voucher or charter), however, students with disabilities and students with poorly educated parents are somewhat underrepresented.

- Education tax subsidy programs are disproportionately used by middle- and upper-income families.

Integration

- In communities where public schools are highly stratified, targeted voucher programs may modestly increase racial integration in that they put minority children into voucher schools that are less uniformly minority without reducing integration in the public schools.

- Limited evidence suggests that, across the nation, most charter schools have racial/ethnic distributions that probably fall within the range of distributions of local public schools. In some states, however, many charter schools serve racially homogeneous populations.

- Evidence from other school-choice contexts, both in the United States and abroad, suggests that large-scale unregulated-choice programs are likely to lead to some increase in stratification.

Civic Socialization

- Virtually nothing is yet known empirically about the civic socialization effects of voucher and charter schools.

WHAT IS NOT KNOWN

The brevity of our list of knowns should send a note of caution to policymakers and to supporters and opponents of choice. For most of the key questions, direct evaluations of vouchers and charter schools have not yet provided clear answers, and the list of unknowns remains substantially longer than the list of knowns. In particular:

Academic Achievement

Unknowns in the realm of academic achievement include, first of all, an explanation for the (possible) voucher advantage for African-American students. In addition, the academic effectiveness of charter schools must be examined in a larger number of states over a longer period of time. Long-term effects on academic skills and attainment in both voucher and charter programs are as yet unexamined. Moreover, there is little information that would permit the effectiveness of vouchers and charters to be compared with other, more conventional reforms, such as class-size reduction, professional development, high-stakes accountability, and district-level interventions. Finally, the systemic effects—positive or negative—of both voucher and charter programs have yet to be clearly identified. Whether the introduction of vouchers/charters will help or harm the achievement of students who stay in conventional public schools remains for the moment entirely unknown. This is perhaps the most important achievement issue, because most students are likely to be "nonchoosers" and remain in conventional public schools.

Choice

The most important unknown related to parental liberty concerns the quality and quantity of the schools made available by voucher and charter programs. The number of high-quality alternatives that different varieties of voucher and charter programs will produce is for the moment highly speculative.

Access

Critical unanswered questions about access to voucher and charter schools relate to the variability that would result from different kinds of programs. The characteristics of voucher students in existing programs differ from those of charter students, and the characteristics of charter students vary across states. Other programs might differ further still in the access they provide to different groups of students. In particular, many types of vouchers may be used disproportionately by middle- and upper-income families.

Integration

The effects of voucher and charter programs on the sorting of students across schools have not been well explored. Studies have produced extensive amounts of demographic data on the students participating in voucher and charter programs, but very few of them provide school-level information—on both voucher/charter schools and local public schools—that is linked to information on individual students, which is essential to understanding dynamic integration effects. Even a direct comparison of school-level integration in voucher/charter schools and in conventional public schools does not explain how the introduction of a voucher/charter policy changes levels of integration across schools. A full understanding of integration effects requires a clear assessment of all possible counterfactuals. Where would students of different racial/ethnic groups be in the absence of vouchers/charters? Different answers to this question imply very different effects for vouchers and charters. Would they attend local public schools? Would they pay tuition at racially homogeneous private schools? Would their families move to the suburbs to enable them to attend racially homogeneous public schools? Would they be schooled at home? Unfortunately, no studies of vouchers or charters have undertaken the kind of dynamic analysis needed to provide clear answers.

Civic Socialization

Despite the fact that civic socialization is commonly recognized as a critical public purpose of the educational system, next to nothing is known about the relative effectiveness of voucher, charter, and conventional public schools in socializing students to become responsible citizens. The best evidence available is far short of that available for assessing each of the other outcome dimensions, for two reasons: existing measures of civic socialization are thin, and they have been applied only to broad comparisons of public and private schools, rather than to schools actually participating in voucher and charter programs. This slim evidence provides little support for the view that existing private schools are on average any worse than public schools at socializing citizens.

IMPLICATIONS FOR POLICY

The Significance of Scale

Specific variations in the details of voucher/charter policies are likely to make a big difference in many of the empirical outcomes. Program scale is one variable likely to be especially important.

Nearly all of the existing empirical evidence on the effects of vouchers and charters comes from relatively small-scale programs. Many existing voucher programs are "escape valves"—i.e., targeted to a small number of at-risk children. For these programs, most of the evidence is neutral or somewhat favorable: they provide valued new choices to low-income families and may provide achievement benefits to African-American students. Although little is known about empirical effects with respect to integration and civic socialization, it seems likely that escape-valve programs would not result in major harm to either. Nor does it seem likely that they have larger financial costs. In brief: in some contexts—such as high-poverty cities with substantial African-American populations, or communities that have underperforming public schools—targeted voucher programs may produce discrete benefits. Such programs will not be the silver bullet that will rescue urban education, but they are unlikely to produce the negative consequences that voucher opponents fear.

Evidence on existing charter laws is harder to summarize, because variation across states is dramatic in terms of both the provisions of the laws and the observed empirical effects. Existing charter schools frequently satisfy a parental demand and are producing mixed but promising academic results. Other effects are ambiguous or unknown.

The implications of the existing findings for larger-scale choice programs, however, are unclear. Using evidence from small voucher/charter programs to infer the outcomes of large-scale choice programs is not easy, for several reasons. First of all, the voucher experiments providing some of the best evidence on achievement effects are "black boxes"—i.e., they do not allow a look "inside" to explain the mechanisms that produce what appears to be an achievement advantage for low-income African-American students who use vouchers. The possible explanations for the observed achievement difference are wide ranging, and different explanations have profoundly different implications for whether the effect is reproducible in a larger-scale program. If, for example, these voucher students benefited only because the program put them in classrooms with high-achieving peers, then the effect might disappear in a larger-scale program that puts large numbers of low-achieving students in voucher classrooms together. Similarly, if the experimental advantage is attributable to a context of underperforming public schools, then a universally available alternative might show no advantage when compared to a broader range of higher-performing public schools. Other mechanisms that could explain the experimental findings may be more easily duplicated on a larger scale. Until the source of these findings is known, however, there is no way to know whether they apply to larger-scale programs.

Similar issues arise with respect to achievement in charter schools. The existing studies show mixed results, with some agreement that academic achievement is lowest in the first year of a charter school's existence. Programs that seek to open large numbers of new charters should not expect high achievement in the short term.

The empirical effects on the dimensions of access and integration will almost certainly differ for large-scale programs. Most existing voucher programs serve low-income or other at-risk students because they are explicitly designed to do so, with eligibility tied to income or to performance of the local public school. Universally available voucher programs, by contrast, may disproportionately benefit highly educated and upper-income families that have the means to take advantage of them, particularly if the programs are funded at low levels and permit supplemental tuition payments. This is especially likely to be true of education tax subsidies that provide support for private-school tuition through income-tax credits, deductions, or exclusions. Similarly, large-scale choice programs (whether voucher or charter) are more likely to undermine school-level integration than are escape-valve vouchers that put low-income children in existing private schools.

The economic costs of large-scale voucher/charter programs are also highly unpredictable. They depend not only on the program's design details, but also on the "take-up rate"—i.e., the number of students who switch schools to participate in the program. Costs will go up if students switch into higher-cost schools, but costs could actually decline if students switch from higher- to lower-cost schools. The existing escape-valve programs provide little guidance on what the take-up rate of universally available programs would be.

But even if the findings of small-scale programs are theoretically generalizable, programs in the process of scaling up may encounter unexpected difficulties. Scaleup often results in a distortion of the original conditions that made treatment effective. Newly established voucher/charter schools may or may not be as effective as pre-existing private schools. High-quality, nonprofit providers (including religious institutions) may lack the capacity and incentive to expand, and the supply may be filled largely by for-profit school operators, whose effectiveness is as yet unknown.

Vouchers and charters may in some respects be relatively easy to scale up, however, because they are not programmatic and can be uniquely sensitive to local needs and desires. They are fully compatible with all programmatic reforms in that they are chosen and implemented at the school level rather than imposed from above. In consequence, they may bypass at least a few of the implementation and scaleup problems that have undermined various types of educational reforms over the past 30 years. Whether they will succeed in doing so—and in producing the achievement, access, liberty, integration, and civic socialization outcomes desired from America's schools—remains to be seen.

A Note on Universal-Choice Systems

The most ambitious voucher/charter programs would replace the existing system of educational governance and finance with an entirely new system in which all schools are autonomous and every family must choose a school. Direct evidence on such programs is very limited, however, because they have never been fully implemented in the United States.

Universal-choice systems would, of course, encounter many of the implementation challenges described above. In addition, because such proposals would directly change the entire educational system, they have the potential to create larger effects—both positive and negative—than do other varieties of programs. Systemic effects would not merely stem indirectly from competition or from "cream skimming" (i.e., the drawing away of high-achieving students), but would follow directly from the changes to all public schools. These proposals therefore could create either the greatest benefit or the greatest harm. Care in the design details might permit construction of a universal-choice program that could avoid negative consequences and perhaps produce substantial benefits—but predicting such benefits depends for now on theory rather than existing evidence.

Considerations in Policy Design

Despite the large number of remaining uncertainties about the empirical effects of vouchers and charters, it is possible to provide some guidance on how to intelligently design the details of voucher/charter programs. Policymakers considering voucher or charter laws can maximize program benefits and mitigate harm through thoughtful policy design. We consider a series of questions that address the relationship between policy details and empirical effects in each of the five key outcome dimensions. Because tradeoffs among desired outcomes may sometimes be necessary, the ideal design depends to some extent on how policymakers value the various outcomes promoted by the educational system. Nevertheless, the relationship among outcomes is sometimes complementary rather than competitive: a few of the same policy prescriptions can serve multiple purposes.

The following prescriptions should be considered tentative rather than definitive. They are promising policy options based on plausible inference from the available evidence.

How might policymakers maximize the likelihood that voucher/charter schools will be academically effective?

- Include existing private and parochial schools
- Enforce requirements for testing and information dissemination
- Do not skimp on resources

How might policymakers maximize the likelihood that systemic effects on nonchoosers will be positive rather than negative?

- Establish communication among schools
- Impose consequences on schools that do not perform at acceptable levels
- Give public schools the autonomy to act competitively
- Require open admissions
- Require all students to choose

How can policymakers ensure that a substantial number of autonomous schools will be available?

- Permit existing private and parochial schools to participate
- Provide generous funding
- Avoid overregulation
- Create multiple chartering authorities, including but not limited to the local school board

How can policymakers ensure that autonomous schools will serve low-income and special-needs students?

- Actively disseminate information about schools
- Target specific students
- Forbid tuition add-ons
- Provide generous funding
- Use a direct funding method rather than funding through the income-tax system
- Provide supplemental funding for students with special needs
- Require open admissions

How can policymakers promote integration in programs of autonomous schooling?

- Require open admissions

- Target communities with racially homogeneous public schools
- Include existing private and parochial schools
- Reward integration financially

How can policymakers ensure that voucher/charter schools will effectively socialize their students to become responsible citizens of our democracy?

- Disseminate information about mission, values, curriculum, and outcomes

CONCLUSION

Our review of the evidence leaves us without a crisp, bottom-line judgment of the wisdom of voucher and charter programs. Prudent observers will note that, at the current scale of things, many important questions cannot be answered at all, notably those concerning total demand, supply response of educational providers, and school characteristics and performance at scale—or final impact on public schools in the new equilibrium. Moreover, in important respects—notably civic socialization—the effects of current or proposed autonomous schools are virtually unknown. And design is crucial: autonomous school policy can be targeted or not, regulated or not, generously funded or not, inclusive of existing providers or not. Each of these policy levers has important implications for student outcomes. A program of vigorous research and experimentation is called for, but not one confined to choice programs. Better information on the performance of conventional public schools and alternative reform models is needed as well. In the meantime, political decisions will undoubtedly be made, for and against vouchers and charter schools. They will be informed by good evidence, one hopes, but will not be fully justified by it for many years to come.

ACKNOWLEDGMENTS

We are grateful to our technical reviewers—Paul Hill, Henry Levin, David Myers, and Bernie Rostker—and to a number of individuals who provided valuable input at various stages of the project: Patrick McEwan, Gina Schuyler, Christopher McKelvey, John Coons, Jennifer Lerner, Stephen Sugarman, J. Michael Ross, Richard Shavelson, Shelley Wiseman, Jeri O'Donnell, and the members of the Pew Forum on Standards-Based Reform. We also thank the foundations that generously funded the work: the Gund Foundation, Spencer Foundation, Annie E. Casey Foundation, and Carnegie Corporation of New York.

Chapter One

FAMILY CHOICE AND THE COMMON SCHOOL

How can the education of the nation's children be improved? Although experts disagree about whether the average performance of American public schools has declined over time, it is clear that their range of effectiveness varies greatly—from excellent to disgraceful. Public dissatisfaction is widespread: only 20 percent of Americans believe the nation's public schools deserve A or B grades, and education was the most important policy issue among voters in the 2000 election campaigns.[1] Americans are eager to reform their schools.

In this context, various reforms have been proposed to improve educational outcomes. One of the most controversial of these is to provide parents with a financial grant, or "voucher," for use at any public or private school.[2] Proponents argue that students using vouchers would be able to attend more-effective and more-efficient schools; that the diversity of choices available would promote parental liberty and, if properly designed, would benefit poor and minority students; and that the competitive threat to public schools

---

[1] Rose and Gallup, 2000; Gallup Organization, 2000. It should be noted, however, that poll respondents gave the schools in their own communities substantially higher grades than they gave schools across the country (Rose and Gallup, 2000).

[2] *Voucher* has become a politically loaded word. It has a negative connotation in some circles and is often associated specifically with the conservative/libertarian ideas of Milton Friedman, perhaps the first to use it in the context of public subsidies for private-school tuition (see Friedman, 1955, 1962/1982). Some supporters of vouchers have sought to abandon the word, instead describing their proposals as "scholarship" or "school choice" programs. We chose to use *voucher* throughout this book because it is commonly recognized. Descriptively, it is the best word available; we intend no normative connotation in using it.

would induce them to improve. Everyone would then be better off. In what has become a fiercely contentious and highly political debate, opponents claim that vouchers would destroy public schools, exacerbate inequities in student outcomes, increase school segregation, breach the constitutional wall between church and state, and undermine the fabric of democracy by promoting narrow, particularistic forms of schooling.

Another proposal for educational reform, less controversial among policymakers and the public, is to establish "charter" schools—i.e., schools that are funded by public money but that are self-governing (rather than operating within the traditional system of public-school governance) and operate under a quasi contract, or "charter," issued by a governmental agency such as a school district or a state education authority. The few voices raised in opposition to charter schools have expressed concerns about their possibly leading to stratification in student placement and balkanization in curriculum. For the most part, however, charter schools have achieved considerable popularity across the political spectrum, with policy arguments centering on the terms and conditions of public oversight—collective bargaining provisions, applicability of assessment and accountability programs, admissions policies, etc. Charter-school advocates argue that they will serve as laboratories for pedagogical innovation, provide havens for students who have been poorly served by traditional public schools, promote parental involvement and satisfaction, improve academic achievement, and save public education.

Taken together, vouchers and charters raise fundamental questions about the provision of public education in the United States. Although they are often perceived as opposing alternatives, we believe that they pose a similar challenge to the conventional system of public education and that they are likely to produce similar empirical effects with regard to a number of important outcomes.

This book has four aims. First, we identify and articulate the range of empirical questions that ought to be answered to fully assess the wisdom of policies promoting vouchers or charter schools, thereby establishing a theoretical framework that accounts for the multiple purposes of public education. Second, we examine the existing empirical evidence on these questions, providing a broad assessment of what is currently known about the effects of vouchers and charter schools in terms of academic achievement and otherwise. Third, we discuss the important empirical questions that are as yet unresolved and consider the prospects for answering them in the future. Fourth, we explore the design details of voucher and charter policies, concluding with recommendations for policymakers considering their enactment.

THE MOVEMENT FOR CHOICE IN EDUCATION

Interest in both vouchers and charters is motivated by frustration with the existing system. Many strategies have tried to improve and reform the system from within. Back-to-basics curricula, teacher professional development, class-size reduction, raised graduation requirements, comprehensive school reform, high-stakes testing, abolition of social promotion, site-based management, and innumerable reading and math programs—these are only a few examples of strategies implemented in public schools since *A Nation at Risk* sounded the alarm about the quality of the American educational system nearly two decades ago.[3]

But some observers of America's schools doubt that these strategies add up to enduring and comprehensive improvement. Those who support vouchers and charters have lost patience with traditional avenues of reform. In their view, policymakers have tried one school reform after another, for decades on end, without notable success.[4] Vouchers and charter schools differ from other reform strategies because they are not programmatic. Rather than establishing a new program, imposing a new mandate, or injecting new resources into the existing public schools, vouchers and charters aim to induce reform by changing the fundamental organization of the school system. They share a belief in decentralization and accountability to parents; they reject a "one size fits all" approach to schooling. These characteristics are consistent with those of other forms of educational choice increasingly popular within the existing structure of the public system, including open enrollment and interdistrict enrollment policies, magnet schools, theme schools, and schools-within-

---

[3]National Commission on Excellence in Education, 1983.

[4]On the difficulty of changing actual teaching practice in schools, see, e.g., Cuban, 1993; Berman and McLaughlin, 1978.

schools. Vouchers and charters, however, go well beyond other forms of choice in the extent to which they inject market forces into a policy arena traditionally governed by political and bureaucratic forces.

The belief that tinkering with the system is fruitless has garnered support from some academics. John Chubb and Terry Moe, for example, applying public-choice theory, argue that reform is impossible in the existing system of public schools. In their view, direct democratic (and bureaucratic) governance turns schools into incoherent institutions dominated by interest groups rather than by a shared sense of educational mission and public purpose.[5] Chubb and Moe propose a regulated voucher system as an alternative. Paul Hill, Lawrence Pierce, and James Guthrie agree that the existing system is too heavily bureaucratized and unresponsive to the needs of students and parents.[6] They propose that all public schools be autonomous institutions operated by independent organizations under contracts issued by school boards, rather than being directly operated by school districts.

Economic theorists, notably Milton Friedman, have long argued that more choice in education will lead to improved outcomes by permitting students to transfer to better schools, by introducing competitive pressure for schools to improve, and by permitting a better match between the needs of the individual student and the program offered by the school. Friedman initiated the American debate over vouchers in 1955 when he proposed replacing the existing system of educational finance and governance with a voucher system.[7]

Legal scholars such as John Coons and Stephen Sugarman meanwhile have supported vouchers as a matter of justice for the poor. In their view, educational choice is a basic parental right that the existing system grants only to those who can afford private-school tuition or a home in the suburbs. A voucher system, they argue, would be a

---

[5]Chubb and Moe, 1990.

[6]Hill, Pierce, and Guthrie, 1997.

[7]Friedman, 1955; see also Friedman, 1962/1982. Friedman was certainly not the first to propose a voucher-like system; much earlier proposals can be found in the writings of Adam Smith and John Stuart Mill.

step toward equal access to educational choices.[8] Similarly, 30 years ago, Christopher Jencks and colleagues, responding to the revelations of educational inequality in the Coleman Report,[9] proposed to replace the existing system of public education with a highly regulated voucher system specifically designed to favor low-income families and their children.[10]

The move to vouchers and charters also builds on a generation of experience with policies expanding the degrees of choice within public education: alternative schools, magnet schools, theme and examination schools, and, in a few instances, districtwide and interdistrict choice. These varieties of "public-school choice" accustomed the public, policymakers, and educators to the idea that widespread choice is an important and possibly beneficial policy option. Many educators themselves, moreover, have long believed that choice programs offer opportunity on the supply side to create innovative instructional programs of a kind that traditional public systems would rarely countenance. Prominent educators involved in creating the most-ambitious public-school choice programs in the 1970s—such as Anthony Alvarado and Deborah Meier in New York—clearly held this view.[11] Later proponents of even more-ambitious public-school choice programs (Hill, Pierce, and Guthrie, for example) agree.[12] Many of the founders and staff of charter schools are simply the most recent cohort of persons seeing and seizing this opportunity to create distinctive educational programs under public auspices, with the hope of enabling educators to act as more-creative professionals.[13]

In recent years, support for vouchers and charter schools has grown among some African-American educators, political leaders, and parents. Their support for choice is based primarily on a conviction that

---

[8]Coons and Sugarman, 1978, 1999.

[9]Coleman, 1966.

[10]Center for the Study of Public Policy, 1970. This proposal is commonly identified by the name of its first author, Christopher Jencks.

[11]See, e.g., Meier, 1995.

[12]See Hill, Pierce, and Guthrie, 1997.

[13]See, e.g., Meier, 1995; Hill, Foster, and Gendler, 1990; Finn, Manno, and Vanourek, 2000.

schools responsive to parents will serve their children better than conventional public schools do. This is thought to be especially true in inner cities where public schools have not lived up to the hopes engendered by desegregation and antipoverty policies, even nearly half a century after *Brown v. Board of Education* and 40 years after federal programs for the education of disadvantaged students were created.[14]

In sum, public frustration and academic theory have together produced a situation in which alternatives to the conventional system of public education are under serious consideration. Conceptually, public funding for schooling does not require public operation of schools. The American standard—in which public funding is limited to government-operated schools—is neither logically necessary nor universally followed. In many countries (Australia, Canada, France, the Netherlands, and Chile, to mention a prominent few), public funding is provided to nongovernment schools. In the United States, the federal government operates a voucher system in higher education: government-subsidized grants and loans are used by students at public and private institutions alike—including church-affiliated colleges and universities. Even at the K–12 level, school districts sometimes pay specialized private providers (generally selected and/or approved by parents) to provide educational services to students with serious disabilities.

Moreover, the historic political barriers toward public funding of private K–12 schools seem to be weakening, despite the defeat of two voucher initiatives on state ballots in November 2000. Opinion polls indicate considerable public support for providing public funds for private-school tuition, as well as for charter schools (although the extent of support and opposition depends on how the question is asked).[15] A new organization called the Black Alliance for Educa-

---

[14]On the opinion of minority parents, see Rose and Gallup, 2000, which we discuss in more depth in Chapter Four. African-American leaders who support a variety of school-choice options, including some varieties of vouchers, include Polly Williams, a Wisconsin state legislator who was largely responsible for Milwaukee's voucher program; Floyd Flake, a former congressman who is now senior pastor of the Allen African Methodist Episcopal Church in Queens and an official of Edison Schools, Inc.; and Howard Fuller, a former superintendent in Milwaukee who now leads a new organization called the Black Alliance for Educational Options (BAEO).

[15]See Rose and Gallup, 2000; Moe, 2001.

tional Options has started disseminating information about vouchers and other forms of school choice to African-American parents, undeterred by the failure of voucher ballot initiatives in California and Michigan—and surely inspired by the opinion polls suggesting that African-American parents are among the strongest supporters of vouchers. Finally, the tax cut initiated by President George W. Bush and passed in the spring of 2001 includes private-school tuition among the expenses that can be paid from tax-free education savings accounts (ESAs).

Several state legislatures have created voucher programs in the past ten years, and more may follow.[16] The states of Wisconsin and Ohio established voucher programs for low-income students in Milwaukee and Cleveland; and the state of Florida established one statewide voucher program for students in low-performing public schools (the Opportunity Scholarship Program) and another for students with disabilities (the John M. McKay Scholarships for Students with Disabilities Program).[17] Arizona and Pennsylvania chose to support vouchers indirectly by creating income-tax credits for charitable contributions to privately operated voucher programs.

Meanwhile, the political significance of charter schools—which represent another kind of market-based approach—is unquestionable. They are the fastest-growing sector of the K–12 education market and one of the most popular reform strategies in education today. They have been celebrated by policymakers from all points on the political spectrum. Charter-school legislation has passed in 36 states and the District of Columbia. Although the first charter schools in the nation opened their doors only as recently as 1992, over 2,000 charter

---

[16]The establishment clause of the U.S. Constitution may or may not pose a barrier to the further growth of voucher programs that include religious schools (see Choper, 1999). We discuss the constitutional issue briefly later in this chapter but take no position on its merits.

[17]Our discussion of Florida in this book focuses on the Opportunity Scholarship Program because the McKay Scholarships Program is very new and has not yet been seriously examined by researchers. Ultimately, however, the McKay program may be substantially larger: 4,000 students are expected to participate in 2001–02, and as many as 350,000 are eligible (Fine, 2001).

schools were operating in the 2000–01 school year, enrolling half a million students.[18]

The political barriers to voucher and charter programs in K–12 education are being reduced within a broader policy environment that is favorable to programs promoting consumer choice and market-based accountability. Outside of education, voucher-like programs that use markets to achieve public-policy goals have become increasingly common—child-care and food-stamp programs, Section 8 housing subsidies, health-care financing, and even the tradable pollution credits of the Clean Air Act. Policymakers look with increasing favor on programs that use private, charitable—and even religious—organizations to deliver public services.[19] Within education, some school districts have begun contracting with profit-making firms to operate public schools. Edison Schools, the largest for-profit educational management organization (EMO), has been growing rapidly and now operates over 100 public schools in 21 different states, enrolling over 60,000 students. Meanwhile, privately funded voucher programs have grown exponentially in recent years: at least 65 such programs are in place or starting up around the country.[20] The largest program, the nationwide Children's Scholarship Fund (CSF), distributed 40,000 scholarships in 1999.[21]

In short, both charters and vouchers are now prominent educational reform proposals. Policymakers need empirical information on their likely effects in order to assess their merits. Although both sides of the debate about vouchers and charters occasionally attempt to bolster their claims with research evidence, the debate is too often conducted without a sound empirical underpinning. Our intention is to illuminate the empirical evidence relevant to the debate. We believe (and argue later in this chapter) that, unlike other reform proposals, charters and vouchers pose fundamental challenges to America's

---

[18]Wilgoren, 2000b. For various descriptive statistics on charter schools through the 1999–2000 school year, see RPP International, 2000.

[19]See Urban Institute, Brookings Institution, and Committee for Economic Development, 1998.

[20]See the list compiled by the Center for Education Reform, available on its Website at http://edreform.com/research/pspchart.htm.

[21]See Pool, 1999.

existing system of K–12 schooling. In consequence, a thorough and objective empirical assessment of their likely effects is even more important—indeed, essential—for determining whether they will make good public policy.

COMMON FEATURES OF VOUCHER AND CHARTER SCHOOLS

Vouchers and charters are not always recognized as comparable in terms of the fundamental issues of public values that they raise, so it is important to begin by explaining why we address them together. They are not, of course, identical. One notable difference is the charter itself: charter schools require the approval of a public body to begin operation, whereas voucher schools are often existing private schools that require no explicit government endorsement to operate. This distinction leads to a second difference: charter schools are not permitted to promote religion, whereas voucher schools often have a sectarian affiliation (to the extent that this is constitutionally permissible, which is not yet settled). We discuss the policy significance of these and other differences between vouchers and charters in Chapter Two.

As a political matter, vouchers are far more controversial than charters are. Because charter schools receive government approval and are nonsectarian, they have come to be regarded as a species of "public-school choice"—a concept that has great popular appeal. Vouchers, by contrast, are often regarded as a threat to the very existence of public education. This dichotomy, however, obscures important common elements underlying the two. Both share three essential characteristics that distinguish them from conventional public schools:

1. *Admission by choice:* Students or their parents are permitted a choice of schools; no student is assigned to attend a voucher or charter school.

2. *Market accountability:* The choice is partially or completely subsidized by public funds tied directly to student enrollment; funds

reach the schools only as a result of a family's decision to enroll a child.[22]

3. *Autonomous, nongovernment operation:* The choice includes schools not operated by local school districts or other government agencies. The schools involved have substantial autonomy, relative to conventional public schools, to control their curriculum, instructional methods, and staffing.

Not all of these characteristics are entirely unique to voucher and charter schools. Admission by choice, for example, is also a feature of magnet public schools. But vouchers and charters push choice beyond the options available in magnet and alternative schools, introduce a level of market accountability that is unparalleled in K–12 public education, and take the novel step of providing direct public support for schools operated by nongovernment organizations outside the direct control of local school boards. We discuss each of these characteristics in turn.

Admission by Choice

The first characteristic that distinguishes charter and voucher schools from conventional public schools is that students/parents choose them rather than accepting assignment based on place of residence. Voucher students, like their tuition-paying classmates, must *actively* choose (or their parents must choose) the school they attend. Similarly, charter-school proponents universally agree that no student should be assigned to a charter school without a family decision to attend.[23]

---

[22]Privately funded scholarship programs are presently operating under the auspices of charitable organizations in many cities across the United States; they are sometimes described as "private voucher" programs. Although these programs may produce relevant evidence about the likely empirical effects of publicly funded programs, they do not directly raise the large questions of public policy that are raised by government-established voucher programs.

[23]See, e.g., Kolderie, 1990; Kolderie, 1993; Hassel, 1999; Finn, Manno, and Vanourek, 2000. Admittedly, charter schools that have been converted from conventional public schools add a complication. At the time of conversion, it is generally assumed that students previously assigned to the school will remain. Nevertheless, they are permitted to opt out. (Finn, Manno, and Vanourek, 2000, p. 15.)

Whether the school has a choice in admitting students is another matter, one that depends on the details of the law authorizing the vouchers or charters. In some cases, attendance at a charter or voucher school may depend on the school's choice as well as the family's. Charter laws in a number of states permit schools to establish enrollment criteria consistent with their educational missions.[24] A national survey conducted for the U.S. Department of Education found that 59 percent of charter schools report that they have primary control over their student admissions policies.[25] Voucher students, meanwhile, often enroll in existing private schools that may practice selective admission of their tuition-paying students, favoring or disfavoring applicants on the basis of behavior, academic performance, religious identity, sex, or ability to pay. But most of the publicly funded voucher programs currently in place (in Milwaukee, Cleveland, and Florida) require participating schools to admit voucher students without regard to race, religion, grades, or test scores (though critics have complained that some schools may be violating the open-admission requirement). A number of charter laws likewise require open admissions in participating schools.[26] In sum, the specifics of the enabling laws determine whether schools are permitted to select students: both voucher and charter programs can be designed either to permit selective admission or to require open access. This policy decision may have important implications for the empirical effects of a choice program; we discuss these implications in the concluding chapter.

Admission by choice distinguishes voucher and charter schools from the conventional public school in which enrollment is determined solely by a student's home address. But this characteristic is not unique to voucher and charter schools: magnet and alternative

---

[24]Ted Kolderie, one of the founders of the charter-school movement, says that an essential characteristic of charter schools is that they do not practice selective admissions (Kolderie, 1990, 1993). In fact, however, some states permit charter schools to set admissions standards. Charter schools are permitted to establish enrollment criteria consistent with their particular educational focus in CT, DE, NH, NJ, PA, RI, and VA. Charter legislation in various other states does not specify whether admissions requirements may be established but does not specifically preclude them (RPP International, 1999). We return to this issue in Chapters Two, Four, and Five.

[25]RPP International, 2000, p. 46.

[26]RPP International, 1999.

schools and intra- and interdistrict choice plans also permit parents to choose. Vouchers and charters, however, increase the range of choice beyond that contemplated by these public-school choice programs in that they expressly include schools not initiated and operated by local school districts.

Market Accountability

The second common characteristic distinguishing voucher and charter schools from conventional public schools is that they receive public funding only if parents decide to enroll their children. Funding follows students. For conventional public schools, including most other forms of choice schools, budgets are determined by the administrative and political decisions of district officials and school board members.[27] Although public taxes provide funding for charter and voucher schools, the market mechanism of parental choice directs the public funds to particular schools. Charter and voucher schools cannot survive unless parents choose to send their children to them. A primary avenue of accountability for charter and voucher schools therefore runs directly to parents, whereas the primary avenue of accountability for conventional public schools is the school district's direct governance.

Autonomous, Nongovernment Operation

The feature of voucher and charter schools that is perhaps most distinctive—as compared with both conventional public schools and "choice" public schools (e.g., magnets)—is the fact that they are publicly funded but operated outside the direct control of a government agency. First, consider vouchers. Although voucher programs may include conventional public schools among the choice set, their distinguishing feature is the inclusion of schools operated by nongovernment organizations. Voucher programs include existing private schools, in which the majority of students may be paying tuition rather than receiving public subsidies. In Milwaukee and Cleveland,

---

[27]To be sure, a part of the funding for public schools—from state and federal sources—is tied to enrollment. But the local revenues that typically provide a large portion of school-district funding are insensitive to enrollment.

voucher programs have led to the opening of new schools designed primarily to serve voucher students. In both cases, however, these schools would typically be described as "private" because they are not operated by the school district or any other government agency. In practice, most of the voucher schools in Milwaukee and Cleveland are operated by religious organizations. Neighborhood organizations, other nonprofits, and profit-making firms may also operate voucher schools.

As for charter schools, like voucher schools, most are not directly operated by school districts, which traditionally have operated all public schools within their geographic boundaries.[28] As a recent book by three prominent charter-school advocates notes, charter schools resemble private schools in that they are "independent . . . self-governing institutions."[29] Like voucher schools, they can be established and operated by groups of teachers, groups of parents, nonprofit organizations, and (in many states) for-profit companies known as EMOs. Indeed, as is also true for most voucher schools, their reason for existence is to offer an alternative to the district-run public school.

Partly because they are not operated directly by government agencies, voucher and charter schools are able to offer education programs different from those offered in the public schools and to employ and deploy staff with more flexibility and fewer constraints. Charter schools are intended to have "wide-ranging control over their own curriculum, instruction, staffing, budget, internal organization, calendar, schedule, and much more."[30] This is also true for voucher schools. Charter schools are typically exempt from some of the procedural regulations that constrain conventional public schools, and they are not subject to the day-to-day political direction of a local school district. This freedom attracts support from many educators, both inside and outside the public schools. It is intended to allow more imaginative, innovative curricula, more tailoring of program to specific students, less rigid application of bureaucratic

---

[28]Local school districts are often responsible for authorizing charters and occasionally choose to operate charter schools themselves.

[29]Finn, Manno, and Vanourek, 2000, p. 15.

[30]Finn, Manno, and Vanourek, 2000, p. 15.

norms and procedures (including collective bargaining rules)—in short, greater opportunity for professional education decisionmaking. The actual extent and effect of such opportunities are, of course, key empirical questions.

Charters and vouchers differ substantially from more-limited forms of public-school choice. Magnet schools, alternative schools, and interdistrict choice have significantly expanded the range of public-school options available in various places around the country over the last quarter-century. In some communities, these different public-school choices permit families to select schools with programs similar to those that may be offered in charter schools. But unlike voucher and charter schools, all schools available under such plans are operated by conventional school districts. They permit choice only among a range of options determined and supplied by the school board. Charters and vouchers, by contrast, create opportunities for parents, teachers, nonprofit organizations, and private businesses to operate publicly funded schools outside the direct control of the local school district and board. Still, the historical record of older forms of school choice can inform an understanding of the likely effects of vouchers and charter schools, and we address evidence on these kinds of school choices where relevant in various later chapters.

Finally, it should be noted that, despite basic similarities, there is considerable variation among voucher and charter policies. The specific details of such policies vary widely on a raft of dimensions related to the financing and regulation of voucher and charter schools. We discuss these policy variations in depth in Chapter Two, and we discuss throughout the book, especially in the concluding chapter, how differences in voucher and charter policies are likely to produce different empirical outcomes.

PUBLIC POLICY AND PRIVATE CHOICE: A NOTE ON THE SCOPE OF OUR INQUIRY

In this book, we are concerned with public policies that promote parental choice among privately operated, autonomous schools. Many families exercise school choice in the absence of government intervention, either by choosing a school district or attendance zone in which to live or by paying private-school tuition. We take for granted that the U.S. Constitution places these kinds of choices beyond the realm of government regulation.[31] Voucher and charter programs, our focus, are public policies with the specific purpose of increasing the range of educational choices available.

Scholarship programs that are privately funded presently operate under the auspices of charitable organizations in many cities across the United States. These programs, sometimes described as "private voucher" programs, merit considerable attention in this book because, although they do not directly raise the large questions of public policy that are raised by government-established voucher programs, they do provide important empirical evidence about the likely effects of publicly funded programs.

The tax-credit programs for contributions to private voucher programs—now operating in Arizona and Pennsylvania—represent a special case. They blur the line between public and private funding by allowing taxpayers to be reimbursed for charitable contributions made to private voucher programs.[32] As a result of the Arizona tax credit, funding for private voucher programs in the state has increased exponentially, from $2 million in donations in 1998 (the first year the law was in effect) to $13 million in 1999.[33] (The Pennsylvania tax credit was newly created in 2001.) Although the Arizona and Pennsylvania voucher programs are privately operated and nominally privately funded, in economic terms the tax credits create an implicit transfer from the state's coffers to the voucher programs. In this respect, the tax credits in Arizona and Pennsylvania are functionally equivalent to publicly funded voucher programs.

Other tax-system initiatives, such as the education savings account (ESA) passed by Congress in 2001, create tax benefits (in the form of

---

[31] Citizens' freedom to reside where they wish and their freedom to send their children to private school are clearly settled in constitutional jurisprudence. This is in marked contrast to the Supreme Court's stance on the extent of permissible public funding for religiously affiliated schools, which is rapidly evolving and not yet clear.

[32] The Arizona credit is available to individual taxpayers and is 100 percent of the amount contributed, up to a maximum of $500 per taxpayer. The Pennsylvania credit is available only to businesses and is a maximum of 90 percent of the amount contributed, up to a maximum of $100,000 per business.

[33] Wilson, 2000; Bland, 2000.

deductions, credits, or tax-free earnings) that subsidize parental payments for private-school tuition.[34] We label these programs "education tax subsidies."

Tuition subsidy programs that operate through the income-tax system may be the wave of the future, for legal and political reasons.[35] The constitutionality of state-operated voucher programs that include religious schools is not settled: the Milwaukee voucher program has withstood all constitutional challenges, but voucher programs in Cleveland and Florida are currently under challenge in the courts by opponents who argue that they represent an impermissible establishment of religion.[36] Programs in which funding does not come directly from the public treasury are less likely to be found unconstitutional.[37] Income-tax subsidies may be more politically viable than direct vouchers, as well. Pennsylvania's income-tax credit for businesses' contributions to privately operated voucher programs passed the state legislature in the spring of 2001 without difficulty, despite the legislature's repeated failures to pass a state-operated voucher program. At the federal level, a proposed voucher program for low-income students in low-performing public schools failed in

---

[34]On programs that operate through the tax system, see James and Levin, 1983.

[35]A recent paper from the Cato Institute, a libertarian think tank, endorses the Arizona model of tax credits as the best way to promote educational choice (Olsen and Brouillette, 2000). Politically, income-tax subsidies usually generate more support and less opposition than vouchers do. For the differences in terms of public opinion, see Rose and Gallup, 1999.

[36]In September 2001, the U.S. Supreme Court agreed to examine the constitutionality of the Cleveland voucher program in its 2001–02 term. The mechanism of family choice distinguishes voucher programs from previous legislative efforts to aid private schools: in a voucher system, public funds go to religious schools only to the extent that individual families direct their scholarship funds to those schools. Although the Supreme Court's ultimate decision on these matters is not certain, related rulings over the last two decades suggest that voucher programs that include religious schools may pass constitutional muster, as long as public funds follow the choices of individual families and students who may choose nonreligious as well as church-affiliated schools. (See Choper, 1999.) But lower courts have disagreed on this issue, as the divergent rulings on the Milwaukee and Cleveland programs indicate. The Supreme Court's decision may ultimately depend on the vote of a single swing justice (Choper, 1999). Meanwhile, some state constitutions have establishment clauses that require a more rigorous separation of church and state than does the federal constitution. In such states, a voucher program may require an amendment to the state constitution.

[37]See *Mueller v. Allen,* 463 U.S. 388, 1983. Arizona's tax-credit voucher program has been upheld by the state's highest court (*Kotterman v. Killian,* 972 P.2d 606 (1999)).

Congress, but the ESA plan passed easily (as part of a larger package of tax cuts).

These constitutional and political issues are beyond the scope of this book, which focuses on the empirical effects of voucher and charter policies. Although education tax subsidies may differ from vouchers in political and constitutional terms, they raise the same public-policy questions as voucher programs that operate through explicitly publicly funded scholarships. They are therefore included in the scope of our study. Unfortunately, however, little evidence is available on their effects because it is difficult to track the students who benefit from such programs. In consequence, they appear in the empirical record less often than their policy importance merits.

CHALLENGING THE COMMON SCHOOL MODEL

The Common School Model

A public responsibility to provide education for all children is a deeply held American value, with roots going back to the founding of the nation.[38] In economic terms, public support for education makes sense because education is (in part) a "public good": it benefits not only those who are students, but society as a whole, which stands to gain from having a well-educated population.[39] In principle, government might support education through a variety of mechanisms that do not necessitate government operation of public schools. In practice, the public responsibility to support education has been executed for most of the nation's history through a system built on the model of the "common school." As this model has developed over the last two centuries, it has come to mean an institution operated by the government, under the democratic auspices of the local school board, which aims to serve all students in the locality with a common curriculum (permitting some variation in content at

---

[38]Thomas Jefferson, for example, was a prominent early advocate of public support for education (see Gilreath, 1999). A national public commitment to education was made explicit in the Northwest Ordinance of 1787.

[39]Even libertarian-leaning neoclassical economists such as Milton Friedman assume that education is a public good that merits government support (Friedman, 1955).

the secondary level).[40] This model implies that both the financing of education and the direct operation of the schools are government functions.

Historically, under this model, American public and private schools have operated in almost entirely separate worlds. American policy-makers have often been suspicious of private schools. Legislative hostility toward private schools peaked early in the 20th century, when strong nativist sentiments brought forth efforts in a few states to require all children to attend public schools. (The Supreme Court preserved the private-school option in 1923 with *Pierce v. Society of Sisters*, which invalidated the state of Oregon's attempt to abolish private schools.) In the 1940s and 1950s, early efforts to establish federal funding for schools repeatedly foundered when advocates, motivated by concerns about the establishment of religion, refused to include funding for religious (mostly Catholic) schools. From the 1950s through the 1970s, the Supreme Court solidified the separation between public and private schooling. When state legislatures tried to provide direct aid to private religious schools, the Supreme Court invalidated the programs as violative of the First Amendment's pro-hibition on government establishment of religion. The result of this history is a compromise: parents can spend their own money, but not public money, to send their children to private school. When it comes to publicly funded education, local school districts have maintained the exclusive franchise that the common school model has entailed.

In pre-industrial America, one factor favoring the common school model was efficiency. Population was distributed widely, and few communities were large enough to support multiple schools. Setting up a single public school was an ambitious undertaking that stimu-lated the tradition of local control still persisting today. Now, how-ever, most Americans live in suburbs and cities that have sufficient population density to support a wide variety of schooling.

Other rationales for providing education via common schools are more relevant to 21st century America. The common school model is intended to promote not only academic achievement, but also sev-

---

[40]See Tyack, 1974; Cremin, 1961.

eral public purposes: equal access, social integration, and civic socialization. Ideally, the common school provides access to high-
quality education for all children in the community—poor as well as
rich, African-American as well as white, and students with disabilities
as well as those with unusual talents. Ideally, the common school involves a healthy social mixing of children from all races and classes.
Ideally, the common school educates children in the virtues of
democratic citizenship. Those three purposes, it has been argued,
require a local public-school system that is under the control of
democratic institutions such as school boards.[41]

Whether the common school model in fact serves its avowed purposes is an empirical question. Champions of the common school
celebrate it as a uniquely democratic and American institution. They
point to its service in offering opportunity to immigrants (in successive waves), minorities, and disabled children; in serving as the
cockpit of social policy surrounding issues of race, class, and gender;
in helping to produce the world's most productive, creative, and en-
trepreneurial economy; and in sustaining the world's oldest democracy. To other observers, however, the historical and contemporary
realities mock the stated ideals of the common school. Allegedly
"common" schools have often segregated and tracked children by
race and class; and despite a generation of integration efforts, many
urban systems remain highly stratified, and levels of racial integration may actually be declining across America.[42] Historically, public-
school efforts at socialization have often been more doctrinaire than
tolerant. Early public-school advocates sought to use the public schools to "Americanize" children who might otherwise be ex-
cessively influenced (in the reformers' view) by their immigrant
(often Catholic or Jewish) parents—i.e., "Americanization" meant
that 19th century public schools espoused a generic, least-common-
denominator Protestantism.[43] More recently, the public-school
perspective has become nonsectarian, indeed nonreligious; but it is

---

[41]On the democratic purposes of public schools, see, e.g., Guttman, 1987; McDonnell,
Timpane, and Benjamin, 2000.

[42]Orfield and Yun, 1999; Orfield and Eaton, 1996. For longer-term critical perspectives
on sorting and stratification in public schools, see Bowles and Gintis, 1976; Spring,
1976.

[43]This stance, it should be noted, led directly to the establishment of Catholic
parochial-school systems (Tyack and Hansot, 1982, pp. 74–83).

now criticized by those who believe schools have abandoned the imparting of specific virtues and values in favor of relativistic, therapeutic perspectives.[44]

The Challenge

In sum, the record of the common school in meeting its own ideals is ambiguous. Despite its shortcomings, however, the common school has provided the standard model for American public education since the mid-19th century. In this context, voucher programs—which would provide public funding for nongovernment schools, including those with sectarian religious affiliations—represent a significant departure for American public policy. Charter schools are less frequently recognized as a departure because they avoid the most politically volatile aspect of private schooling: affiliation with a particular religious sect. But in key respects—by embracing parental choice, pluralism in curriculum and pedagogy, and nongovernment operation—charters represent as much of a challenge to the system as vouchers do. Implicitly or explicitly, the supporters of vouchers and charters assume that these decentralized, autonomous schools of choice will be more effective than conventional public schools—perhaps even in advancing the public goals that the common school model is specifically intended to promote.

Supporters of both vouchers and charters propose that families should be able to choose the educational program they want for their children without having to move to a different school district or pay private-school tuition. These supporters assume that public schooling might exist in diverse forms: charter schools are often organized to serve particular educational visions that may be in opposition to the educational philosophy of the local public-school district; voucher schools often include a sectarian religious focus unavailable in government-operated schools. And supporters of vouchers and charters suggest that the provision of education using public funds need not be the sole province of the local school district. Moreover, many of these supporters believe that these changes can promote both academic achievement and parental choice with-

---

[44]See, e.g., Grant, 1988; Bellah et al., 1985; Bloom, 1987; Glenn, 2001a.

out serious harm (and perhaps with substantial benefit) to the public goals associated with the common school, including equal access, integration, and the socialization of effective citizens.[45] *In sum, both charters and vouchers challenge the model of the common school—in which all students are educated together with a common curriculum in a government-run school—in favor of the model of family choice—in which individual families are permitted to select autonomous, nongovernment schools that reflect their needs and values.*

To be sure, not all voucher and charter schools are innovative or unique. Indeed, most of the educational programs and philosophies adopted by charter schools can be found in conventional public schools somewhere in the country. But in an individual community, charters and vouchers can create more choices than those presently available solely in conventional public schools. Charters and vouchers aim to give families the option of choosing schools that the local school district might not create on its own.

It should be noted that market accountability does not necessarily involve the abandonment of public oversight. Charter schools are subject to public accountability through the charter-granting process. Moreover, both charter and voucher schools may be subject to varying degrees of government regulation in all sorts of areas, including admissions, facilities, finances, testing, teacher credentials, and even curriculum. In Chapter Two, we explore how these regulations vary in different voucher and charter policies.

But even when voucher and charter schools are regulated, market accountability, nongovernment operation, and self-governing autonomy are key characteristics, all representing a significant departure from the traditional American system of public education. Vouchers and charters are unique in creating publicly funded alternatives to the offerings of the local school district. Under the traditional framework, government accepts responsibility not only for subsidizing education, but also for providing the schools (through the local school district). Both vouchers and charters separate the

---

[45]John Coons, a long-time supporter of vouchers as a means of fairness to the poor, notes that the appropriate task is "to ask whether school choice, properly designed, can serve a range of democratic and human values—including efficiency—in a manner superior to the traditional school monopoly" (Coons, 2000).

function of subsidizing education from the function of operating schools—they seek to eliminate the local district's exclusive franchise in publicly funded schooling.[46] Voucher and charter laws assume that government remains responsible for subsidizing education but need not be responsible for running schools (though government-run schools may be included among the choices).[47] Governance and accountability are radically different in voucher and charter schools than in conventional public schools. While conventional public schools are operated by local districts through political and bureaucratic channels, voucher and charter schools avoid (to a great extent) the political and bureaucratic governance of the district in favor of self-governing autonomy and direct market accountability to parents.[48]

This book systematically examines contemporary empirical evidence to determine the effects of this difference in governance and accountability in terms of basic goals of the educational system. Opponents of vouchers and charters fear that privatizing the governance and operation of schools will undermine their public purposes; supporters believe that the public purposes of the educational system will be served even though voucher and charter schools are not owned and operated by government. Policymakers need empirical information on the effects of vouchers and charters in order to assess their merits and resolve this dispute.

---

[46]The public-school establishment clearly recognizes the challenge. Teachers' unions and other public-school interest groups have overwhelmingly expressed strong public opposition to vouchers, and their view of charters is often one of suspicion, occasionally leaning to qualified support when they perceive their own interests and those of public education to be sufficiently safeguarded. (See Finn, Manno, and Vanourek, 2000, pp. 170–186.)

[47]From an economics perspective, education's status as a public good implies the necessity for government subsidy, but not necessarily government operation, of schools (Lamdin and Mintrom, 1997). Some theorists have argued that government should get out of the business of operating schools (see, e.g., Mill, 1859/1978; Friedman, 1955; Hill, Pierce, and Guthrie, 1997).

[48]The terms *political* and *bureaucratic* are intended to be descriptive rather than evaluative. The fact that public schools operate under political and bureaucratic accountability rather than market accountability does not mean that they are necessarily less flexible than voucher, charter, or private schools. In some instances, political and bureaucratic institutions may be more responsive than market institutions.

"Private" or "Public"?

Advocates of charter schools often distinguish them from voucher schools by declaring that charter schools are "public" and voucher schools are "private." Unfortunately—apart from the issue of religious affiliation—this distinction obscures more than it illuminates. Indeed, charters and vouchers demand a reconsideration of what makes a school public.

Americans have traditionally defined public schools as those owned and operated by government. If operation by an agency of government is the critical characteristic of a public school, then neither charter schools nor voucher schools qualify as public. Charter schools nevertheless reasonably claim to be public because they do not charge tuition and (usually) are required to admit all applicants (if space is available). But voucher schools such as those in Milwaukee might make the same claim, because the regulations of their voucher program forbid them from charging tuition to voucher students (above the level of the voucher) and require them to admit all applicants (if space is available). Thus, if open access is the critical characteristic, some charter schools and some voucher schools qualify as public, whereas others (and, indeed, some district-operated public schools) fail to qualify because they impose admissions standards.[49]

In sum, vouchers and charters blur traditional distinctions between public and private schools because they are hybrids including both public and private elements. Indeed, they help to point out that conventional public schools also have both public and private elements, in terms of purposes, funding, and access. Conventional public schools simultaneously serve the private purpose of teaching marketable skills and the public purpose of promoting citizenship. Many conventional public schools benefit from supplemental private funding through local education foundations. And most public schools permit access only to those who live in their district—which

---

[49]These ambiguities already exist in higher education, where "private" universities enroll students supported by government-funded financial aid, and many "public" universities charge tuition, receive substantial amounts of private funding, and impose selective admissions standards.

frequently excludes low-income urban students from attending suburban public schools.

Given these ambiguities, we have chosen to use terminology that may prevent confusion and sidestep the value-laden baggage implicit in terms such as *public* and *private*. Mere labels should not carry weight in the debate. There are reasonable grounds for disagreeing about whether charter and voucher schools are public or private, so we describe them as "autonomous" in the hope of preempting a semantic debate. The key issue is not the language used to describe the programs, but their empirical effects. Vouchers and charters have enough features in common that policymakers will need to assess some of the same empirical questions.

DEFINING THE RELEVANT EMPIRICAL ISSUES

This book seeks to define the full range of questions that policymakers should ask about the empirical effects of school choice. Defining those questions and assessing the wisdom of a voucher or charter law require a complete understanding of the varied goals that a system of schooling should promote. The goals that are explicit or implicit in the arguments of both supporters and opponents of educational choice, and more generally in the philosophical positions of those who have supported a public role in education over the last two centuries, can be divided into five broad outcome dimensions:[50]

- Academic achievement

- Choice

- Access

---

[50]Henry Levin recently proposed an evaluative framework similar to ours, with minor organizational differences (Levin, 2000). He posits four criteria on which vouchers should be evaluated: productive efficiency, freedom of choice, equity, and social cohesion. Productive efficiency addresses the same questions we discuss regarding academic outcomes and includes a concern for the costs of the system. (We address costs only briefly, in the concluding chapter.) Levin's freedom-to-choose category is addressed by our chapter on choice. We discuss equity in Chapters Five and Six, where we address the equitable distribution of choice and concerns about segregation, respectively. Finally, Levin's social cohesion seems to be similar to our civic socialization.

- Integration
- Civic socialization

As should be clear from the preceding pages, these outcome dimensions are derived from the various goals that provide motivation for the advocates of the traditional common school and the advocates of vouchers and charters. We regard all five as legitimate ends of public policy. We recognize that these goals are sometimes in tension with each other, and that individuals will differ in prioritizing them; we do not attempt to resolve such philosophical disputes. Nevertheless, performance on all five can be empirically evaluated, and empirical evidence can help to clarify the debate.

We have used these five categories to structure this book. Following Chapter Two, which sets out key policy variables and provides basic descriptive data on voucher and charter schools, each of the next five chapters is devoted to empirical evidence concerning one of the outcome dimensions.

Academic Achievement

Academic achievement—which includes not only the skills and knowledge measured by standardized tests, but also long-term educational attainment (measured as advancement in school, graduation, and later participation in higher education)—is the appropriate outcome measure with which to begin an assessment of voucher and charter programs. In the case of vouchers, the research literature now includes a number of studies that examine how publicly and privately funded voucher programs operating in cities around the United States have affected the test scores of participating students. Our discussion of academic achievement in Chapter Three begins with these studies. We also examine the evidence on achievement in charter schools, which is less extensive to date than that on vouchers. And we provide an overview of the literature on achievement in private schools, which may provide suggestive, if not definitive, evidence on the effects of vouchers and charters over the long term. This is particularly important with respect to outcomes such as high school graduation and college attendance, which have not yet been measured directly for the new voucher and charter programs. Finally, we address evidence from school-choice programs operating in other countries. Using all of the available evidence, we examine the academic effects on both participating students (those who attend voucher and charter schools) and nonparticipating students (those who remain in conventional public schools).

Choice

Family choice is not merely the mechanism that supports the operation of autonomous schools, it is also a valued outcome in its own right. Indeed, for many advocates of vouchers and charters, their primary virtue is that they give parents the opportunity to choose a school for their children. Supporters of autonomous schooling often assume that expanded parental liberty follows automatically from the establishment of charter or voucher programs. In fact, however, the schooling options created by voucher and charter programs, the number of families who have access to those options, and the subjective benefits that parents derive from choice are all empirical issues. In Chapter Four, we address a range of empirical questions related to the choices made available to families by vouchers and charters. This involves first examining empirical evidence about the demand for autonomous schools and the supply of schools that vouchers and charters make available. To determine whether the new choices are meaningful to parents, we then explore evidence of the satisfaction levels of parents whose children attend voucher and charter schools.

Access

Chapter Five addresses the distribution of choice: Will vouchers and charters create additional choices solely for the middle and upper classes, or will they open up autonomous school options to those who presently have the fewest choices? This question is hotly debated by the polemicists on both sides. Proponents argue that vouchers and charters are necessary if low-income (and minority) parents are to have the choices now available to upper-income (and white) families; opponents claim that autonomous schools will largely benefit upper-income families. Fortunately, considerable empirical evidence is available to address this dispute. We examine data on the income, race/ethnicity, parental education level, and disability status of students who attend voucher and charter schools.

Integration

The question of whether voucher and charter programs provide access to disadvantaged students is distinct from the question of how those students are sorted to individual schools. The common school model (in its ideal) aims not only to provide educational access to all students, but also to mix students from different racial and socioeconomic backgrounds in the same schools. In Chapter Six, we examine the empirical evidence about the sorting effects likely to be produced by school choice. We seek to understand whether vouchers and charters will lead to increased or decreased integration in terms of race/ethnicity (and, to a lesser extent, socioeconomic status).[51] Theoretically, it is possible that school choice could lead to either outcome, so an empirical examination is critical. Some evidence on integration is available from existing voucher and charter programs, as well as from other school-choice programs in the United States and other countries.

Civic Socialization

Vouchers and charters involve a substantial decentralization of the educational system, and they contemplate the creation of a wide variety of autonomous schools, each with its own curriculum, pedagogical style, and values. Opponents fear that voucher and charter schools will be dominated by private purposes and parental desires, neglecting the public function of schools to socialize students into good citizens. This concern is especially prominent among those who oppose voucher programs that include religious schools. Some supporters of vouchers and charters, by contrast, argue that autonomous schools are likely to be more effective than conventional public schools at the task of civic socialization.[52] In Chapter Seven, we ask what is known about whether vouchers and charters are likely to promote or detract from the inculcation of the civic values necessary for the functioning of a healthy democracy. Unfortunately, the

---

[51]The extent to which vouchers and charters promote or reduce stratification by academic ability is another key empirical question. Because it directly relates to academic performance (via peer effects), we address it in Chapter Three rather than Chapter Six.

[52]See, e.g., Coons, 1998.

existing evidence on civic socialization is very limited and largely indirect. We examine the little that is available, which is mostly from comparative studies of public and private schools.

VALUES AND KNOWLEDGE IN THE SCHOOL-CHOICE DEBATE

The challenge to the common school model that is implicit in vouchers and charters ultimately relates to the basic values that the educational system is intended to serve. Admittedly, American society lacks a universal consensus on these values. Americans argue about the relative importance of music and social studies, God and Darwin, multiculturalism and patriotism, vocational training and college preparation—as well as about the priority of values such as academic achievement, choice, access, integration, and civic socialization. In the debate over vouchers and charters, the tension between family choice and common schooling is especially striking. Some advocates of school choice believe that parents have a paramount right to direct their children's education. Some opponents believe that the common school should not be compromised under any circumstances, and that a key purpose of public education is to expose children to a broader range of ideas and values than that espoused by their parents. To the extent that Americans disagree about the basic priority of values such as these, our attempt to assess empirical issues will be irrelevant. Resolving such fundamental disputes is a matter for philosophers and politicians, not researchers.

Fortunately for us, however, Americans in general are not especially ideological. Most Americans respect both parental liberty and the values associated with the common school—as well as the more mundane value of academic achievement. Indeed, many of those who support increased choice in schooling do so largely for pragmatic rather than ideological reasons.[53] We believe that there is enough consensus on basic goals that a clarification of the empirical evidence will substantially advance the debate. Many of the arguments about vouchers and charters—regardless of whether they ap-

---

[53]Democratic Senator Joseph Lieberman, for example, once supported vouchers as an option for low-income urban children in failing public schools.

peal to the values of achievement, choice, access, integration, or civic socialization—involve direct disputes about empirical effects.

This book aims to be nonideological, driven by the assumption that the empirical questions about vouchers and charters are what is critical. The debate over school choice has produced two streams, each problematic for its own reasons: (1) an advocacy literature—both pro and con—that is uninterested in empirical evidence except when it can be used as ammunition on the rhetorical battlefield, and (2) an empirical literature that is focused too narrowly on a limited range of questions. We hope to broaden the empirical debate to include the full range of questions that must be addressed if wise public policy is to be made regarding vouchers and charters.

We do not claim to introduce new empirical evidence. Indeed, we rely heavily on prior empirical efforts. The research literature evaluating voucher experiments, in particular, has grown rapidly in recent years; in some cases, the same data have been analyzed and re-analyzed by several groups of researchers. Systematic evaluations of charter schools are also beginning to appear. We examine these evaluations in the chapters that follow, but we also use empirical evidence from other literatures—including comparisons of public and private schools and studies of school choice in other countries—to assess a broader range of questions than have typically been addressed in the direct evaluations of vouchers and charters.

The first limitation of the empirical debate is that it concentrates largely on achievement test scores, often ignoring the other key outcome dimensions. A few researchers have addressed an additional issue related to access, asking whether vouchers and charters are serving disadvantaged students. But these measures reflect only a few of the many outcomes that may be affected, positively or negatively, by vouchers and charters. In particular, the structural shift from a model of common schooling to a model of family choice is not merely a matter of ideological preference—it raises a number of serious empirical issues. Although vouchers and charters appeal to the ideal of family choice, the extent to which they create real alternatives, the quality of those alternatives, and the availability of those alternatives to a wide range of families are all empirical questions. Although vouchers and charters challenge the model of the common school, the extent to which they impact the underlying values associated with that ideal—social integration and civic socialization—is an empirical question. All of these empirical questions are important to public policy independent of their effects on academic achievement per se.

A second problem with the existing debate is that evaluations of voucher and charter programs focus largely on students attending autonomous schools and neglect students who remain in conventional public schools (except as those peers form a control group). Because vouchers and charters potentially represent a transformation of the entire system for distributing schooling, evaluations of empirical evidence must consider that effects may be felt by nonparticipating as well as participating students. If the supporters of school choice are correct, nonparticipants will benefit from the competition created, which will induce improvement in the public schools. If the opponents of school choice are correct, nonparticipants will be harmed by the removal of voucher and charter students from the conventional public schools. In either case, the effects of school choice will not be limited solely to students who switch to autonomous schools.

SUMMARY: KEY POLICY QUESTIONS IN BRIEF

In sum, policymakers should answer a series of questions in assessing the wisdom of vouchers and charters:

- *Academic achievement*: Will vouchers/charters promote the academic skills, knowledge, and attainment of their students? How will they affect the achievement of those who remain in assigned public schools?

- *Choice*: What is the parental demand for vouchers/charters? Will they induce a supply response that makes a variety of desirable school options available? What do voucher/charter parents think of their children's schools?

- *Access*: Will voucher/charter programs be available to those who presently lack educational options, notably low-income (frequently nonwhite) residents of inner cities? Will they provide any options for students with special needs?

- *Integration:* Will vouchers/charters increase or reduce the integration of students across and within schools by race/ethnicity and socioeconomic status?

- *Civic socialization:* Will vouchers/charters contribute to the socialization of responsible, tolerant, democratically active citizens, or will they promote intolerance and balkanization?

One voucher/charter policy may have radically different effects than another in terms of achievement, choice, access, integration, and civic socialization. Throughout our explication of these empirical issues, we consider important differences between and among voucher and charter policies. In Chapter Two, prior to addressing the empirical questions in depth, we discuss in detail the wide range of variation among voucher and charter programs on dimensions such as the level of public subsidy, regulation of admissions and curriculum in participating schools, and targeting of programs to at-risk populations. Our concluding chapter (Chapter Eight) explicitly considers how these policy variations should be expected to influence the outcomes resulting from voucher and charter programs.

Ultimately, whether charters or vouchers are good public policy depends not only on the outcomes on the five dimensions discussed, but also on the costs incurred by adopting such reforms. Tallying the direct fiscal costs of vouchers and charters may be relatively straightforward, but an accurate assessment requires a full accounting of all economic costs, which may include costs (or cost reductions) borne by existing public schools and by private parties. As yet, very few researchers have systematically addressed the costs of voucher and charter programs.[54] We do not address costs in depth, but we do discuss them briefly in Chapter Eight.

Compared with other educational reforms, voucher and charter programs are more challenging to evaluate because they are not programmatic; their purpose is to create a wide variety of distinguishable schools rather than to implement a singular, consistent program. As will become clear in the chapters that follow, the evidence on most of the policy questions is quite limited. Nevertheless, direct evidence on some of the questions is accumulating rapidly, and vari-

---

[54]One early attempt can be found in Levin and Driver, 1997.

ous kinds of indirect evidence are available to inform the debate. Although few publicly funded voucher programs exist, and charter schools are very new, suggestive evidence can be found in studies of privately funded voucher programs, the international experience with public funding of private schools, and research comparing private and public schools. We focus first of all on evidence from evaluations of existing voucher and charter programs. Where these evaluations leave important questions unanswered, we consider whether further research on existing programs might be beneficial.

Further research on existing programs, however, is not likely to answer several of the most important empirical questions about vouchers and charters. We therefore consider in Chapter Eight the possible utility of a new choice experiment and the design elements that such an experiment would need in order to permit researchers to answer further questions.

Some of the empirical questions may be unanswerable in the absence of large-scale implementation of voucher or charter programs. Policymakers, however, are often required to make decisions with incomplete information. In the interest of ensuring that decisions are made with the best information available—even if it is incomplete—we conclude Chapter Eight by exploring the relationship between the details of policy design and outcome measures. Our aim in doing so is to provide policymakers with a guide to designing programs able to produce the greatest benefit (or least harm) in terms of their desired outcomes in the dimensions of achievement, choice, access, integration, and civic socialization.

Chapter Two

VOUCHERS AND CHARTERS IN POLICY AND PRACTICE

Chapter One points out that vouchers and charters have several fundamental similarities. Nevertheless, voucher and charter programs can vary widely in terms of policy details. Some of the key policy variables distinguish vouchers from charters, but many apply to both. Differences in policy details are critical for the answers to the key empirical questions raised in Chapter One concerning the five outcome dimensions: achievement, choice, access, integration, and civic socialization. The evidence in Chapters Three through Seven demonstrates that the impact of vouchers and charters cannot be assessed in the abstract; dramatic variations in policy details are likely to produce equally dramatic variations in empirical effects. In Chapter Eight, we discuss in depth the ways that specific policy-design dimensions of voucher/charter programs can produce very different outcomes.

This chapter enumerates an array of variations in policy design both between voucher and charter programs and among them, and illuminates those variations using examples drawn from existing or proposed programs.[1] The chapter concludes with a broad comparative picture of some of the descriptive characteristics of voucher, charter, and conventional public schools.

---

[1]Here and throughout the book, our primary interest is in publicly supported voucher and charter programs. Nevertheless, we sometimes use privately funded programs as illustrative examples, because their design dimensions could be reproduced in publicly funded programs and are therefore relevant to public policy.

POLICY-DESIGN DIMENSIONS COMMON TO VOUCHER AND CHARTER PROGRAMS

We begin with the extensive list of policy-design dimensions, related to regulation and financing, that policymakers can consider in designing both voucher and charter laws.

Regulatory Dimensions

The extent of government regulation of voucher and charter schools varies widely. Different voucher and charter programs place different restrictions on participating schools. Some voucher proposals are completely unrestrictive, imposing no more requirements than are currently placed on private schools. Milton Friedman's original 1955 voucher proposal is one such unregulated plan. In practice, the only notable choice programs that impose no regulations on participating schools are education tax subsidies, which are voucher-like programs funded through the income-tax system. The new federal tax shelter for education savings accounts (ESAs), for example, subsidizes tuition payments to any private school (as well as other educational expenses). It is difficult to create and enforce regulations for programs administered through income taxes because the benefit is not received at the time the child enrolls in school. The only regulation that education tax subsidies sometimes impose is a limitation on eligibility based on family income.

Apart from education tax subsidies, school choice programs—whether voucher or charter—rarely are designed to rely exclusively on market-based accountability. Existing and proposed voucher and charter programs have sought to place constraints on student eligibility, admissions, hiring, curriculum, physical plant, and other characteristics of participating schools. As we show in later chapters, these policy variables often have important implications for the effects of a choice program. Policy details turn out to be critical: differences in the specifics of voucher/charter programs can produce profound differences in empirical outcomes in terms of all five key outcome dimensions. The following is a description of regulatory dimensions that policymakers may consider when enacting voucher/charter programs.

Eligible schools. Voucher and charter policies vary as to the kinds of schools that are eligible to participate. Different policies have different rules with respect to religious schools, same-sex schools, and for-profit schools. Charter policies, by definition, exclude private schools, but in a number of states they permit pre-existing private schools to convert to charter status (if they are nonreligious). Charter laws also require all participating schools to be approved by a chartering authority. Voucher laws typically require no such approval but may include other limitations: Florida's Opportunity Scholarship Program, for example, requires participating private schools to be accredited.

Number of schools/students permitted. Policymakers sometimes choose to limit the total size of a choice program by placing a cap on the number of schools or students that may participate.

Deregulation of existing public schools. Some comprehensive choice proposals would permit all schools to operate under the same kind of deregulated system that applies to charter/voucher schools. Student assignment would be abolished, every student (or parent) would choose a school, and all schools would operate autonomously. Although no state has implemented such a system, a few states have taken small steps in this direction by permitting districts to convert all of their schools to charter status.

Student eligibility. Some charter/voucher programs are open to all students in a state, some favor students in the local school district, and others are targeted to specific populations, typically low-income or other at-risk students. A few plans (e.g., the Cleveland voucher program) vary the amount of public subsidy inversely with the income level of the student's family.

Student admissions. Unregulated-choice programs permit schools to establish their own admissions criteria, subject only to standard anti-discrimination laws. Other programs require participating schools to admit all applicants, allocating spaces by lottery if applications exceed available space. A few proposals have suggested hybrid solutions in which schools would be permitted to select a fraction of their students (on the basis of, for example, a special talent consistent with the school's curricular focus) and would be required to admit the rest by lottery. Along with regulating admissions, policymakers might choose to regulate student suspension and expulsion procedures in participating schools.[2]

Students with disabilities. In the case of charter schools, existing federal laws, including the Americans with Disabilities Act (ADA), Section 504 of the Rehabilitation Act, and the Individuals with Disabilities Education Act (IDEA) apply just as they do in conventional public schools. IDEA does not automatically apply to voucher schools, however, and some voucher schools (if they are operated by religious organizations and do not receive federal funding) may not be required to adhere to ADA and Section 504.[3] Policymakers designing voucher programs, however, may choose to go beyond the requirements of federal law, imposing nondiscrimination, accommodation, and service requirements on participating voucher schools. Few existing voucher programs have addressed this issue.

Family contribution. Unregulated-voucher programs would permit schools to charge additional tuition above the value of the government subsidy. All charter laws and some voucher laws prohibit tuition add-ons. Under some programs, schools may require parents to provide an in-kind contribution by performing service at the school.

Teacher certification. Policymakers have the option of deciding whether teachers in participating autonomous schools must meet the same certification level as teachers in conventional public schools (or something short of that level, including no certification).

School performance requirements. Policymakers may choose to let the market regulate performance, or they may choose to set explicit performance requirements for participating schools. These can be defined generally for all participating voucher/charter schools or specifically for individual schools in their charters. They can include any variety of performance measures (typically related to student outcomes).

---

[2]To be sure, regulation of suspensions and expulsions might be logistically more difficult and intrusive than regulation of admissions.

[3]Rothstein, 1999.

Student testing requirements. Even if policymakers do not require participating schools to meet specific performance standards, they may require them to administer standardized tests to their students.

Information dissemination. Choice programs vary in how much information they require schools to report. Unregulated programs require no reporting, whereas regulated programs may require the reporting of standardized test scores, graduation rates, teacher qualifications, class sizes, and various other school characteristics (these are now sometimes disseminated via the World Wide Web). The most aggressive proposals would actively disseminate information to parents, not only through electronic media, but also through mailings and staffed parent-information centers.

Curriculum requirements. Unregulated programs, including some charter programs, impose no general requirements for the content of a participating school's curriculum. Policymakers may, however, choose to impose standards similar to those in conventional public schools or to adopt standards used by private-school accrediting agencies.

Fiscal accountability. The extent to which the government supervises the finances of participating schools can vary substantially.

Facility standards. Policymakers can decide whether participating schools will have to operate in facilities comparable to those of public schools or will be permitted to use less-conventional buildings.

Financing Dimensions

Policymakers have a variety of options available not only with respect to regulation, but also with respect to financing. The range of funding in voucher and charter programs is very wide. Funding is relevant not only as a matter of general operating expenses, but also in terms of supplemental money that is typically available to conventional public schools for facilities, transportation, special education, and other functions. Any of these might or might not be included in a voucher/charter program. These variations have very different consequences for the supply of schools and the distribution of benefits (as we discuss in Chapters Four and Eight). The following is a list of financing dimensions:

General operating funds. Per-pupil funds in actual and proposed programs vary from an amount that is insufficient to pay private-school tuition up to an amount that is comparable to per-pupil expenditures (PPE) in conventional public schools. Moreover, formulas used to calculate funding vary widely.

Facilities. While many programs provide no funding for facilities, policymakers may choose to subsidize facilities either through access to additional funding or through access to unused buildings.

Startup. Programs that seek to create substantial numbers of new schools (rather than relying on existing private schools or converted schools) may offer supplemental funding for school startup costs. We know of no voucher programs that provide such funding. The funding provided by state programs for charter-school startup varies widely, but federal assistance for charter-school startup is often available.[4]

Special needs. Many programs provide a flat per-student funding rate, whereas others provide additional funding for students with special needs. Of those that provide the additional funding, some use an average special-needs rate and some vary funding with the actual costs required to serve specific needs.[5]

At-risk adjustment. Policymakers can choose to provide additional funding for low-income and other at-risk students. A number of proposals and programs do so.

Grade-level adjustment. Most voucher programs and many charter laws provide fixed per-pupil funding amounts that do not vary by the grade levels served in the school, even though high-school students in conventional public schools tend to cost more to educate than do students in lower grades. A few charter laws recognize these differences and provide differential funding.[6]

---

[4]Nelson, Muir, and Drown, 2000.

[5]Nelson, Muir, and Drown, 2000.

[6]Nelson, Muir, and Drown, 2000.

Transportation. Some programs expect students to find their own transportation to their chosen schools; others subsidize or directly provide transportation.

Examples of Regulatory and Financing Differences

Tables 2.1 and 2.2 explore regulatory and financing dimensions of voucher and charter programs more systematically. Table 2.1 maps each of the regulatory dimensions on a continuum measuring the degree of government regulation involved; Table 2.2 maps each of the financing dimensions on a continuum describing the generosity of funding provided. Various examples of proposed and existing voucher and charter programs are used to illustrate cells in each table.[7] Later in the chapter, we describe a few of the specific programs and proposals in greater detail.[8]

Note that Table 2.1 demonstrates that charter programs are not necessarily more regulated than voucher programs. In terms of student eligibility, for example, most existing voucher programs are targeted to low-income students or students in low-performing schools, whereas charter programs generally have no such requirements. For most of these variables, existing and proposed voucher and charter programs may fall anywhere along a wide continuum.

Although we provide examples of actual and proposed programs to illustrate the design differences among voucher and charter policies, Tables 2.1 and 2.2 are not intended to provide a comprehensive characterization of all existing voucher and charter laws. The purpose of the tables is to illustrate the wide range of policy details available to policymakers who are considering whether to establish a program promoting autonomous schools.

---

[7]As noted in Chapter One, Arizona's voucher law does not create a state-operated voucher program; instead, it creates an income-tax credit for contributions to privately operated voucher programs. The Florida voucher program referenced in these tables is the Opportunity Scholarship Program for students in low-performing public schools, not the McKay Scholarships Program for students with disabilities.

[8]For more detailed information on the charter laws noted in Tables 2.1 and 2.2, see RPP International, 1999; Nelson, Muir, and Drown, 2000; RPP International, 2000; Center for Education Reform, 2000b.

Table 2.1

Regulatory Dimensions of Voucher and Charter Programs

Dimension	Degree of regulation →			
Eligible schools	New and existing schools, including for-profit, religious, and same-sex institutions: *Milwaukee, Cleveland, FL(v), AZ(v), Bush Title I, federal ESA*[a]		New and existing (or converted) nonsectarian schools: *Milwaukee in 1990-95, AZ(c), DC, MI*	New schools and converted public schools only: *CA, CO, MA*
Number of schools/students permitted	Unlimited: *Cleveland, FL(v), AZ(c), AZ(v), CO, PA, CA Prop 38, federal ESA*	Annual startups limited: *DC (20), NY (100)*	Total enrollment capped: *Milwaukee (15% of district enrollment)*	Total number of schools limited: *MA (50), CT (24)*
Deregulation of existing public schools	All schools become autonomous, deregulated schools of choice: *Jencks, Hill/Pierce/Guthrie*		Partial deregulation: *CA and FL allow "charter districts"; mandatory choice in East Harlem*	No deregulation: *Milwaukee, Cleveland, charters in most states*
Student admissions	School has discretion subject to civil rights laws: *TX, VA, AZ(v), CA Prop 38, federal ESA*	School selects half, other half selected by lottery: *Jencks, Coons/Sugarman*	All subsidized students admitted by lottery: *Milwaukee, Cleveland, FL(v), AZ, CO, MA*	By lottery and school expected to reflect district's racial/ethnic proportion: *KS, CA, CT*
Students with disabilities	Existing federal requirements only: *Milwaukee, Cleveland, federal ESA*		Admission required: *FL(v)*	Admission and services required: *All charter laws*

Table 2.1 (continued)

Dimension	Degree of regulation →→→			
Family contribution	Family pays part of tuition: *Cleveland (10%), federal ESA, CA Prop 38 (anything > $4000), Coons/Sugarman (based on ability to pay)*	No tuition charged but in-kind contribution may be expected: *Charters in most states, FL(v)*		Tuition may not be charged and in-kind contribution may not be required: *Milwaukee*
Teacher certification	No requirements beyond those for private schools: *CA Prop 38, AZ(v), Milwaukee, Cleveland, AZ(c), DC, FL(c), TX, federal ESA*	Limited requirements: *PA (25% of teachers may be uncertified), CT (50% of teachers may have temporary certification), FL(v)*		Equivalent requirements for public school teachers: *Charters in CA and most other states*
School performance requirements	None (market accountability only): *Cleveland, FL(v), AZ(v), Bush Title I, federal ESA*	Limited general standards (e.g. advancement in grade, attendance): *Milwaukee, MN (same as public)*	Specific standards of charter (e.g. test-score outcomes, graduation, attendance, attention to special needs): *MA, CA*	Participation in state high-stakes accountability system, including general standards for academic performance: *GA*
Student testing requirements	None: *Milwaukee, Cleveland, federal ESA*		State public-school testing requirements: *FL(v), CA Prop 38, AZ(c), CA, CO, MA, MI*	
Information dissemination	No requirements: *AZ(v), federal ESA*	Information made publicly available: test results, teacher qualifications, finances, class size, program and philosophy: *FL(v), AZ(c), FL(c)*		Information publicly available and actively disseminated to parents: *Jencks, Hill/Pierce/Guthrie, Coons/Sugarman*

Table 2.1 (continued)

Dimension	Degree of regulation →			
	None beyond those for private schools: *CA Prop 38, AZ(v), federal ESA*	Accreditation standards: *FL(v), DC*	State standards: *TX*	State and school district standards: *CO*
Curriculum requirements				
Fiscal accountability	Minimal: *AZ(v), FL(v), federal ESA*		Substantial auditing requirements: *MI, MN, MA, DC*	
Facilities	Minimal building safety requirements: *Milwaukee, FL(v), CA, AZ(c)*		Equivalent to standards for conventional public schools	

NOTE: State postal abbreviations are used to refer to charter programs, except in the cases of Florida and Arizona, which have both charter (c) and voucher (v) programs. Other voucher and charter proposals are referred to by the names of their authors.
[a]Education savings account.

Table 2.2

Financing Dimensions of Voucher and Charter Programs

Dimension	Level of public subsidy →→→		
General operating funds[a]	<60% of public-school PPE: *Cleveland (1/3 of district PPE), Bush Title I ($1500), federal ESA* [b]	60–95% of public-school PPE: *Milwaukee (state share), PA (70–82% PPE), CO (minimum 80% PPE), NJ, FL(v)*	Equivalent to full PPE in existing public schools: *FL(c), MI, DC, WI, Jencks*
Facilities	None provided: *Milwaukee, Cleveland, FL(v), PA, NJ, Bush Title I, federal ESA*	Limited funding available: *CA and many other charter states*	Substantial funding available: *Bond funding in CO and NC, buildings in CO and DC, lease payments in MN and FL*
Startup funding	None (except federal grants): *Milwaukee, Cleveland, FL(v), CO, MI, DC, federal ESA*	Available: *Charters in AZ, CA, MA, MN*	
Special needs	No additional funds available: *AZ(v), federal ESA*	Some supplemental funds provided: *Cleveland, FL(v), MA, NC*	Funding based on severity of disability: *MN, AZ(c), DC, CA*
At-risk adjustment	None: *Milwaukee, Cleveland, federal ESA, DC, CT*	Additional funding: *Jencks, CO, MI, TX*	

Table 2.2 (continued)

Dimension	Level of public subsidy	
Grade-level adjustment	None: *Milwaukee, Cleveland, federal ESA, PA, MI, TX*	Varies by grade level: *AZ(c), DC, MN*
Transportation	None provided: *Milwaukee, MI, MN, AZ(v), CA Prop 38, federal ESA*	Subsidized or provided: *Cleveland, CT, DC*

NOTE: State postal abbreviations are used to refer to charter programs, except in the cases of Florida and Arizona, which have both charter (c) and voucher (v) programs. Other voucher and charter proposals are referred to by the names of their authors.

[a]As Henry Levin points out, direct comparisons of expenditures in voucher, charter, and district public schools may be deceptive because the mix of services they provide may be different. Average per-pupil expenditures (PPE) in district public schools include funding for transportation, food service, vocational education, and other services that may not be provided by charter or voucher schools. Special education programs represent a disproportionate share of district PPE, including very expensive services for children with the most severe disabilities. These kinds of services are unlikely to be provided in voucher schools and may be underrepresented in charter schools as well. (Levin (1998.) Similarly, a recent report on charter-school funding points out that charter schools often receive services from school districts (e.g., transportation) free of charge (Nelson, Muir, and Drown (2000). These differences suggest that funding comparisons should be made cautiously. Nevertheless, district PPE is a reasonable benchmark to use for rough comparisons of funding among voucher and charter programs.

[b]Education savings account.

DIFFERENCES BETWEEN VOUCHER AND CHARTER PROGRAMS

Although voucher and charter laws share a number of essential features, they have a few systematic differences, both in principle and in the practice of existing state and local programs. These are briefly summarized in Table 2.3 and discussed below.

Table 2.3

Features Distinguishing Charter Programs from Voucher Programs

Feature	Charter Programs	Voucher Programs
Public accountability	Charter authorization and government regulation (variable extent)	Government regulation (variable extent)
Religion	No	Usually permitted
Participation of existing "private" schools	No (but conversions possible in some states)	Yes

Public Accountability

As noted in Chapter One, one form of accountability for both voucher and charter schools lies in the market: both types of schools survive only to the extent that parents choose to enroll their children in them. In addition, as the preceding pages make clear, policymakers can impose a variety of different kinds of regulatory accountability on both voucher and charter schools. But charter schools have another accountability mechanism that is absent in voucher programs—the charter itself. Charter schools operate under a quasi contract (the "charter") granted by a public body—i.e., they cannot be established unless they meet the approval of a chartering authority. Approved charter schools are usually expected to meet a variety of standards, which include not only process-oriented legal requirements in areas such as auditing and safety, but also substantive standards for educational outcomes spelled out in the charter. Charters are typically granted for a designated period of time, with renewal required at the end of the period. Chartering authorities—known as "sponsors"—can refuse to renew the charters of schools that have not met their stated goals. Five years is a common charter length, but charters may run for as little as three years (as in Kansas) or as long as 15 (as in Arizona).

Chartering authorities vary in different states, but they typically include local school boards and may also include universities and state-level bodies created specifically for the purpose of chartering schools. The designation of the chartering authority represents a key variable distinguishing charter laws in different states. Charter schools generally proliferate more rapidly in states where local school districts are not the exclusive sponsors. Not surprisingly, local school districts are often reluctant to sponsor their own competition, particularly if charter funding comes out of the school-district budget.[9]

Theoretically, then, all charter schools are subject to substantial government oversight through their sponsors. A study of California charter schools suggests, however, that this oversight more often involves attention to fiscal accountability than to the educational results promised in the charter.[10] Similarly, a national survey finds that the most common areas in which charter schools are monitored are finances and compliance with regulations.[11] Other evidence suggests that when charter schools have been shut down by their sponsors, failure to meet educational standards has rarely been the reason.[12] If the sponsoring authority's oversight is largely procedural and regulatory, it is not clear that the chartering process serves a purpose beyond what could be accomplished by explicit regulations. Regulations, however, can apply to voucher policies as well as charter policies.[13] In sum, although the quasi-contractual accountability

---

[9]Hassel, 1999; Nathan, 1999.

[10]Wells et al., 2000b.

[11]RPP International, 2000, p. 50. Monitoring of student achievement was next on the list, according to the survey.

[12]Rothstein, 1998.

[13]For example, the existing (publicly funded) voucher programs in Milwaukee, Cleveland, and Florida require open admissions for voucher students; Milwaukee's voucher schools are additionally required to demonstrate some evidence of performance. To further confuse the issue, consider the example of New York State. For two centuries, all private schools in New York have operated under "charters" issued by a public authority, the State Board of Regents. Despite the existence of charters and the oversight of the Regents, however, no one confuses these private "charter" schools with public schools. (In 1998, New York passed a law permitting the

of charter schools distinguishes them from voucher schools, it is not clear how much difference this makes in practice.

Religion

On the issue of religious affiliation, there is an important legal difference between charters and vouchers. Charter schools, like conventional public schools, are not permitted to promote religion.[14] Voucher programs, in contrast, do not necessarily exclude religious schools, although policymakers may choose to limit the programs to nonreligious institutions.[15] Most voucher proposals, and the existing programs in Milwaukee, Cleveland, and Florida, include religious schools.[16] Whether the provision of publicly funded vouchers to religious schools passes constitutional muster is not yet settled, as noted in Chapter One. We take no position on the constitutional question; for the purposes of this book, the inclusion or exclusion of religiously affiliated schools is relevant only to the extent that it affects empirical outcomes—an issue which we explore in later chapters.

---

creation of new, publicly funded charter schools that resemble those in other states and are distinguished from the long-standing, chartered, private schools.)

[14]Some charter schools are closely affiliated with religious institutions even though they do not explicitly teach religion and are nominally independent of religious groups. A charter school in Fremont, California, for example, operates in a building that also houses a local Islamic congregation. The students are taught a secular curriculum in the morning; in the afternoon, they are taught the tenets of Islam by the same teachers in a nominally separate religious school. (Fuller et al., 1999.) In short, although charter laws explicitly exclude religious schools, some charter school operators may bring religion in through the back door.

[15]Milwaukee's voucher program excluded religious schools in the first several years of its operation. A few rural school districts in Maine and Vermont, lacking sufficient enrollment to operate their own schools, send their children to nonreligious private schools at public expense. (See Greene, 2000a.) The federal courts have denied parental appeals to include religious schools among the options (see *Strout v. Albanese,* 178 F.3d 57 (1st Cir., 27 May 1999)).

[16]The voucher programs in Cleveland and Florida are currently under challenge in the federal courts on grounds that the participation of church-affiliated schools violates the establishment clause. Cleveland's program was found unconstitutional by a federal appeals court; the U.S. Supreme Court will decide the appeal in its 2001–02 term. In contrast, Milwaukee's program, which now permits the participation of religious schools, has withstood all establishment clause challenges, and the Supreme Court has declined to review a lower court decision that found the program constitutional.

Participation of Existing Private Schools

Voucher and charter laws differ not only in whether they include religious institutions, but in whether they include existing private schools more generally. Charter schools are not permitted to charge tuition; all of their students are subsidized by public funds. Existing private schools, which include tuition-paying students, therefore cannot participate in charter programs. In some states (such as Arizona, which has an unusually unrestrictive charter law), existing private schools may apply to a sponsoring agency to convert to charter status. Charter laws in many states, however, forbid such conversions. Voucher laws, by contrast, make use of existing private schools by subsidizing voucher students' tuition in schools that also include nonsubsidized, tuition-paying students. Existing private schools are permitted to participate as long as they agree to the conditions imposed by the voucher law (which, as the preceding pages have shown, may be minimal or substantial). Throughout the remaining chapters of the book, we address the effects that inclusion or exclusion of sectarian and other private schools may have on academic achievement, choice, access, integration, and civic socialization.

Funding

Voucher and charter policies often have another difference in practice, although not in principle: charters are usually funded more generously. Privately funded vouchers usually cover only part of the cost of low-tuition private schools (which also operate with tuition levels set below true costs). Publicly funded vouchers are sometimes set at similar levels (as in Cleveland, for example). Education tax subsidies, such as the federal ESA, generally create implicit "vouchers" that are quite small. Charter-school funding, by contrast, is sometimes based only on the state's contribution, but is often linked to the per-pupil expenditure of the local district.[17] To be sure,

---

[17]Direct comparisons of the average PPE of conventional school districts with school-level figures from voucher and charter schools may be deceptive. Special-education students, who are expensive to educate, are underrepresented in voucher and charter schools, and the underrepresentation is likely to be more extreme for students with more-serious disabilities. Moreover, district-level figures include costs such as

the amount of charter funding varies substantially across states, not only in terms of operating funds, but also in terms of the availability of facility and startup funding.[18]

The incentives created by the differentials in voucher and charter funding have been clearest in Cleveland, where per-pupil public funding is twice as much for charter schools as for voucher schools.[19] Not surprisingly, an entrepreneur who had opened two Cleveland schools aimed at voucher students (the Hope schools) subsequently chose to reconstitute them as charter schools in order to benefit from the substantially higher funding given to charter schools.[20] In principle, however, voucher-program funding could be just as generous as charter-school funding.

Milwaukee, which has perhaps the most generous voucher program in the country, is a partial exception to the usual rule. The voucher is tied to the state's contribution to public-school funding and is nominally equivalent to about 60 percent of the per-pupil expenditures of the Milwaukee public schools. As Henry Levin points out, however, this comparison ignores the fact that public schools are responsible for additional services that voucher schools need not provide, including special education, transportation, food services, and vocational education.[21] Moreover, a disproportionate number of voucher students are enrolled in elementary and middle grades, which are generally less expensive than high school.[22] In consequence, Levin believes that Milwaukee's vouchers are approximately equivalent to the costs of educating similar students with similar services in the Milwaukee public schools.[23]

---

transportation, which is normally not included in voucher- and charter-school expenses.

[18]See Nelson, Muir, and Drown, 2000.

[19]While the maximum per-pupil payment was $2,250 for voucher students, Cuyahoga County charter schools received a minimum of $4,537 per student in grades 1–8 and $4,195 for kindergarteners (Greene, 1999a).

[20]Archer, 1999.

[21]Levin, 1998.

[22]Wisconsin Legislative Audit Bureau, 2000; Levin, 1998.

[23]Levin, 1998.

In sum, even the Milwaukee voucher program, which is relatively generous, only provides funding that is comparable to what public schools spend for limited services to relatively low-cost students. These differences suggest that policymakers setting funding levels for both voucher and charter programs should consider the mix of services they want participating schools to provide.[24]

EDUCATION TAX SUBSIDIES

As noted in Chapter One, policymakers sometimes choose to provide indirect support for private-school tuition in the form of income-tax subsidies. These education subsidies often are not labeled as voucher programs, but they raise the same public-policy questions as vouchers do and thus are included in our analysis.

Education tax subsidies can work in several different ways. Some states permit families to deduct private-school tuition charges from their income. This creates a subsidy (which could be viewed as an implicit "voucher") equal to the deduction times the taxpayer's marginal state income tax rate. Most tuition tax deductions are capped at low levels, and most states have relatively low marginal income-tax rates, so deductions typically create only very small subsidies. Other programs permit a credit on income tax for private-school tuition. These programs create a subsidy equal to the full value of the tuition payment, limited only by a cap placed on the credit (which is usually fairly low) and by the taxpayer's total tax liability (unless the credit is refundable). As of 1999, small state-level income-tax deductions or credits were in place in Arizona, Illinois, Iowa, and Minnesota.[25]

A new wrinkle on income-tax subsidies for private-school tuition is the federal education savings account (ESA), which works like a Roth IRA in excluding income from federal taxation if that income goes into and then is drawn from an account intended for a specific pur-

---

[24]Many charter laws provide additional funding for students with special needs, as shown in Table 2.2. The second of Florida's two voucher programs, which is known as the McKay Scholarships Program and is aimed specifically at children who need special-education services, provides funding that can vary with student needs. For details, see http://www.opportunityschools.org/osas/spswd/.

[25]Education Commission of the States, 1999.

pose—in this case, to pay educational costs. Although ESAs already existed for higher-education tuition, the 2001 federal tax cut expanded them to include K–12 tuition. The new law permits parents to place up to $2,000 per year in accounts that earn interest tax-free and can be used for private-school tuition payments.[26] As is true for tuition tax deductions, the size of the subsidy (or implicit voucher) associated with the ESA depends on the taxpayer's marginal tax bracket (though in the case of the ESA, it also depends on the rate of return earned by the account). Taxpayers in higher tax brackets benefit from larger subsidies (although eligibility for the ESA eventually phases out when annual family income exceeds $190,000).

Arizona broke new ground in 1997 by creating a voucher credit—i.e., an income-tax credit that applies not to private-school tuition, but to charitable contributions made to privately operated voucher programs. The law permits taxpayers to claim a credit on their state income tax of up to $500 annually for donations to organizations providing scholarships to private schools. Arizona parents thus cannot take a tax credit for their own children's tuition charges, but they can take a tax credit for contributing to the tuition costs of other children.[27] In May 2001, Pennsylvania followed Arizona's lead, establishing a law that creates up to $20 million annually in tax credits for businesses that contribute to private voucher programs.[28] As we note in Chapter One, tax credits may become an increasingly important method of funding voucher programs because they are more politically palatable and less susceptible to constitutional challenge than are publicly operated voucher programs.

SAMPLE VOUCHER AND CHARTER POLICIES

To make the significance of these regulatory and financing variables concrete, we describe here a number of actual and proposed voucher

---

[26]See Rothstein, 2001.

[27]See Bland, 2000.

[28]See Potts, 2001. Pennsylvania's voucher credits are worth a maximum of 90 percent of the amount contributed to the scholarship, which can be up to $100,000 per business. Moreover, Pennsylvania's law has an income restriction: vouchers are available only to students with a family income below $50,000 plus $10,000 per child (e.g., $70,000 for a family with two children). (See 2001 Pennsylvania House Bill No. 996.)

and charter programs that vary along many of the dimensions discussed above.

Sample Voucher Programs

"Escape valves" for low-income students. The existing voucher programs in Milwaukee and Cleveland can be characterized as escape
valves because they are intended to enroll only a small minority of
the students in a community and are targeted to low-income students, much like the privately funded voucher programs now operating in many cities.

The Milwaukee Parental Choice Program (MPCP) offers scholarships
of approximately $5,300 to low-income students in Milwaukee to at-
tend private and religious schools of their choice. Eligibility is limited to families below an income threshold (approximately $25,000
for a family of three in 2000–01). Unlike schools receiving students
from privately funded voucher programs, however, schools participating in MPCP are expected to conform to a number of program
regulations. They are not permitted to charge additional tuition,
must demonstrate minimal performance based on one of a number
of general outcome standards,[29] and are required to admit all applicants as long as space is available. Schools with a shortage of space
must allocate spaces by lottery.[30] In the 2000–01 school year, the
program included 103 schools serving over 9,500 students.[31]

The Cleveland Scholarship and Tutoring Grant Program began operating in the 1996–97 school year, allowing students in kindergarten
through grade 3 (to be expanded by one grade each subsequent year,

---

[29]Students are not required to take standardized tests, so little information is available
on the academic performance of voucher students and schools.

[30]For more on the Milwaukee program, see the program's Website at http://www.
dpi.state.wi.us/dpi/dfm/sms/choice.html.

[31]Fletcher, 2001. When the program was inaugurated in 1990–91, it included only 330
students in seven schools. This tremendous expansion is due in large part to the
legislative changes made in the program in 1995. Prior to 1995, religious schools were
not permitted to participate, no more than 49 percent of a school's enrollment could
consist of voucher students, and overall program participation was capped at 1,500
students. Today, religious schools are permitted to participate, schools may be
composed entirely of voucher students, and the program cap is 15,000 students.
(Witte, 1998.)

up to grade 8) to attend any participating private school in the city, including religious schools. Scholarship recipients are selected by lottery, with priority given to low-income families. A proportion of the scholarships were allocated to students already attending private schools. The scholarship covers a maximum of 90 percent of private-school tuition up to $2,250, with smaller scholarships for higher-income families. Parents are required to make up the difference in tuition. As of the 1998–99 school year, 59 schools were participating in the program, enrolling 3,674 students.[32] (Federal courts have held the program unconstitutional, and an appeal to the U.S. Supreme Court is in progress.)

Incentive-based voucher programs. Florida's Opportunity Scholarship Program, which became law in June 1999, is an integral part of the state's educational accountability act, which grades all public schools each year on students' academic progress. The program's primary purpose is to induce improvement in low-performing public schools, rather than to send large numbers of students to voucher schools. Any student attending a public school that receives a failing grade for two years of a four-year period on the state's A–F grading system is eligible to receive a tuition voucher of approximately $4,000 to attend any participating private school. Participating schools cannot require families to pay additional tuition beyond the scholarship. In the 1999–2000 school year, students from two public schools became eligible for scholarships; 57 of those students used the scholarships to enroll in five private schools.[33] In 2000, all of the state's "F" schools improved their performance enough that no additional students were given vouchers. (We discuss this result in Chapter Three.)

The Florida model may have influence elsewhere. Recently, before abandoning the idea in the face of substantial congressional opposition, President George W. Bush proposed that Title I funding for low-income students in low-performing public schools be converted to

---

[32]Greene, 1999b.

[33]American Civil Liberties Union of Florida, 1999. The Opportunity Scholarship Program is distinct from the McKay Scholarships Program, a second Florida voucher program that is aimed specifically at students with disabilities.

vouchers as an incentive for improving academic achievement in those schools.

Wide-eligibility vouchers. Other voucher proposals and programs are intended to be widely available to a large number of students rather than to be targeted to at-risk children. A prominent recent proposal, rejected by voters in the fall of 2000, was California's Proposition 38. It proposed a universal program that would grant $4,000 scholarships to all children in the state that could be used to pay tuition at any private school in California. Proposition 38 approached Milton Friedman's 1955 proposal in terms of its minimal regulations. Participating schools would retain control over their own admissions and would be permitted to charge additional tuition if they chose to do so. The only substantial regulation was that, like public schools in California, participating schools would be required to administer the Stanford Achievement Test to their students.[34]

Income-tax programs, such as the Arizona voucher credit and the federal ESA, also generally make benefits widely available to large numbers of children and families (though the size of the benefit to any particular family may be small). These programs usually impose no constraints on the private schools that participating students attend.

Sample Charter Laws

Broadly speaking, charter laws vary from highly restrictive to highly unrestrictive in terms of the limitations they impose on charter-school startup and operation. To illustrate the range of possibilities, we discuss two charter laws—that of Kansas and that of Arizona—as representatives of the extreme ends of the spectrum. Some states have charter laws very similar to these; other states fall on a continuum between the extremes. (Additional examples can be found in Tables 2.1 and 2.2.)

Restrictive charter law. One example of a highly restrictive charter law can be found in Kansas, which was early to adopt charter schools

---

[34]For more details and analysis of Proposition 38, see Fuller, Huerta, and Ruenzel, 2000.

when it passed its law in 1994. The Kansas law caps the total number of schools at 15, and schools are granted only three-year charter terms. Local school boards are the only eligible authorizers, private schools are not permitted to convert to charter status, and charter schools may not be operated by for-profit management companies. Schools must hire certified teachers and are not automatically waived from state and district regulations; exemptions must be negotiated with the authorizing agency and specified in the charter. A charter school's student body must reflect the racial and socioeconomic makeup of the district in which it is located. Charter schools receive no startup funding from the state.[35]

Unrestrictive charter law. Arizona is generally viewed as having the nation's least restrictive charter law.[36] Charter schools may be authorized by local school boards, the state board of education, or the state board of charter schools. No evidence of local support for the school is required in the application process. The law allows both public and private schools to convert to charter status, and charter schools can be operated on a profit-seeking basis. Arizona's charter schools are initially approved for a term of 15 years, the longest term of any state, and are automatically waived from most state and district regulations, including teacher certification requirements. All students in the state are eligible to attend. Operating funds for Arizona charter schools are equivalent to the state per-pupil allocation that conventional public schools receive. The state also provides $1 million annually in startup funds for charter schools, as well as substantial funding for charter facilities.[37]

Universal-Choice Systems of Autonomous Schools

Other school-choice programs are more ambitious than any of those described above. These programs—which may be called voucher systems, contract systems, or universal chartering—would replace the existing system of educational governance and finance with an entirely new system in which all schools are autonomous and every

---

[35]Center for Education Reform, 2000b; see also RPP International, 1999.

[36]See Center for Education Reform, 2000b; see also RPP International, 1999.

[37]Center for Education Reform, 2000b; Nelson, Muir, and Drown, 2000.

family must choose a school. They are designed not to set up alternatives to the conventional system of public education, but to replace it entirely. They propose that school boards and districts get out of the business of operating schools, instead becoming regulatory and contractual authorities providing oversight to independently operated voucher/charter schools. Although universal-choice systems have been proposed in different forms for at least 30 years, they have never been tried in the United States.

A 1970 proposal by the Center for the Study of Public Policy (which we refer to here in text by the name of its first author, the Harvard scholar Christopher Jencks) would have converted the entire system of public education to a highly regulated voucher system. All schools would compete for students because family choice would determine student assignment. Schools could be operated by a wide variety of organizations, including religious groups. Participating schools would be permitted to select applicants for up to half of their spaces, the other half would be open to all applicants, and lotteries would determine admission to overenrolled schools. Schools would not be permitted to charge supplemental tuition; low-income students would receive larger subsidies to encourage schools to seek them out. Schools would be required to make publicly available an extensive amount of information about themselves, including their students' outcomes. This information would be actively disseminated to families by a public agency.[38] A similar proposal (with some variations) has been made at various points over the last 30 years by John Coons and Stephen Sugarman.[39]

More recently, Paul Hill, Lawrence Pierce, and James W. Guthrie likewise proposed to revolutionize the system of educational governance and finance. Their proposal would permit all schools to operate autonomously under contracts granted by the school district. Funding would follow students to the schools of their choice. The school district itself would get out of the business of operating schools, instead acting as a contracting authority with responsibility

---

[38]Center for the Study of Public Policy, 1970.

[39]Coons and Sugarman, 1971, 1978, 1992, 1999. Indeed, the Jencks proposal may have been influenced by conversations with Coons and Sugarman (private correspondence with John Coons, April 2001).

for ensuring that the community has an array of high-quality schools operated by a variety of independent organizations.[40]   Similarly, Hugh Price of the National Urban League has proposed that all urban schools across the country be converted to autonomous charter schools.[41]

The only existing examples of universal-choice systems of autonomous schools are outside the United States. New Zealand's system of public education, in place for the last decade, permits parental choice among all public schools, each of which is operated independently by its own school board. Schools that are in demand are permitted to choose among the students who apply. Some schools charge student fees in addition to their public subsidy.[42] Meanwhile, Chile's national voucher system, established in 1980 under the influence of the ideas of Milton Friedman, provides equivalent per-pupil funding to all public and private schools willing to accept the voucher without charging additional tuition. For-profit private schools have dramatically increased their market share under the program.[43]   We examine evidence on the effects of these programs where relevant in subsequent chapters.

These examples should make clear both that the variation among programs of autonomous schooling is vast and that the boundary between voucher and charter programs is permeable. For example, although Jencks proposed a voucher system and Hill, Pierce, and Guthrie proposed a system of contracting, the proposals have far more similarities than differences—and both look much like a system of universal charter schools. Consider, also, that the Milwaukee Parental Choice Program is generally regarded as a voucher program and yet is more regulated than some charter laws (in that it imposes an income restriction and requires open admissions). Arizona's voucher tax credit, by contrast, promotes privately operated voucher programs that are largely unregulated. Tables 2.1 and 2.2 (shown earlier) further suggest how voucher and charter policies can be

---

[40]Hill, Pierce, and Guthrie, 1997.

[41]Price, 1999.

[42]See Fiske and Ladd, 2000.

[43]McEwan, 2000b.

characterized on the same policy continuum. Voucher and charter proposals should not be evaluated by their labels; instead, each should be assessed in terms of its details.

CHARACTERISTICS OF VOUCHER AND CHARTER SCHOOLS

Having illustrated the extent to which choice programs may vary on key policy dimensions, we now turn to the schools that have emerged to offer different types of choice options for students. To the extent that voucher and charter programs make a difference for students, they do so through differences in the characteristics of the schools themselves. Although some of the most important differences among schools may not be readily apparent in a statistical summary, a broad characterization of the differences among the schools should nevertheless help to provide context for the empirical assessment that follows in Chapters Three through Seven. We therefore end this chapter by comparing the general characteristics of public, charter, voucher, and private schools.

Table 2.4 spells out a few of these comparisons at the national level. This table has two omissions that are noteworthy. First, there is no column on voucher schools, because there are no national figures on them. In the text below, we discuss what is known about schools now participating in voucher programs, pointing out how those schools differ from typical private schools across the country. It is unfortunate that little is known about schools participating in pub- licly funded voucher programs, especially in light of the tremendous attention and controversy surrounding those programs. To date, most of the research done on voucher programs has focused intently on achievement outcomes, often overlooking the characteristics of schools themselves.

Second, Table 2.4 does not include information on student charac- teristics. In this case, the information is omitted because it is the subject of extensive attention in Chapter Five, where we discuss dis- tributive questions about access to vouchers and charter schools.

Separate columns for Catholic, other religious, and independent (nonsectarian) private schools are included in Table 2.4 because these schools have important differences that are relevant to voucher programs. The popular image of private schools is one of elite, inde-

Table 2.4

Characteristics of Schools, by Sector

Characteristic	Conventional Public	Charter	Catholic	Other Religious	Independent Private
			Private		
Enrollment					
Percentage of all students	88	1	6	4	2
Median enrollment	475	140	~250	~130	~90[a]
Pupil-teacher ratio	17	16	19	14	10
Special services (percentage of schools)					
Special education	89	95	26	16	42[a]
English as a second language	43	Unknown	12	9	14
Bilingual	18	Unknown	3	5	4
Gifted	71	Unknown	28	23	24
Teachers					
Percentage with less than bachelor's degree	1	Unknown	3	12	5
Percentage with master's or higher	47	Unknown	34	30	41
Percentage certified	97	72[b]	85	70	74
Years of teaching experience	~15	7[b]	~10 (overall median in private schools)		
Base salary ($/year)	34,189	Unknown	21,652	19,356	25,052

SOURCES: Choy, 1997; RPP International, 2000; Finn, Manno, and Vanourek, 2000.
[a]Note that close to one-quarter of nonsectarian schools are special-education schools.
[b]From a survey of charter schools in ten states (Finn, Manno, and Vanourek, 2000).

pendent, college-preparatory high schools that charge high tuition rates and admit students selectively based on academic achievement. As the table shows, however, such schools represent only a small minority of the total private-school market. Approximately half of all private-school students are enrolled in Catholic schools. For the relatively small-scale, urban-focused voucher programs now in operation (both publicly and privately funded), Catholic schools are critical because they are overrepresented in cities and tend to charge relatively low tuition rates (and are generally willing to admit non-Catholic students[44]). Systematic national data on tuition rates are dated, but they clearly demonstrate the differences among the private-school sectors. At the elementary level in 1993–94, average tuition was $4,700 at independent private schools, $2,600 at non-Catholic sectarian schools, and $1,600 at Catholic schools. At the same time, secondary tuition was $9,500 at independents, $5,300 at non-Catholic sectarian schools, and $3,600 at Catholic schools.[45] Although tuition levels have undoubtedly risen since 1993–94, relative differences among the sectors should have remained similar.[46]

Enrollment, School Size, and Pupil-Teacher Ratio

As Table 2.4 makes clear, charter schools and all varieties of private schools tend to be substantially smaller than conventional public schools. Variation in pupil-teacher ratio is less dramatic than variation in school size (except for the category of independent private schools, which includes many schools that focus on special education and have very small classes). For conventional public schools, pupil-teacher ratio may substantially underestimate class size, because it includes sizable numbers of specialist teachers who are not assigned to regular classes.

Charter schools are the fastest-growing sector of the K–12 education market. In 1991, Minnesota was the first state to pass legislation permitting the existence of charter schools. As of the fall of 1999, 36 states and the District of Columbia had enacted legislation, and charter schools were operating in 32 states.[47] The number of operating charter schools has grown from two in 1992 to approximately 2,000 in the 2000–01 academic year, enrolling about half a million

---

[44]Of the 2.6 million students enrolled in Catholic schools today, 13.4 percent are non-Catholic, which is four times the proportion of non-Catholic students enrolled in 1970 (Egan, 2000). In many urban Catholic schools, the proportion of non-Catholic students is far higher.

[45]Choy, 1997.

[46]Other data from 1997–98 indicate that median tuition was $1,500 in Catholic elementary schools and $4,100 in Catholic high schools (Youniss and McLellan, 1999). Catholic schools are likely to be especially prominent in the privately funded voucher programs, where scholarship amounts tend to be only around $1,500.

[47]RPP International, 2000.

students.[48] The largest numbers of charter schools are in Arizona, California, Michigan, and Texas.[49]

As of the 1998–99 school year, 72 percent of charter schools had been started from scratch (often referred to as new startups), 18 percent had been converted from conventional public schools, and the remaining 10 percent had been converted from private schools. Among charter schools, enrollment is considerably lower in new startups and private conversions, with median number of students at 128 and 159, respectively, compared to 368 for converted public schools. Although charter schools will surely remain smaller than conventional public schools, their average size is likely to increase somewhat as more of them reach maturity (charter schools often open with only a few of the planned grades in operation).

Milwaukee's voucher program saw dramatic growth only after religious schools were permitted to participate: the number of schools accepting choice students increased from 23 in the 1997–98 school year to 86 in the 1998–99 school year. In that same time period, the number of students attending choice schools increased from 1,497 to 5,758. Nevertheless, Milwaukee's voucher schools remain quite small, with the average school serving 200 students, 70 of whom receive vouchers (while the others pay tuition through other means).[50] Cleveland's voucher schools are also small, enrolling an average of 201 to 300 students, compared to an average of 401 to 500 in public schools. Cleveland's voucher schools have smaller classes than its public schools do—21 students on average per class versus 24.[51]

Parental surveys from private voucher programs suggest that true class sizes in voucher schools are often smaller than those in public schools, even if overall pupil-teacher ratios are not lower. In the Edgewood school district, outside of San Antonio, Texas, there is no significant difference in class size between voucher and public

---

[48]Wilgoren, 2000b.

[49]RPP International, 2000.

[50]Wisconsin Legislative Audit Bureau, 2000.

[51]Metcalf, 1999.

schools, but this result is unusual.[52]   Parents report classes being smaller by four students in Washington (18 versus 22), four in Dayton (21 versus 25), and two in New York (25 versus 27).[53]   Voucher parents also report smaller class sizes in Charlotte.[54]   In all five cities, voucher schools are far smaller than local public schools.

Grade-Level Configuration

Not included in Table 2.4, but a matter of substantial difference between conventional public schools and the other sectors, is the configuration of grade levels in individual schools. The conventional public-school pattern of three levels of schooling (elementary, middle, high) is often ignored by both charter and private schools. Even though their average enrollments are much smaller, private schools are far more likely than public schools to include a wide range of grade levels (such as K–8 or K–12).[55]   Such configurations are also common in charter schools, of which only half have traditional grade structures, compared to 78 percent of public schools.[56]

The limited information available on voucher schools is consistent with the general private-school pattern. In Milwaukee, a majority of voucher schools (59 percent) serve either grades K–8 or 1–8.[57]   In Cleveland, most voucher schools serve a greater number of grades (usually K–8) than public schools do.[58]   Voucher students tend to be overrepresented in grades K–8, perhaps because private-school tuition is substantially higher in high school.

Teachers

As Table 2.4 indicates, private-school teachers are somewhat less likely to have master's degrees than are teachers in conventional

---

[52]Peterson, Myers, and Howell, 1999.

[53]Wolf, Howell, and Peterson, 2000; Howell and Peterson, 2000; Myers et al., 2000.

[54]Greene, 2000b.

[55]Choy, 1997.

[56]RPP International, 2000.

[57]Wisconsin Legislative Audit Bureau, 2000.

[58]Metcalf, 1999.

public schools. In addition, teachers in both private and charter schools are less experienced and less likely to be fully certified than are conventional public-school teachers.

Information on charter-school teachers at the national level is difficult to find. One survey, however, provides information on charter-school teachers concentrated in Arizona, California, Colorado, and Michigan.[59] It found that charter-school teachers had taught an average of 5.6 years in public schools and 1.7 years in private schools, and that 72 percent were state certified. While 41 percent of charter-school teachers had previously been members of the teachers' union, only 24 percent reported that they were current members.

In Cleveland, public-school teachers are significantly more experienced than voucher-school teachers (14.2 versus 8.6 years) and are more likely to have completed course work beyond their undergraduate degree.[60]

Table 2.4 also shows that conventional public-school teachers are paid substantially more than private-school teachers in all sectors. National salary data on charter-school teachers are unavailable, but the more limited experience and certification of these teachers suggest that they, too, would earn lower salaries (on average) than their counterparts in conventional public schools. In some instances, however, they may have salary schedules similar to those in public schools, in which case they would make more money than their private-school counterparts. Moreover, many charter schools are not bound by conventional salary schedules, giving rise to the possibility that teachers' pay is not directly tied to seniority.

In the past, Catholic schools could pay very low salaries because many of their teachers were religious-order members who had no dependents to support and often had taken vows of poverty. Today, however, Catholic schools can no longer rely on a supply of inexpensive teachers. Of 157,000 teachers in Catholic schools nationally,

---

[59]Finn, Manno, and Vanourek, 2000. Although the survey responses come from 521 teachers in 36 schools in ten states, 82 percent of the respondents taught in the four states listed.

[60]Metcalf, 1999.

5.5 percent are nuns, less than 1 percent are brothers, less than 1 percent are priests, and 93 percent are lay teachers.[61]

Program Content

Some of the most interesting questions about charter and voucher schools relate to the educational programs they provide. For many private schools, adherence to a particular educational philosophy—whether based on Roman Catholic faith or the teachings of Maria Montessori, for example—is their primary reason for existence and their primary focus of difference from conventional public schools. Charter schools, too, have been touted as a way for educational mavericks to pursue their pedagogical visions.

There is little systematic evidence on program content available for charter schools. Anecdotally, however, it is clear that they are pursuing a wide range of programs. Some focus on mathematics and science, others on the arts; some have adopted the "world-class" curriculum of Edison Schools, others the "Core Knowledge" program of E. D. Hirsch. Some develop curriculum aimed at African-American children; others seek to promote leadership in girls. The proportion of charter schools across the nation using innovative or alternative programs, however, is not clear.

More evidence is available for voucher schools; it comes from programs in Milwaukee, Cleveland, and Florida. In all three cases, religious schools predominate. Of the 86 schools participating in the Milwaukee voucher program in 1998–99, 63 were religious, serving 69.9 percent of students, and 23 secular schools served the remaining 30.1 percent. Catholic schools accounted for almost two-thirds of the religious schools and 45.1 percent of all participating students. Other types of religious schools participating in the program included Lutheran (11 schools, 9.7 percent of voucher enrollment), other Christian schools (nine schools, 11 percent of enrollment), two Islamic schools (3 percent of enrollment), and one Jewish school (1.1 percent of enrollment). The remaining secular schools were quite diverse, including Montessori schools, one Waldorf school, and sev-

---

[61]Egan, 2000.

eral schools based on the theory of multiple intelligences. Several high schools provided vocational education, school-to-work programs, and college-preparatory programs; a small number of voucher high schools were specially designed to serve at-risk students. Many other schools had an ethnic focus or provided bilingual or multilingual education. Two-thirds of the participating schools, serving approximately the same proportion of voucher students, had or were seeking accreditation. The most common sources of accreditation were the Wisconsin Nonpublic School Accrediting Association and the Catholic Archdiocese of Milwaukee.[62]

In Cleveland, as in Milwaukee, religious schools dominate the voucher program. In the first year of the program, 1,994 students attended 55 schools, 46 of which were religious schools.[63] Of those religious schools, 35 were Catholic, nine Protestant, and two Christian Fundamentalist, and together they served 77 percent of voucher students. After the Hope schools converted to charter status, the proportion of voucher students in religious institutions rose. In the 1998–99 school year, the third year of the program, 3,674 students were attending grades K–5 in 59 schools. Ninety-seven percent of voucher students attended religious schools.[64] As Jay Greene points out, the high proportion of religious schools involved in the voucher program is clearly influenced by the availability of greater funding for nonsectarian schools that choose to operate as charters (as well as the existence of nonsectarian public magnet schools in Cleveland).[65]

In Florida, only 57 students used vouchers to attend private schools in the first year of the Opportunity Scholarship Program. Of these, 53 attended four Catholic schools, and four attended a Montessori school.[66]

---

[62]Wisconsin Legislative Audit Bureau, 2000.

[63]Murphy, Nelson, and Rosenberg, 1997.

[64]Greene, 1999a.

[65]Greene, 1999a.

[66]See American Civil Liberties Union of Florida, 1999.

Complementary Programs and Resources

Table 2.4 makes it clear that public schools are more likely than private schools to offer special services for gifted students, students with disabilities, and English-language learners. This difference reflects legal obligations, larger school sizes, and generally higher levels of resources in public schools. Charter schools, like conventional public schools, have a legal obligation to serve students with disabilities: 95 percent of charter schools responding to a voluntary survey reported that they provide special-education services. Approximately half coordinate with either the district (29 percent) or an outside provider (22 percent) for these services. However, even though most charter schools say they offer special-education services, the proportion of charter-school enrollments that are special-education students is smaller than that in public schools (8 versus 11 percent).[67]

Voucher schools are less likely than public schools to offer special services, probably because they are not required to do so by law and because they have limited resources. On average, students with disabilities cost 2.3 times as much as other students to educate, and the cost is substantially more for students with severe disabilities, such as autism or blindness.[68] The limited resources of most inner-city voucher schools are apparent not only in the relative lack of special services, but also in that they are less likely than public schools to have libraries, computer laboratories, and cafeterias.[69] Even the publicly funded voucher programs in Milwaukee and Cleveland do not require participating schools to offer special-education services. A survey of voucher schools in Milwaukee found only seven out of 86 schools participating in the program reporting that they offered special education.[70] In New York, Washington DC, and Charlotte, parental reports indicated that voucher schools were less likely than public schools to offer services for special education and English-

---

[67]RPP International, 2000.

[68]Moore et al., 1988.

[69]The advantages of public schools over voucher schools in terms of physical facilities is apparent in Washington DC, Dayton, New York, Edgewood, and Charlotte (Wolf, Howell, and Peterson, 2000; Howell and Peterson, 2000; Myers et al., 2000; Peterson, Myers, and Howell, 1999; Greene, 2000b).

[70]Wisconsin Legislative Audit Bureau, 2000, p. 26.

language learners—though substantially more likely than the national averages in Table 2.4 would suggest.[71]

These results might be quite different under voucher programs—such as Florida's McKay Scholarships Program—that are specifically designed to serve students with disabilities. The McKay program, however, is quite new, and we have seen no data on the services provided in participating schools.

The fact that most voucher schools are less likely than public schools to offer special-education services does not necessarily mean that they do not admit students with disabilities. In Chapter Five, we discuss evidence about the enrollment rates of children with disabilities in voucher and charter schools, as well as some (limited) evidence about the satisfaction levels of parents of students with disabilities.

SUMMARY

Voucher and charter schools differ from conventional public schools in a number of significant ways. In some instances, the relationships between these descriptive differences and the outcomes discussed in the next five chapters will be readily apparent. In many cases, however, the relationships will remain speculative—too often the existing studies are "black boxes," providing little insight into the mechanisms that might produce differences in outcomes. Considerable research remains to be done to examine the relationships between inputs and outputs across varieties of schools.

It is likely that the policy-design dimensions discussed in the first half of this chapter will have an influence on the characteristics of voucher and charter schools. In Chapter Four, we discuss how policy

---

[71]Myers et al., 2000; Greene, 2000b; Wolf, Howell, and Peterson, 2000. According to parent reports, voucher schools in New York, Charlotte, Dayton, and Washington DC, were somewhat less likely than the public schools of control students to offer special programs for students with learning disabilities. In New York, 58 percent of voucher parents reported such services offered in their children's schools, compared to 74 percent of public-school parents (Myers et al., 2000). In Charlotte, it was 49 percent vs. 71 percent (Greene, 2000b, Table 7); Dayton, 82 percent vs. 88 percent (Howell and Peterson, 2000, Table 5); and Washington DC, 67 percent vs. 78 percent (Wolf, Howell, and Peterson, 2000, Table 5).

variations may affect the supply of schools participating in voucher and charter programs.

More generally, our discussion of policy variables should make it clear that the range of variation among voucher and charter policies is wide. While reading the discussion of empirical evidence in Chapters Three through Seven, readers should keep in mind that outcomes produced by a specific voucher/charter policy may differ greatly under a different policy. Indeed, some differences in policy details can lead to diametrically opposed empirical outcomes. We note the importance of policy details throughout the book, discussing the relationship between details and outcomes in depth in our concluding chapter.

Chapter Three

ACADEMIC ACHIEVEMENT

The first question that policymakers ask about voucher and charter programs is whether they will improve or harm academic achievement. Vouchers and charters may have positive or negative effects on conventional public schools, so the question about achievement effects should be asked systemically, both for students who choose to attend voucher/charter schools and for students who remain in conventional public schools. We define academic achievement broadly, to include attainment (measured by advancement in school, graduation, and later participation in higher education) as well as academic skills and knowledge. Ideally, achievement measures would include not only assessments of basic skills in reading and math, but broader gauges of knowledge, cognitive skills, and creativity, in wide-ranging domains from science to fine arts. In practice, the available assessments often focus on a relatively narrow range of basic skills. Fortunately, proponents and opponents of vouchers and charters agree that the promotion of basic academic skills is a key function of education.

This chapter summarizes the empirical evidence related to academic achievement under voucher and charter programs for both choosers and nonchoosers. Vouchers and charters are relatively recent innovations that have had little opportunity to be evaluated systematically over a substantial period of time. Nevertheless, a number of evaluations directly address many of the critical empirical questions. Moreover, a variety of nonexperimental studies—of public and private schools, of school-choice programs of older varieties, and of private-school subsidies in other countries—provide additional evidence relevant to both voucher and charter programs. We begin with theoretical arguments on both sides.

THEORETICAL ARGUMENTS

Proponents argue that vouchers and charters will improve academic outcomes because autonomous schools are more effective and focused than are conventional public schools, which, in their view, lack a clear sense of mission and are unduly constrained by politics and bureaucracy. In their 1990 *Politics, Markets, and America's Schools,* John Chubb and Terry Moe use a large national data set on schools and students to develop an organizational theory on democratic governance of schooling, concluding that, whatever the historical intent and experience might have been, contemporary public schools cannot function effectively precisely *because* they are democratically governed.[1] In their view, public schools are paralyzed by a convoluted balancing of the interests of educators, unions, community forces, and politicians. In this web of action, effective educational programs cannot be created and sustained. According to Chubb and Moe, only redirection of authority to parents and families through vouchers (charters did not yet exist at the time they wrote), so that they can choose the schools their children attend, can shatter and replace existing arrangements sufficiently to give hope of improved educational outcomes.

Similarly, Paul Hill, Lawrence Pierce, and James Guthrie argue that conventional public schools are too heavily bureaucratized, rule bound, and interest-group dominated to consistently operate effectively.[2] They believe that the operation of schools by political bodies distracts schools from their basic educational mission, interposing educationally irrelevant concerns about compliance, standardization, and employment. In their view, the existing governance structure of public schools cannot be expected to produce effective education on a wide scale. Motivated by studies of successful schools, they propose to have all public schools operated autonomously, by

---

[1]Chubb and Moe, 1990. Chubb subsequently left academia to join Edison Schools, Inc., where he is now chief education officer.

[2]Hill, Pierce, and Guthrie, 1997; Hill and Celio, 1998.

nongovernment organizations, as schools of choice under contracts with school boards—creating what is essentially a system of universal charter schools.

Opponents of choice, in contrast, argue that conventional public schools are often just as effective as private and charter schools. In their view, the higher achievement often seen in private schools results not from a more effective educational program, but from the private schools' ability to select privileged students from highly motivated, high-income families. Moreover, they argue that public schools are in fact improving their performance through a variety of reform methods, including class-size reduction, district-level governance reforms, state-level accountability systems, and research-based curriculum interventions. Although these arguments challenge the view that conventional public schools cannot be reformed, supporters of choice respond by arguing that improvements to the conventional system are possible in the short term but will not be sustained without basic changes in educational governance.[3]

Much of the debate between supporters and opponents of choice centers on the likely systemic effects on nonchoosing students. It is critical to keep in mind that voucher and charter programs may affect academic achievement not only for students who enroll in voucher and charter schools, but also for students who remain in conventional public schools. Supporters of choice, appealing to the power of the market, often argue that vouchers and charters will provide competition for conventional public schools—in order to survive, they will be forced to improve.[4] If so, students who remain in conventional public schools will benefit from the introduction of vouchers or charters.

---

[3]In their view, the reforms of well-meaning, effective, and charismatic leaders will eventually fade away if schools lack the institutional structure to sustain them. Discussions of the political and bureaucratic constraints on conventional public schools can be found in Hill and Celio, 1998; Hill, Campbell, and Harvey, 2000; Hess, 1999.

[4]This view is not universal among supporters of choice. Milton Friedman, for example, would like government to get out of the business of operating schools entirely (see Friedman, 1955, 1962/1982). Chubb and Moe's view that conventional public schools are bureaucratically and politically constrained suggests that such schools may not be capable of improvement (see Chubb and Moe, 1990).

By contrast, opponents worry that voucher and charter schools will "skim the cream" from the public schools—i.e., will enroll the highest-achieving and most-advantaged students. They argue that students remaining in the conventional public schools will be worse off as a result, because they will lose the benefit of associating with highly motivated, high-achieving peers. Both the competition argument and the cream-skimming argument are theoretically plausible; which effect will dominate is a critical empirical question.

As shown in the pages ahead, the existing empirical literature has a number of weaknesses that preclude comprehensive and definitive answers to all the relevant questions about academic outcomes. Nevertheless, the store of evidence available about both vouchers and charter schools is growing rapidly. Moreover, even where the evidence is less than definitive, guidance can be provided on how specific variations in the details of voucher and charter policies are likely to affect achievement. Here and in later chapters, the details of policy design will be critical to predicting empirical effects. We postpone an in-depth discussion of the implications of policy variation until Chapter Eight.

EFFECTS ON STUDENTS IN VOUCHER AND CHARTER SCHOOLS

We begin with evidence on the academic effects on students attending charter or voucher schools. This evidence is more plentiful and somewhat less fraught with methodological problems than is the evidence on systemic effects on nonchoosers (which we address later in the chapter).

Methodological Issues

Theoretically, the best evidence on the academic effectiveness of voucher and charter schools would come from systematic experimental evaluations using random assignment of students: some students would be sent to voucher/charter schools and other students to conventional public schools, their assignment being based on a lottery. An experimental design with random assignment to the "treatment" and "control" conditions is often regarded as the ideal methodology in social science research because it avoids the problem of selection bias,[5] which, in empirical studies of vouchers and charter schools, is the single thorniest methodological problem: students and parents who choose voucher and charter schools are likely to differ in systematic ways from those who remain in assigned public schools. Any observed differences in outcomes, then, might result from pre-existing differences in the students and their families rather than from differences in the effectiveness of schools. If voucher and charter students come from highly educated and highly motivated families, they may perform better than public-school students even if their schools are no more effective. By the same token, if students entering voucher and charter schools have not done well in conventional public schools, they may perform worse than public-school students even if their schools are just as effective. And even if researchers adjust their findings based on observable background characteristics (such as income and parental education), unobservable characteristics (such as how much parents value education) can have a substantial effect on outcomes.

Random assignment solves the problem of selection bias by ensuring that the treatment and control groups have similar characteristics. If assignment to a school is determined by lottery, the achievement of applicants who win the lottery for vouchers or charters can be directly compared with the achievement of applicants who do not. Because the two groups have similar background characteristics—including unobservable characteristics related to motivation and values—researchers and policymakers can have confidence that any observed differences in achievement result from the voucher/charter program itself.

In practice, for ethical and political reasons, educational programs rarely involve experimental research designs with random assignment.[6] Random assignment is especially unlikely in a school-choice

---

[5]See, e.g., Burtless, 1995; Krueger, 1999. For a discussion of some of the weaknesses of experiments, see Heckman and Smith, 1995. Random assignment cannot solve all methodological problems; moreover, experiments do not necessarily duplicate all of the conditions that would hold in an actual policy implementation. We address these issues later in the chapter.

[6]The Tennessee class-size experiment of the 1980s is one of the rare instances in which an educational reform underwent a large-scale experimental evaluation. Findings from the study are still being mined today. (See Krueger and Whitmore, 2001.)

program, both because choice is itself one of the major goals of the reform and because the creation of a chosen community in the school is postulated as a primary mechanism for improving outcomes. In consequence, fully randomized assignment would defeat the purpose of vouchers and charters.

Although fully randomized assignment of all students would conflict with the basic purposes of vouchers and charters, more-limited randomization is possible when the number of applicants for a program exceeds the number of spaces available. Spaces can be allocated randomly among the applicants. Four of the privately funded voucher programs did exactly that: applicants were selected to receive vouchers by lottery. In consequence, some of the best evidence about the empirical effects of school choice (on students who choose) comes from the private scholarship programs. Our discussion below includes all of the randomized experimental voucher studies.[7]

Many other voucher and charter programs do not incorporate randomized research designs.[8] Researchers therefore have been forced to use other methods to deal with the problem of selection bias. The best nonexperimental studies are those that make use of longitudinal, panel data sets that can follow the progress of individual students over time. Longitudinal data permit researchers to create statistical controls not only for student background characteristics, but also for each student's prior achievement. In essence, this creates

---

[7]In practice, evaluations with random assignment are not as simple as this discussion suggests. Assessments are complicated by noncompliance and attrition. In experimental voucher studies, for example, some lottery winners did not use their vouchers, and some lottery losers found other ways to enroll in private schools; moreover, many members of both treatment and control groups did not return for follow-up study. These issues are discussed in the context of the voucher experiments in the pages below.

[8]Some charter laws require oversubscribed charter schools to admit students by lottery. These lotteries, however, are motivated by a concern for fairness rather than an interest in promoting research. We are aware of no charter-school studies that have attempted to use these lotteries for research purposes. Overenrollment in Milwaukee's voucher program in early years meant that vouchers sometimes were awarded randomly. As discussed below, some researchers have used the Milwaukee lottery to assess outcomes. (See Greene, Peterson, and Du, 1998; Rouse, 1998.)

the opportunity to compare achievement growth trajectories of students in different kinds of schools, factoring out both family background and prior achievement.

In the absence of longitudinal data in nonexperimental studies, the best method that researchers have to control for systematic, unobservable differences between choosers (in voucher/charter schools) and nonchoosers (in conventional public schools) is an "instrumental variable" (IV) approach. Researchers using this approach seek to find variables that are correlated with the likelihood of attending a voucher/charter school but uncorrelated with achievement; these then can be used as "instruments" to adjust for unobserved differences. Unfortunately, it is often very difficult to find variables that unambiguously meet these criteria.

The pages below discuss the best available current evidence relevant to academic achievement in voucher and charter schools. We have included all of the experimental evidence, several nonexperimental studies that use longitudinal data sets, and a few nonexperimental studies that seem to involve robust IV adjustments for selection bias.

It should be noted, however, that many of the studies we discuss— both experimental and nonexperimental—are very new and have not yet been subjected to the scrutiny of extensive academic peer review. Some caution in interpreting their significance is thus needed. The reliability of evaluation findings is ensured in the long term both by the peer review process and by re-analysis of the data by other researchers. Findings on the Tennessee class-size reduction experiment of the 1980s, for example, have become widely accepted over the last decade as a result of extensive re-analysis and publication, not only by the original evaluators, but also by other researchers.[9] To provide the most-current information available, however, we could not wait until all relevant studies had been peer reviewed, published, and re-analyzed. The discussion below therefore includes the best of the studies now (as of July 2001) available.

_____

[9]See, e.g., Krueger and Whitmore, 2001; Krueger, 1999; Rouse, 2000.

Evidence from Voucher Programs

To date, the academic effects of vouchers have been more extensively analyzed than those of charters. Although most American voucher programs began operating only in the last decade,[10] the number of research evaluations of voucher programs is growing rapidly (with the notable exception of education tax subsidies, which, as far as we know, have produced no studies of academic effects). Moreover, every new report on the academic effects of voucher programs has produced a torrent of commentary from both critics and defenders in the research community. Thus, although the intensive scrutiny has helped to clarify the studies' strengths and weaknesses, the blizzard of competing claims and counterclaims has surely left many readers bewildered. This chapter aims to provide a sober assessment of the bottom line.

Recent studies include evaluations not only of the publicly funded voucher programs in Milwaukee and Cleveland, but also of a variety of privately funded, charitable-scholarship programs operating in cities across the United States.[11] From a research perspective, these privately funded scholarship programs—sometimes described as "private vouchers"—are very useful for predicting the empirical effects of publicly funded programs. Privately and publicly funded voucher programs may differ from each other in scale and in the regulations attached, but the funding source per se makes little difference to the student or the school. In consequence, privately funded scholarship programs may produce empirical effects similar to those that would be produced by publicly funded voucher pro-

---

[10]For decades, a few rural school districts in Maine and Vermont have practiced what is sometimes called "tuitioning"—i.e., they have sent small numbers of children to private schools because they lacked sufficient numbers of students to operate schools of their own (Greene, 2000a). We are aware of no evaluations of the effects of these programs. Also, in the early 1970s in Alum Rock, California, the federal government sponsored a public-school choice program that was often described as a voucher experiment. In fact, however, private schools were not permitted to participate, and participating public schools were protected by regulations from any potential negative effects of competition among themselves. In short, the Alum Rock experiment was not a true voucher program. (Levinson, 1976.)

[11]The state of Florida's voucher program has been in operation only for a year (1999–2000), on a very small scale, and has not yet been evaluated.

grams.[12] We begin with the evidence from these programs because they are the only ones that were designed to permit experimental research.

Experimental voucher studies. The most carefully analyzed experimental voucher evidence comes from New York City. In 1997, the School Choice Scholarship Foundation, a nonprofit organization in New York, began offering scholarships (worth up to $1,400) to low-income students in grades 1 through 5, focusing especially on students coming from public schools that have low achievement-test scores. In the first year, the program received 20,000 applications for 1,300 scholarships. The scholarships were awarded by lottery, and a comparably sized group of applicants who were rejected was chosen for comparison. David Myers of Mathematica Policy Research is leading the group of scholars evaluating the program.

Myers and colleagues have reported results from two years of studying the winners and losers of the 1997 lottery (further follow-up reports are expected). The evaluators measured achievement for participants in the New York experiment using math and reading components of the Iowa Test of Basic Skills (ITBS). Comparing the average test scores of students who used vouchers to attend private school for two years with those of a comparable group of students who did not, they found no statistically significant difference in reading or math.[13]

---

[12]Because privately funded scholarship programs do not result in reduced funding to public schools (as do many publicly funded programs and proposals), they may have less of an effect on public schools than do publicly funded programs. This difference, however, is not relevant to their effect on students using vouchers.

[13]Myers et al., 2000, Tables 19, 20. Unless otherwise stated, statistical significance is measured at a level of .05 throughout our discussion. In New York and the other sites of voucher experiments discussed below, comparison of achievement outcomes of voucher users and the control group required statistical adjustments to account for the fact that some lottery winners did not use their vouchers. In New York, 62 percent of those offered vouchers used them to attend private school in both years, 14 percent used them in one of the two years, and 24 percent did not use them at all. Meanwhile, 4 percent of those who lost the lottery found their way into private school for both years, and 4 percent attended private school for one year. (Myers et al., 2000, p. 13.) Most likely, families that actually used their vouchers (because they had the means and motivation to pay the remaining tuition) were a nonrandom sample of all lottery winners. The lottery mechanism, however, created an ideal instrumental variable, permitting an IV adjustment to ensure a fair comparison between voucher winners

Myers's team also analyzed results separately for African-American and Latino students, who together constituted the overwhelming majority of the voucher users in New York. The story for Latino students (half of all participants) was the same as that for the total population: no evidence of a statistically significant private-school effect was observed after two years, in math or reading.[14]

For African-American students, Myers's team found evidence of a possible private-school advantage. Voucher users' scores in reading were higher than those of the African-American control group by statistically significant margins; their math scores were also higher, but the difference did not achieve statistical significance. These results, however, become ambiguous when disaggregated by grade level. Effects were measured in grades 3 through 6, and statistically significant differences were apparent only in grade 6—where the advantage for African-American voucher users was quite large in both reading and math. In short, the advantage on average for African-American students was driven almost entirely by a large effect at one grade level.[15] Myers argues that this is reason for caution in interpreting results.[16] We share his reluctance to read too much into findings focused solely on a single grade level.

The finding of an advantage for African-American students, however, is consistent with reported findings from similar randomized voucher experiments in three other cities. In Dayton, Ohio, and Washington DC (in 1998), and in Charlotte, North Carolina (in 1999), nonprofit organizations distributed tuition scholarships to low-

---

and the control group. The IV adjustment was used for the results we discuss, which Myers describes as a "private school effect."

In addition to reporting a private school effect, Myers' team reports the effect of a voucher *offer*, as measured by a simple comparison of differences in outcomes between lottery winners and losers. The effect of the offer should be relevant to policymakers, because the policy instrument they have available is the offer of a voucher. In general, readers should recognize that the "voucher offer effect" in New York was about 40 percent smaller than the private school effect. (Myers et al., 2000, p. 13.)

[14]Myers et al., 2000, Tables 19, 20.

[15]Myers et al., 2000, Tables 19, 20.

[16]See response to some concerns of David Myers and of critics of the experimental studies in Howell et al., 2000a.

income students, allocating the scholarships by lottery in imitation of the New York program. As in New York, the vouchers were relatively small, with maximum amounts ranging from $1,200 to $2,200; families were expected to contribute a portion of tuition costs. Among African-American students in Dayton and Washington DC, test scores were somewhat higher in reading and math for students who had used vouchers to attend private schools for two years (although in Dayton the differences did not achieve statistical significance).[17] African-Americans constituted over 70 percent of the participants in both cities, and no effect was found for other ethnic groups.[18] In Charlotte, after one year, the evaluator found statistically significant advantages for voucher students in both reading and math. Charlotte results are not disaggregated by ethnicity, but the overwhelming majority of participants were African-American.[19]

Figure 3.1 shows the size of the advantage for African-American voucher users in each of the four cities—in terms of national percentile composite score (combining reading and math) on the ITBS—over their African-American control groups. In Dayton, Washington DC, and New York, the figures are differentials after two years; in Charlotte, they are one-year differentials. All results are statistically significant except in Dayton. To put these figures in context, it should be noted that most students using vouchers (as well as the control group) had very low scores on entering the program, typically around the 30th percentile nationally.[20]

Although these findings look consistently positive—if only for African-American students—caution is necessary in their interpretation. Results in Dayton, Washington DC, and Charlotte were not as fully or carefully reported as those in New York—where the effect is driven by a single cohort of students, with no measurable benefit for those in other grades. Critics have expressed a number of concerns

---

[17]As in New York, the comparison group was students who did not use a voucher for two years, which includes students who attended private school for one year and those who attended public schools for two years.

[18]Howell et al., 2000b, Tables 2B, 2C.

[19]Greene, 2000b, Tables 2, 3.

[20]See Myers et al., 2000; Howell et al., 2000b.

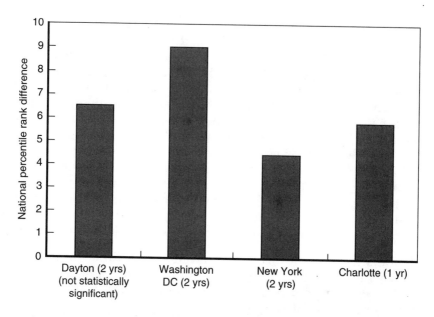

Figure 3.1—Average Composite Percentile Score Advantage for African-American Voucher Students over an African-American Control Group

about the analyses in the other three cities.[21] Two notable issues relate to grade-level differences and attrition among study participants:

- Washington DC is the only city where the private-school effect for African-American students was shown to be fairly consistent across grades. In Dayton, voucher users in three of seven grade-level cohorts showed large advantages over the control group, while three other cohorts showed no substantial difference and one showed a substantial disadvantage.[22] In Charlotte, grade-level results were not reported.

- Substantial numbers of the study participants—both voucher users and nonusers—failed to participate in the follow-up testing. Participant attrition is a problem that plagues all longitudi-

---

[21]An extensive set of criticisms can be found in Carnoy (2001).

[22]Carnoy, 2001, Table 2.

nal studies, and it was particularly acute here: although the New York study lost about a third of its participants after two years, rates of nonresponse were higher in Dayton, Washington DC, and Charlotte, where half to three-fifths of the original participants did not return for follow-up.[23] The researchers adjusted their findings by weighting inversely according to the probability of responding, but it is impossible to know whether this weighting captured unobserved differences.

A high attrition rate is problematic because it is possible that the lottery winners who continued to show up for standardized testing were those who were doing well in their voucher schools. Because biased attrition is always a possibility in social experiments, a nonresponse rate substantially above 30 percent is often regarded as reason for concern.[24] Further analyses could be conducted with existing data to help confirm that attrition did not bias the results.[25] For now, we can say only that the results look positive for low-income African-American children, but that they remain tentative.

Another unanswered question about the experimental studies is this: Why would vouchers have an effect only for African-American students? African-American students constituted the majority of participants in three of the four cities, but the New York study included a substantial number of Latinos, for whom no effect was found.[26] Intensive examination of students' actual experience in public and voucher schools might provide an explanation for the differential ef-

---

[23]Myers et al., 2000, Table 1; Howell et al., 2000b, p. 21; Greene, 2000b, p. 2.

[24]See Orr, 1999.

[25]As Patrick McEwan points out, the first test is to compare baseline characteristics (such as family income and parental education level) for those who remained and those who did not; except in New York, these comparisons have not been clearly and fully reported (with tests of statistical significance). Second, the data could be examined using a statistical regression that controls not only for whether a voucher was used, but also for baseline characteristics. If the results change when baseline characteristics are controlled, then there is reason for concern about biased attrition. (Private correspondence, October 12, 2000.) The latter test has been done only in Charlotte, where it did not substantially change the results (Greene, 2000b).

[26]As Latinos are the fastest-growing ethnic group in the United States, this difference may be important.

fect for African-Americans. Unfortunately, the existing studies have not collected extensive data on the schools and therefore cannot distinguish among a variety of possible reasons for the effect.[27] The specific reason(s) for the effect is critical to understanding its generalizability and its implications for public policy. Later in this chapter we discuss a variety of possible explanations for the effect and their implications.

Despite these various concerns, the findings from the experimental studies could become—with appropriate methodological checks—the most compelling evidence available on the achievement effects of vouchers (for voucher students). It should be noted that these are short-run effects, and it will be critical to see whether they grow or dissipate in the long term. Further follow-up of the experimental and control groups in coming years would provide an extremely valuable source of information on the long-term effects of vouchers—ideally, not only in terms of test scores, but also for other outcome measures, including dropout and graduation rates, college attendance, and future earnings.

Vouchers in Milwaukee. More ink has been spilled over the academic effects of Milwaukee's publicly funded program than over any other voucher or charter program. Unfortunately, however, the furor created by this debate is far disproportionate to the public policy significance of the results.

Milwaukee's voucher program began operating in 1990, opening to both fanfare and controversy. The Wisconsin legislature, which established the program, commissioned a five-year evaluation that was conducted by John Witte of the University of Wisconsin. Comparing voucher students with a sample of Milwaukee public-school students, Witte ultimately found "no consistent difference" in achievement in reading or math.[28] Subsequently, Jay Greene, Paul Peterson, and Jiangtao Du re-analyzed the Milwaukee data using a different comparison group: voucher applicants who were unable to use their vouchers because they could not find space in a par-

---

[27]Future reports on the New York program may partially remedy this limitation by including some information on schools from administrative sources and parental reports. (Correspondence with David Myers.)

[28]Witte, 2000, p. 132.

ticipating school. This team of researchers argued that the thwarted applicants were a more appropriate control group than the one Witte had used because their failure to use the vouchers created a "quasi experiment." Greene, Peterson, and Du found statistically significant advantages for voucher students in both reading and math after four years in the program.[29] Later still, Cecilia Rouse of Princeton University re-analyzed the data once more, in this case using both quasi-experimental and statistical controls. She found that voucher students did better in math but not reading, and that the math advantage accumulated over time, reaching a fairly substantial one-third to one-half of a standard deviation after four years.[30]

In our view, Rouse's analysis is most likely to be accurate. She subjected her findings to a number of statistical tests to confirm their robustness and found similar results using both quasi-experimental and statistical controls. Even so, her results are of minimal relevance to the general debate over vouchers and charters (as Rouse herself has suggested) and even to the current operation of the Milwaukee program.

When the Milwaukee data were collected, the program involved a small number of students concentrated in a few schools. Initially, enrollment in the voucher program was capped at 1 percent of enrollment in Milwaukee public schools; moreover, only nonsectarian schools were permitted to participate. This restriction excluded the great majority of private schools in the city. In its first year of operation (1990–91), only 341 students participated, enrolling at only seven voucher schools. Following the evaluation's completion, however, the Wisconsin legislature amended the program's rules, raising the cap on the number of students who could enroll to 15,000 and allowing religiously affiliated schools to participate. The result was a dramatic expansion in the number of schools and students participating: enrollment more than tripled between 1997–98 and 1998–99, when religious schools joined the program. Suddenly, 70 percent of voucher students were attending religious schools (mostly Catholic institutions). In 2000–01, over 9,500 Milwaukee students used

---

[29]Greene, Peterson, and Du, 1997, 1998.

[30]Rouse, 1998.

vouchers to attend 103 different private schools.[31] Unfortunately, the Wisconsin legislature has eliminated the requirement that voucher students be tested, so more-recent achievement data are unavailable.

Results from a program consisting of a few hundred students attending seven nonsectarian voucher schools are of minimal relevance to predicting the results from a program enrolling 9,500 students at 103 voucher schools, most of which are sectarian.[32] As we show below, the literature on public and private schooling suggests that, compared with other private schools, Catholic schools may have a unique advantage for low-income minority children. In sum, the findings from the early years of the Milwaukee voucher program tell little about the effectiveness of the program as it exists today and tell even less about the effectiveness of voucher and charter programs generally. Rouse's results are methodologically solid, but they speak only to the effectiveness of a handful of nonsectarian private schools in Milwaukee in the early 1990s.

Vouchers in Cleveland. Whereas the achievement results from Milwaukee are controversial and of minimal relevance to broader policy issues, those from Cleveland are even more problematic. Cleveland's voucher program, established by the Ohio legislature and aimed at low-income families, began operating in the 1996–97 academic year. About 3,700 students participated in 1998–99, enrolling in 59 schools. The program is now (July 2001) in legal limbo, awaiting possible Supreme Court review of a federal appellate court's determination that it violates the constitutional wall between church and state. One study of the Cleveland program examined the operation of two schools—the Hope schools—that were established to serve voucher students.[33] Students in the Hope schools showed gains in test scores during the first two years of the program's operation, but the researchers had no public-school group with which to compare gains, and their data included only the two schools, which have since

---

[31]Fletcher, 2001; Wisconsin Legislative Audit Bureau, 2000.

[32]To be fair, both Witte and Rouse have expressed concern about the extent to which the program's findings can be generalized (see Rouse, 1998; Witte, 2000, pp. 150–151). The problem with generalizing from the early Milwaukee results has also been raised in Moe, 1995, and McEwan, 2000c.

[33]Peterson, Howell, and Greene, 1999.

dropped out of the voucher program in order to convert to charter status.[34] The official evaluation of the program has been conducted by an Indiana University team. The reporting of the results, however, leaves a series of unanswered questions about methodology and the validity of the comparison group of nonvoucher students.[35] In sum, existing evidence permits no reliable conclusions, positive or negative, about the achievement effects of the Cleveland voucher program.

Implications of an expanded pool of choosers. Care is needed in interpreting the relevance of the findings of these studies for larger-scale, more generously funded choice programs. First of all, the privately funded experimental programs usually involve only partial scholarships with substantial family co-payments, which may produce an unusual sample of voucher users. Consider the following. Parents who are willing to pay partial tuition are those who are especially motivated to get their children into private school. The most-motivated parents may have three unusual characteristics: (1) they may be especially well informed about options in the educational market, (2) they may value education very highly,[36] and (3) their children may be having unusual difficulty in their current public schools. These children thus may be especially likely to move to high-quality voucher schools, and they may have the greatest potential to improve their achievement in new schools.

This point does not undermine the methodological validity of the experimental studies, because allocation by lottery ensures that voucher winners are comparable to voucher losers, and the eval-

---

[34]See Archer, 1999.

[35]In particular: (1) it is not clear how the research team selected the public-school comparison group; (2) it appears that the researchers underestimated the baseline differences between voucher students and public-school students; (3) their method does not make a statistical adjustment for unobserved differences between voucher students and public-school students; and (4) the accuracy of the baseline test scores is subject to doubt. Other researchers have concluded, as we have, that the official evaluation of the Cleveland program is too problematic for any conclusions about achievement effects to be drawn from it. (See McEwan, 2000c; Peterson, Greene, and Howell, 1998.)

[36]Goldhaber notes that empirical evidence suggests that parents often do select schools based on academic quality, but that nonacademic characteristics, such as the proportion of white students in a school, also motivate parental choices (Goldhaber, 1999; see also Goldhaber, 1997; Lankford and Wyckoff, 1992).

uators use an appropriate statistical technique (the IV approach) to account for the fact that some voucher winners do not use their vouchers. Nevertheless, even if the experimental findings are methodologically sound, they may be imperfect predictors of the achievement effects of more-generous, publicly funded voucher and charter programs that would bring in a larger segment of the population.

In all of the experimental studies, a substantial number of lottery winners did not use their vouchers. In New York, 75 percent of those awarded scholarships used them in the first year; 62 percent used them in both of the first two years.[37] First-year users constituted only 54 percent of voucher winners in Dayton and 53 percent in Washington DC.[38] In Charlotte, less than half used their scholarships in the first year.[39] According to survey responses of parents in New York, Dayton, and Washington DC, the most prominent reason that vouchers went unused was inability to pay additional tuition and associated costs (above the value of the scholarship).[40] This strongly suggests that a larger voucher, by reducing the family's co-payment (perhaps to zero), would produce a higher "take-up rate" among eligible families. The additional students brought into the program, however, might be those with somewhat less to gain by transferring to a voucher school and with less-motivated and less-informed parents. In consequence, average achievement gains for a generous voucher/charter program on a larger scale might be somewhat lower than the achievement gains suggested in these small-scale experimental programs.[41]

The black box of the voucher experiments. An increase in the take-up rate is not the only reason that a large-scale, publicly funded program might produce results different from those of a small-scale

---

[37]Howell et al., 2000b.

[38]Howell et al., 2000b.

[39]Greene, 2000b.

[40]Myers et al., 2000, pp. 15–16; Howell and Peterson, 2000, Table 4; Wolf, Howell, and Peterson, 2000, Table 4. In Dayton and Washington, the survey asked parents why their child was not in their preferred school rather than why the voucher went unused. Although these questions are not identical, we think they address the same issue.

[41]It is also possible, however, that the voucher schools could compensate for lower parental motivation.

experiment. To predict how the results might differ requires an understanding of the mechanisms behind the experimental results. Unfortunately, the experimental evaluations have not told us *why* voucher schools seem to perform better for this population of low-income African-American students. The experimental evaluations have been "black box" research designs and, as such, did not go into the schools to examine the processes that determine outcomes.[42] We are therefore left to theorize explanations for the apparent test-score advantage for African-American voucher students; there are several possibilities:

- *Peers:* Any advantage associated with voucher-school attendance may result (in part or entirely) from attending school with classmates of higher socioeconomic status or higher academic ability rather than from a more-effective school program.[43] Researchers generally have great difficulty disentangling peer effects from program effects, and the voucher experiments were not designed to separate these mechanisms.

- *Class size:* In Milwaukee, Cleveland, New York, Dayton, Washington DC, and Charlotte, voucher schools typically had smaller classes than did nonvoucher schools.[44] Tennessee's widely reported experimental study on class-size reduction demonstrated that reducing class size in primary grades by one-third (from about 23 to about 15 students) results in achievement gains for all students, but especially for low-income and African-American students.[45] In most of the voucher cities, the difference in class

---

[42]Members of the research team that conducted the experimental evaluations are now beginning to use data from their surveys of parents in an attempt to explain the differential effect on African-American students (Peterson and Howell, 2001). Although this is commendable, it is unfortunate that their only available evidence is indirect information, from parent surveys, rather than more-direct information collected in the schools.

[43]See McEwan, 2000a; Levin, 1998; Goldhaber, 1999, 1996.

[44]Rouse, 2000; Metcalf, 1999; Myers et al., 2000; Greene, 2000b; Wolf, Howell, and Peterson, 2000; Howell and Peterson, 2000. In 1993–94, the average self-contained class in private schools across the country had 21.8 students, versus 23.8 in public schools. Catholic schools, however, which constitute a large part of the private-school market in inner cities, had slightly larger self-contained classes, at 25.7 students. (See Choy, 1997.)

[45]Krueger, 1999. More recent work also found an achievement effect (though small) in a statewide class-size reduction program in California (Stecher and Bohrnstedt, 2000).

size between public and voucher schools was not large (two or three students, as reported by school records or parent surveys). Nevertheless, class size may explain some of the advantage for African-American voucher students.[46]

- *School size:* Total enrollments of schools participating in the voucher experiments were not reported, but it is likely that most of the schools are smaller than the urban public schools attended by the control groups. In general, private schools are far smaller than public schools: average enrollment is well under 300 students, compared to 475 in a typical public school.[47] Although there is less evidence on the academic effect of school size than there is on class size, some scholars believe that small schools lead not only to higher achievement, but also to a more equitable distribution of achievement (i.e., small schools have particular advantages for low-income children).[48]

- *Unusually bad local public schools:* As Dan Goldhaber points out, vouchers might help children in communities where public schools are especially low-performing, because it would not be hard for private schools to do better.[49] The relative advantage of Catholic schools for urban residents that was found in some studies (discussed below) is consistent with this possibility.

- *Better matching of student's needs to school's program:* Voucher and charter schools may be better for students with particular needs, even if not for all students. That is, any advantage for voucher students may result not from a general productivity advantage for autonomous schools, but from a coupling of parents' accurate identification of the particular needs of their children

---

[46]Cecelia Rouse believes that, in Milwaukee, the positive effect of vouchers may have been explained by smaller classes (Rouse, 2000). In Charlotte, Jay Greene concluded that even though class size was smaller in the voucher schools, it did not explain the advantage for voucher students (Greene, 2000b). The issue has not been directly explored in Cleveland, Dayton, Washington DC, and New York.

[47]See Choy, 1997; RPP International, 2000, p. 20.

[48]See Bickel and Howley, 2000; Walberg and Walberg, 1994; Stevens and Peltier, 1994; Guthrie, 1979; Fowler, 1995; Mik and Flynn, 1996. On the equity effect, see especially Bickel and Howley, 2000.

[49]Goldhaber, 1999. See also Neal, 1997, which finds that Catholic schools perform better than many urban public schools but only comparably to many suburban public schools.

with the opportunity to choose a school appropriate for their children.

- *Focus, mission, and values:* A variety of scholars have attributed effectiveness to the institutional focus on a basic educational mission and set of values that is characteristic of some private schools—most notably, the Catholic schools that have enrolled a substantial proportion of voucher students in many cities.[50]

- *Higher academic expectations:* One consequence of a stronger focus on educational mission and values may be higher academic expectations for students. In general, Catholic schools are less likely than public schools to stratify students in academic tracks differentiated by perceived student ability.[51] African-American students (as well as other minority students and low-income students) in public schools are disproportionately likely to be placed in low-achieving tracks.[52] The apparent voucher advantage for African-American students may therefore result from uniformly higher academic expectations in voucher schools.

All of these explanations are possible, separately or in combination. (It should be noted, moreover, that only a few of them apply exclusively to African-American students.) Different explanations lead to different predictions about the results that might be produced by larger-scale programs. Existing schools have a limited capacity to absorb new students while maintaining the characteristics that made them effective in the voucher experiments. A larger program may create a number of tensions not evident in the experiments. For example:

- Any positive peer effects from the experimental programs may disappear when scale is increased. A voucher program that fills schools with large numbers of low-income, low-scoring students

---

[50]See, e.g., Hill, Foster, and Gendler, 1990; Hill, Pierce, and Guthrie, 1997; Coleman, Hoffer, and Kilgore, 1982; Coleman and Hoffer, 1987; Chubb and Moe, 1990; Bryk and Driscoll, 1988.

[51]Bryk, Lee, and Holland, 1993; Coleman, Hoffer, and Kilgore, 1982; Coleman and Hoffer, 1987.

[52]Oakes, 1985, 1990; Gamoran, 1987; Braddock and Dawkins, 1993.

may not produce the same benefits as an experimental program that puts a few disadvantaged students into schools with more-advantaged classmates.

- Voucher schools may feel pressure to increase the size of their classes and school enrollments. (However, since smaller classes are one reason parents choose voucher schools,[53] there may be a strong incentive to keep class size from rising even if total demand increases.)

- Benefits may be minimal (or even negative) for voucher schools in communities that already have effective public schools.

- Institutional focus on a mission might be maintained under large-scale voucher programs, but how enrollment pressure will affect school character is unknown. Moreover, a unified focus may derive in part from a deep value commitment by parents, and families who are fully subsidized may be less committed to a school than families who are paying only part of the tuition (as in the experiments).

- Large-scale voucher programs, like charter programs, will rely to some extent on new startup schools. Existing private schools would almost surely be unable to meet the vast new demand for spaces, and newly created voucher schools—perhaps supplied largely by the for-profit sector—might not be as effective as some existing (Catholic, for example) schools.

- The uniformly high expectations that seem to characterize many Catholic schools might be challenged by a large influx of students whose socioeconomic status is low. Egalitarian ideals might be undermined by the challenge of educating a newly heterogeneous student population. Voucher schools might be tempted to lower their expectations or to adopt the kinds of tracking systems often used in conventional public schools.

In sum, then, evidence on the academic achievement of students in existing, small-scale voucher programs can be characterized as promising for low-income African-Americans; showing neither harms nor benefits for other students (with a very small amount of

---

[53]See RPP International, 2000, p. 24; Myers et al., 2000, Table 3.

data); and limited in its scope and breadth of applicability. And even if the results of the voucher experiments are read in their most favorable light, it will be very difficult to use them to predict the academic effects of a large-scale voucher program.

Evidence from Charter Schools

Charter laws have been established in more than 35 states, new schools have been opening at a rapid pace, and total charter enrollments have now reached half a million students. Despite this rapid growth, however, very few systematic evaluations of student achievement in charter schools have been conducted. This scarcity stems partly from the fact that the movement is new and partly from the movement's being geographically and temporally diffuse. Whereas most of the voucher programs (both privately and publicly funded) are in specific cities and began operating in multiple (existing) schools simultaneously, charter schools are spread across states and the nation and have begun operating at different points in time following the passage of enabling legislation. Moreover, we are aware of no one who has attempted to conduct a controlled experiment to measure charter-school outcomes.[54] As a result, the research literature on the achievement effects of charter schools is sparse.

Nevertheless, systematic evaluations of the academic effects of charter schools are growing in number as rapidly as the charter schools themselves. In terms of methodology, some of the strongest studies of charter-school achievement are statewide assessments that have been conducted in Michigan, Arizona, and Texas—three of the states with the largest number of charter schools.

New charters in Michigan. The first of these studies was in Michigan, where Eric Bettinger (then at MIT, now at Case Western) used a statewide data set of achievement test scores to analyze the effec-

---

[54]Such an experiment might be possible, at least for some charter schools. Some states require overenrolled charter schools to admit students by lottery. If data could be collected on lottery winners and losers, an experimental or quasi-experimental evaluation might be possible.

tiveness of charter schools.[55] Michigan has one of the most permissive charter laws in the United States, and by 1999—five years after the state's first charter school opened—already had 170 charter schools operating. This rapid growth made it possible to find a substantial cohort of charter schools opening at the same time. Bettinger examined scores on Michigan's statewide standardized test for charter schools that opened in 1996–97 (there were over 30), comparing them to conventional public schools nearby. He examined school performance longitudinally, controlling for demographic characteristics of school populations. Unfortunately, the data available to Bettinger consisted of school-level averages, which do not permit as precise an analysis as student-level data do.

In Michigan, students are tested in grades 4 and 7. Schools can be compared based on the proportion of students scoring at "satisfactory" and "low" levels on math and reading subject tests. When the new charter schools opened in the fall of 1996, baseline test scores demonstrated that they were enrolling, on average, lower-scoring students than those enrolled in typical public schools. A simple comparison of changes in school test scores a year and a half later, however, seemed to suggest that charter schools were doing better than public schools in terms of improvement—that is, in moving kids from "low" to "satisfactory" scores. Controlling for demographics and baseline test scores, Bettinger compared changes in charter-school achievement to changes in the achievement of public schools in the same communities. For grade 7, he found no statistically significant differences between charter schools and comparable public schools; but for grade 4, he found that charter schools were lagging behind comparable public schools in moving students from "low" to "satisfactory" in both reading and math. Thus, even though most charter schools had improved their scores, the conventional public schools had improved equally as much in grade 7 and more in grade 4.[56]

---

[55]Bettinger, 1999.

[56]Bettinger, 1999.

It would be easy to overstate the importance of these findings.[57] Charter-school defenders might reasonably complain that the key caveat is implicit in the words "newly opened." As most charter-school operators would attest, the primary struggle in the opening months of operation is survival. Judging the long-term effectiveness of the charter-school movement based on outcomes of infant schools in their first two years of operation may be unfair, or at least premature. Nevertheless, Bettinger's findings suggest that a school-choice program that relies on new startup schools may not produce stellar academic results, at least in the short term.

Charters in Texas. A more recent study of charter schools, this one conducted in Texas by Timothy Gronberg and Dennis Jansen of Texas A&M University, had data available to it on changes in the test scores of individual students, permitting a more finely tuned analysis than was possible for Bettinger.[58] Gronberg and Jansen examined scores on the Texas Assessment of Academic Skills (TAAS) between 1997, when the state's first charter schools opened, and 2000. Using an "individual fixed-effects" analysis that controls not only for students' prior test scores, but also for school-level demographic characteristics,[59] they separately analyzed results for charters serving predominantly "at-risk" students and for all other charters.[60] This analysis found that at-risk charters provided slightly more "added value" than did conventional public schools in terms of student achievement—i.e., a difference of three-quarters of a point on the Texas Learning Index (TLI), for which the average score statewide is about 80 points. However, conventional public schools slightly out-performed non-at-risk charters, producing an "added value" of

---

[57]A more recent study of Michigan's charter schools using data updated to 1999–2000 and a larger set of charter schools reached similar conclusions, but its methodology does not permit clear quantification of aggregate results (Horn and Miron, 2000).

[58]Gronberg and Jansen, 2001.

[59]The adjustment for the school's demographic characteristics may help to separate a peer effect from a school-productivity effect.

[60]The authors conducted separate analyses for "at-risk charters" and other charters because the Texas charter law establishes a distinction and makes it easier to establish a charter school focusing on at-risk students. The law provides a number of reasons that a student can be counted as at-risk; they relate to course failure, low scores on the TAAS, and unusual personal circumstances (e.g., pregnancy). (Gronberg and Jansen, 2001, pp. 10–11.)

about a point and a half by comparison.[61] In short, Texas charter schools showed mixed achievement results in their first three years of operation.

Additional analyses conducted by Gronberg and Jansen suggest that the newness of the charter schools was important—which is relevant to Bettinger's Michigan results, as well as to the Texas results. First, Gronberg and Jansen found that continuing charters—those in their second and third year of operation—produced better academic outcomes than did new charters—those in their first year of operation.[62] Since a substantial proportion of the data used in the overall analysis described above came from new charters, it is possible that results will improve over time as charter schools mature. Second, Gronberg and Jansen found that charter students' academic achievement was lowest during their first year in charters and improved in subsequent years.[63] This finding is consistent with well-known research indicating that student mobility across schools has a negative effect on academic achievement.[64]

The individual fixed-effects analysis conducted by Gronberg and Jansen to assess the value-added of Texas charter schools factors out student mobility but does not account for the newness of charter schools. Together, Gronberg and Jansen's findings suggest that states may see improvements in academic outcomes in charter schools as schools mature and as students spend more time in them.

Charters in Arizona. A recent study of achievement in Arizona charter schools used student-level test scores longitudinally linked over three years.[65] Lewis Solmon (an economist at the Milken Family Foundation; formerly dean of the UCLA School of Education), Kern Paark (of Arizona State University), and David Garcia (of the Arizona Department of Education) used methods similar to those of Gronberg and Jansen in Texas, but their results are more consistently

---

[61]Gronberg and Jansen, 2001, pp. 42–43. The authors do not report how these results translate into fractions of a standard deviation, but the differences (in both directions) appear to be statistically significant.

[62]Gronberg and Jansen, 2001, pp. 40–41.

[63]Gronberg and Jansen, 2001, pp. 40–41.

[64]See Pribesh and Downey, 1999; Swanson and Schneider, 1999.

[65]Solmon, Paark, and Garcia, 2001.

favorable to charter schools. Solmon's team found that, compared with students remaining in conventional public schools, students spending two to three years in charter schools could expect gains in their Stanford Achievement Test reading scores. In math, students spending two to three years in charter schools did at least as well as, and perhaps better than, students in conventional public schools (depending on model specifications). The reading advantage for three-year charter students was not large (about one-tenth of a standard deviation) but was statistically significant. As in Texas, a student's first year in a charter school typically had a negative effect on test scores—apparently the cost of changing schools. Nevertheless, over time "the positive effect of charter schools outweighed the negative effect of moving."[66]

Summary and implications. In sum, evidence on the academic effectiveness of charter schools is mixed. A Michigan study found charters to be less effective in grade 7 and holding their own in grade 4 compared with conventional public schools; a Texas study found at-risk charters to be slightly more effective and other charters to be slightly less effective than conventional public schools; and an Arizona study found charters to be slightly more effective in reading and at least holding their own in math compared with conventional public schools. These different results may stem from the examinations taking place at different stages in the schools' development. When examined closely, the findings of the three studies suggest reason for cautious optimism.

As noted above, the Texas study demonstrates that newly opened charters are less effective than older charters. This finding seems likely to hold true for charter schools everywhere and may explain the unimpressive results of the Michigan study, which limited its examination to charter schools in their first two years of operation. The finding may also explain why the Arizona results are more favorable than those in Texas. Arizona's charter law was passed in 1994, two years earlier than the one in Texas. The Arizona study therefore examined a state with a more mature charter sector. If charter-school maturity predicts effectiveness, then policymakers in many states

---

[66]Solmon, Paark, and Garcia, 2001, p. 20.

may need to wait a few years if they are to get an accurate, long-term picture of how charter schools will affect student achievement.

It should also be noted that Arizona is one of the few states that permit existing private schools to convert to charter status. To the extent that experience is relevant to effectiveness, states that permit conversions may see better results than states that rely largely on new startups to build a charter sector. Future studies could make a useful contribution to the research base by comparing the effectiveness of charter schools converted from public schools, charter schools converted from private schools, and charter schools that are new startups.

More generally, as Chapter Two demonstrates, charter laws vary from state to state on a wide variety of policy-design dimensions. Additional studies of charter-school performance in other states are necessary to determine whether the Arizona result is generalizable to charter schools across the country. If other states continue to see results like those in Michigan and Texas, it will be critical to determine the characteristics of charter laws that lead to better academic achievement.

Except for the valuable information from the Texas study on the importance of experience, these charter-school evaluations, like the voucher evaluations, have been black boxes, making no attempt to explain the reasons for any measured effect on student achievement. Getting inside the black box is especially important, because charter schools (like private schools) are by their nature diverse. Some are undoubtedly more effective than others, and the next step of analysis might seek to identify the characteristics of especially effective charter schools. If the Arizona result is correct, however, a sectorwide explanation for the average advantage of charter schools is also needed. Some of the possibilities mirror those that may explain the experimental voucher results:

- On average, charter-school classes are slightly smaller than conventional public-school classes, and school enrollments are substantially smaller.[67]

---

[67]RPP International, 2000, p. 24.

- Given their small size, it seems unlikely that most charter schools engage in much academic tracking (though this has not been confirmed systematically).

- Charter schools are popular in some communities where the public schools seem to be performing especially poorly.[68]

- New charter-school options give more parents the opportunity to match their children's needs to a school's program.

- Most operators of charter schools aim to create an institutional focus on a specific educational mission.[69]

The Arizona study provides no evidence to suggest that the favorable results were produced by a peer effect; on average, Arizona charter students have slightly lower levels of academic achievement than do students in conventional public schools.[70] Interestingly, the Texas study suggests that charters serving at-risk students can be effective despite the absence of high-achieving peers.

Finally, it should be noted that, despite some promising evidence on achievement scores, there is as yet no evidence on the long-term academic effects of charter schools. In this respect, voucher programs have the advantage of including existing private schools with a track record, including Catholic schools, which may have unique advantages in promoting the academic attainment of African-American children. In future studies, researchers should seek evidence about long-term attainment outcomes in charter schools. In particular, it is not yet known whether newly created nonreligious charter schools can succeed in becoming "focus schools" that are effective not only at raising test scores, but also at promoting long-term academic outcomes such as high school graduation and college attendance.

---

[68]Washington DC may be the most prominent case, with 10 percent of its students enrolled in charter schools.

[69]See Finn, Manno, and Vanourek, 2000; Hassel, 1999.

[70]Solmon, Paark, and Garcia, 2001, Table 8.

Evidence from School Choice in Other Contexts

A variety of studies have attempted to examine the achievement effects of school choice in contexts outside the voucher and charter programs that are the focus of this book. Public-school choice programs have increased in a variety of guises in the United States, and the international scene provides a wide array of school-choice policies that include both public and private schools. These kinds of evidence are less directly relevant to our inquiry than are the evaluations of existing U.S. voucher and charter programs given the differences in policies or institutional context. On the American scene, previous public-school choice policies (whether interdistrict choice, magnet schools, or alternative schools) did not involve the participation of autonomous schools operating outside traditional district governance. Some other countries have school-choice policies that more closely resemble vouchers or charters, but the institutional and historical context is usually quite different, and the "public" and "private" sectors are often not directly comparable to those in the United States. Despite these differences, international and U.S. experiences with school choice may provide two kinds of evidence that are sparse or absent in existing voucher and charter evaluations: evidence about long-term effects and evidence about the effects of choice being implemented on a large scale.

In fact, the literature on school choice in other contexts provides a few suggestive pieces of evidence but no findings sufficiently consistent to provide clear guidance about the effects of vouchers and charters in the long term or on a large scale. Here we describe findings from a number of these contexts:

- Despite extensive experience with public magnet schools in many communities across America over the last three decades, researchers have been unable to reach a consensus on clear findings on the academic effectiveness of these schools. The problem of selection bias is at least as much of a methodological morass in the case of magnet schools as it is in nonexperimental evaluations of voucher and charter schools, because magnets often impose academic standards in their admissions processes.[71]

- The public-school choice program enacted in Alum Rock, California, in the early 1970s—commonly, if questionably, described as a voucher program—produced no conclusive results on academic achievement (the inconclusive findings resulted in part from data limitations and changes in program implementation).[72]

- A number of school districts that have adopted choice plans internally (e.g., Cambridge, Massachusetts; Montclair, New Jersey; New York City's District 4 in East Harlem) have seen test scores improve.[73] Unfortunately, it is very difficult to demonstrate whether these single-district improvements are caused by the choice plans or by other factors, such as an influx of additional resources, changes in student demographics, or the operation of inspired leadership. We have seen no studies that can definitively demonstrate a causal link to the school-choice policies in these districts.[74]

- Although many nations in Western Europe and elsewhere outside the United States subsidize private schooling through a variety of mechanisms, few of the studies of these programs have adequately dealt with the selection bias problem.[75]

---

[71]For summaries, see Goldhaber, 1999; Orfield, 1990. A 1996 article using a national database found some positive effects for magnet schools, but the instrumental variables used in the analysis were probably flawed and may have biased results upward (Gamoran, 1996). On the problems with the instrumental variables used, see McEwan, 2000a.

[72]See Capell, 1981; Levinson, 1976.

[73]See Schneider, Teske, and Marschall, 2000; Henig, 1994.

[74]Schneider, Teske, and Marschall make a valiant effort to factor out some of the nonchoice factors in analyzing performance in District 4 (Schneider, Teske, and Marschall, 2000). We do not believe, however, that the demographic variables they use are sufficient to control for possible changes in the unobserved characteristics of the students. In particular, the substantial number of students attracted to District 4 from other parts of New York City are likely to come from families who value education highly.

[75]We are indebted to Patrick McEwan for providing an exhaustive analysis of the international literature on school choice (private correspondence, July 3, 2000). Studies include West and Pennell, 1997; Glenn, 1989; Ambler, 1994; Fiske and Ladd, 2000; Angus, 2000; Bashir, 1997; Calderon, 1996; Cox and Jimenez, 1991; Daun, 2000;

- We know of three studies of school choice outside the United States that address academic achievement and seem to make effective adjustments for selection bias:

  — The first of these is in Chile. For the last 20 years, Chile has had a voucher program that is strongly based on Milton Friedman's market-oriented proposal. A recent study by Patrick McEwan and Martin Carnoy, which controlled for student background characteristics, unobserved differences, and school socioeconomic status, found that test scores were slightly higher in Chile's Catholic schools than in its public schools. In nonreligious private schools (most of which are for-profit institutions that came into existence with the establishment of the voucher program), however, achievement was no better than in public schools and perhaps slightly worse.[76]

  — The second study comes from Indonesia. Indonesia has no voucher program per se, but many private schools receive government subsidies. The study examined the long-term effects of private schooling, adjusting for background characteristics and unobserved differences, and found that graduates of nonreligious private schools had significantly higher earnings than graduates of public schools.[77]

  — The third study comes from Colombia. This most recent addition to the international literature looked at a program that provided vouchers to 125,000 children from low-income neighborhoods. Many of the vouchers were awarded by lottery, giving the researchers the opportunity to use an experimental methodology. After three years, lottery winners

---

Edwards, Fitz, and Whitty, 1989; Fuller and Clarke, 1994; Gauri, 1998; Glewwe and Patrinos, 1999; James, 1984; Jiminez, Lockheed, and Wattanawaha, 1988; Jiminez et al., 1991; Jiminez and Sawada, 1999; Kim, Alderman, and Orazem, 1999; King, Orazem, and Wohlgemuth, 1999; Kingdon, 1996; Knight and Sabot, 1990; Lassabille, Tan, and Sumra, 2000; Louis and Van Velzen, 1991; Miron, 1993, 1996; Mizala and Romoaguera, 2000; Psacharopoulos, 1987; Riddell, 1993; Toma, 1996; Vandenberghe, 1998; Walford, 2000; Walford, in press; Williams and Carpenter, 1991; Wylie, 1998.

[76]McEwan, 2000b.

[77]Bedi and Garg, 2000.

were less likely to have repeated a grade, and their test scores were 0.2 standard deviations higher than those of lottery losers.[78]

In sum, the evidence on public-school choice policies in the United States is equivocal, and the best international evidence—limited as it is—is somewhat favorable to choice schools, except in Chile, where the results are mixed. We think that, ultimately, these evaluations have only tangential relevance for debates over vouchers and charters, because institutional contexts are so varied, especially in the case of international studies. In Chile, for example, Catholic schools outspend public schools to produce their superior outcomes;[79] in the United States, by contrast, Catholic schools typically spend substantially less than public schools do. Similarly, the institutional characteristics of public and private schools in Indonesia and Colombia are likely to be quite different from those in the United States. Meanwhile, American studies of other forms of school choice do not produce consistent results and are likely to be influenced by variations in policy details and local context.

Literature on Public and Private Schools

In addition to the literature on subsidized school choice in other contexts, there is extensive research literature comparing the effectiveness of public and private schools in the United States. The literature comparing test-score results in public and private schools remains hotly contested. After a number of early studies based on national data sets had found an advantage for private schools in general and Catholic schools in particular, more-recent studies, typically employing more-sophisticated statistical tools, found mixed

---

[78]Angrist et al., 2001. Because this study compared lottery winners with lottery losers, the effects described are those of a voucher offer, rather than voucher use. The effects of actually using a voucher to attend private school for three years would be larger, because not all lottery winners used their vouchers (like the private voucher programs in the United States, the Colombia voucher program covered only part of tuition costs). The study's methodology does not rule out the possibility that the benefits may have resulted from a peer effect.

[79]McEwan, 2000b.

results.[80] We will not discuss these studies in depth, for two reasons: the findings remain controversial, and the voucher experiments provide more-direct evidence on specific voucher effects.

In one respect, the research literature on public and private schools provides evidence beyond what is available from the voucher experiments. The academic outcomes addressed by the experimental studies have thus far been limited to test scores, while some of the nonexperimental research literature has also compared the academic attainment—high school graduation and college attendance—resulting from public and private high schools. In contrast to the literature on achievement, the literature on attainment is relatively consistent: most studies find that Catholic high schools produce higher educational attainment and that the size of the effect is larger for minority students in urban areas. That is, most studies find that urban minority students are more likely to graduate from high school and attend college if they attend Catholic high schools.[81] One recent study, however, using a different set of instrumental control variables, found somewhat less-positive outcomes, suggesting that private high schools (religious and nonreligious) may increase the likelihood of attending a selective college and persistence in college, but not the likelihood of attending college generally or the likelihood of graduating from high school. This study is consistent with the others in suggesting that the positive effects are larger for urban African-American students.[82]

---

[80]Early studies that favored private schools included Coleman, Hoffer, and Kilgore, 1982; Coleman and Hoffer, 1987; Chubb and Moe, 1990. The more-recent studies that reached mixed conclusions include Goldhaber, 1996; Neal, 1997; Altonji, Elder, and Taber, 2000; Sander, 1996; Jepsen, 1999a; Toma, 1996. For a detailed review, see McEwan, 2000a.

[81]See the summaries of the literature in McEwan, 2000c, 2000a. Studies include Altonji, Elder, and Taber, 2000; Neal, 1997; Evans and Schwab, 1995.

[82]Figlio and Stone, 1999. Patrick McEwan argues persuasively that the Figlio and Stone study uses a more appropriate set of instrumental variables than the other studies do (McEwan, 2000c). Nevertheless, Figlio and Stone also use slightly different school categories (religious schools rather than Catholic schools) and do not separately examine effects for African-American students in all cases. Although this does not undermine the validity of their findings, a more direct comparison of variables is necessary to determine whether a direct conflict with other studies exists.

Final Thoughts on Achievement in Voucher and Charter Schools

What are policymakers to make of this array of evidence related to the academic effectiveness of voucher and charter schools? Strong evidence on the issue is still fairly limited, but new evidence is accumulating at a steady pace. In the near future, there should be more evaluations of achievement in charter schools and additional follow-up at the sites of the experimental voucher programs. Even now, evidence is accumulating that suggests that small-scale targeted voucher programs may help low-income urban African-American children: both nonexperimental studies of attainment in Catholic schools and experimental voucher studies of achievement point in this direction. The implications for larger-scale voucher programs, however, are far less clear. In the case of charter schools, the evidence on academic achievement is mixed but can be interpreted as promising for the future as the schools mature. Still, it is not yet known whether the favorable results in Arizona's charter schools will become the pattern nationally; nor is there any indication about long-term effects on academic attainment in charter schools.

Large-scale programs—whether voucher or charter—generate further uncertainties. The experimental voucher programs have been conducted on a very small scale, and charter programs, though usually larger, have yet to enroll even 10 percent of the school-age population in more than a handful of cities. Perhaps the greatest uncertainty associated with scale concerns the supply of school spaces. Under both voucher and charter laws, the entities with the largest incentives to fill the demand for new schools are for-profit companies (where they are permitted to participate). The participation of such companies in K–12 schooling is so new in the United States that there is as yet no systematic evidence on their effectiveness. In Chile, where for-profits filled much of the demand after a nationwide voucher program was created, evidence suggests that they have been no more effective than public schools and less effective than Catholic schools.[83] For-profits may, for example, have an unusually strong incentive to operate large schools with large classes. Edison Schools, America's largest for-profit operator of public schools, is attempting

---

[83]McEwan, 2000b.

to create autonomous, focused schools with high expectations for all students, but it is not yet clear whether Edison is succeeding in raising academic achievement.[84] Moreover, other for-profits may prefer schooling on the cheap to Edison's comprehensive, research-based design. We discuss issues related to the supply of voucher and charter schools in more depth in Chapter Four. More generally, Chapter Eight further examines how policy variations in voucher and charter programs may lead to different outcomes.

EFFECTS ON STUDENTS REMAINING IN ASSIGNED PUBLIC SCHOOLS

Having exhausted the available evidence on the academic effects on students who choose voucher and charter schools, we move on to the systemic academic effects of vouchers and charters on nonchoosing students. The question of systemic effects is at least as important as the question of direct effects, and it represents the heart of the political battle over vouchers and charters. Under most proposed choice plans (with the notable exceptions of those that would change how all schools operate, such as the Hill/Pierce/Guthrie universal-choice proposal), the majority of students are likely to remain in conventional public schools. In consequence, the sum total of effects on these students—whether positive or negative—may well outweigh the effects on students who actively choose voucher or charter schools.

Although the political dispute about systemic effects is clear, the empirical information needed to decide the debate is very difficult to find. One problem is that the debate involves at least four different possible mechanisms of influence. Supporters of choice argue that vouchers and charters will be good for the public schools because (1) market competition will induce improvement and (2) innovation will induce imitation. Opponents of choice argue that vouchers and charters will harm the public schools because (3) they will drain the

---

[84]A few studies have attempted to assess outcomes in Edison schools, but all published attempts have been limited by two difficulties: that of finding good data for all Edison schools across the country and that of choosing an appropriate comparison group (see, e.g., American Federation of Teachers, 1998; Nelson, 2000; Miron and Applegate, 2000). RAND is now undertaking a three-year evaluation of Edison Schools that is to be completed in 2003.

public schools of their best students, reducing the positive influence of high-achieving peers, and (4) they will permit the most-motivated parents to exit the public system, reducing parental pressure for improving the schools.[85] Separating the effects of multiple mechanisms of influence is not easy.

It might be possible to design an evaluation that assesses the net effect of all of the mechanisms. But the methodological challenges of measuring and understanding systemic effects on nonchoosers are great—even more daunting than challenge of dealing with the selection bias associated with interpreting direct effects on choosers. The experimental voucher studies, for example, have no way of determining whether vouchers are having positive or negative effects on local public schools. Nevertheless, a few creative efforts have attempted to assess the systemic effects of competition on conventional public schools.

Systemic Effects of Vouchers

Studies of the effectiveness of voucher schools for voucher students are proliferating rapidly, but evidence about the systemic effects of vouchers is scant. We have seen no systematic studies of the effects on public schools of the voucher programs in Milwaukee or Cleveland, despite the extensive number of reports on these two programs. Nor have systemic effects been a component of the experimental studies in New York, Washington DC, Dayton, or Charlotte. To be sure, the methodological challenges are even greater here than with respect to charter schools. The privately funded experimental programs are quite small and may not have any measurable effects on public schools.[86] The publicly funded programs in Cleveland and (especially) Milwaukee are larger, but the fact that they focus on

---

[85]Note that the extent of peer effects on student achievement is itself a topic that has generated substantial research literature that has not yet produced a definitive consensus (see, e.g., Argys, Rees, and Brewer, 1996; Jencks and Mayer, 1990; Gaviria and Raphael, 1997). This literature is summarized in McEwan, 2000c.

[86]The privately funded voucher program in Edgewood, Texas, is unusual because it makes vouchers available to nearly all students in the district. It is therefore far more likely to produce a systemic effect on the public schools. We hope Edgewood's evaluators will examine this issue.

single districts makes it difficult to assess whether any changes that occur are attributable to the voucher programs.

Systemic effects in Florida. The prospects for assessing systemic effects of vouchers may be better in Florida, because Florida's Opportunity Scholarship Program is specifically designed to provide an incentive to low-performing public schools to improve their students' academic achievement. In the first half of 2001, the possible systemic effects of this Florida voucher program were the hottest topic of debate among voucher researchers and interest groups.[87] The voucher policy is tied to the state's high-stakes testing program (known as the "A+ Accountability" system), which rates all public schools in the state on an A–F scale. The fact that the incentive focuses on a subset of schools creates a kind of quasi experiment (though without random assignment, to be sure): schools that have received an F in the past are given the voucher "treatment" if they receive a second F, while all other schools are not subject to this voucher "threat" (at least in the current year).

In the program's first year of operation (1999–2000), the statewide A–F assessment system was new, and only two public schools performed poorly enough so that their students became eligible for vouchers.[88] Most observers anticipated that the number of vouchers would grow dramatically in later years, however. Seventy-six other schools received their first F in 1999 and therefore would have triggered the voucher provision if they had earned another F in 2000. In fact, however, the low-performing public schools in Florida performed far better than anticipated on the state assessment in the spring of 2000: statewide, every one of the 78 schools that had earned an F in 1999 improved its grade in 2000, thereby avoiding the voucher threat.[89]

---

[87]In contrast, Florida's McKay Scholarships Program, which is for students with disabilities, has received little attention, even though it will soon be substantially larger, with 4,000 participating students expected in 2001–02 (Fine, 2001).

[88]Since this was the program's first year, the previous year's performance was considered for all schools. Two schools were assessed as having performed at a level equivalent to an F and thus were, in essence, receiving their second F in the program's first year.

[89]Greene, 2001. Results were similar a year later: in the the spring of 2001, not a single Florida public school earned an F (Fine, 2001).

Some voucher supporters immediately pronounced this improvement as evidence that the threat of vouchers had succeeded in inducing dramatic improvements in low-performing public schools across the state. The first scholar to systematically analyze the data on school choice in Florida was Jay Greene, a senior fellow at the Manhattan Institute and one of the researchers involved in several of the experimental voucher studies.[90] Greene compared 1999–2000 gains in the reading, math, and writing components of the Florida Comprehensive Assessment Test (FCAT)—performance on which is a major component of the A–F grading system—for schools that had earned a high F in 1999 and schools that had earned a low D in 1999. In reading, he found no statistically significant difference in gains the following year. In both math and writing, however, "F" schools improved substantially more than "D" schools, by margins that were statistically significant.[91] In Greene's view, this strongly suggests that public schools effectively responded to the voucher threat.

Already, three other studies have challenged Greene's analysis of the Florida program. The first two—by Gregory Camilli and Katrina Bulkley of Rutgers, and by Haggai Kupermintz of the University of Colorado—convincingly argue that Greene misunderstood the need to account for the effect of "regression to the mean," a statistical artifact that causes overestimation of the improvement of low-scoring schools.[92] The intuition behind the regression to the mean is that, on any scale, scores at the extreme ends are relatively unlikely; in consequence, subjects (schools) that score very low in one measurement are likely to score a bit higher in the next. In the Florida context, this means that "F" schools will, on average, show larger improvements than other schools. Even so, both studies suggest that "F" schools show a real, program-driven improvement in writing scores, and one of the two suggests a possible program-driven

---

[90]Greene, 2001.

[91]Greene, 2001, Table 3. The differences in math and writing were statistically significant at $p < .01$. Effect size was 0.30 standard deviations in math and 0.41 standard deviations in reading. These cannot be directly compared to effect sizes in the voucher experiments, however, because they are school-level effects (with school-level standard deviations) rather than student-level effects.

[92]Camilli and Bulkley, 2001; Kupermintz, 2001.

improvement in math as well.[93]   Assessing the findings of these two studies alongside Greene's original evidence, we conclude that Florida's A+ Accountability system induced modest short-run improvements in the scores of low-performing schools in writing and probably in math as well.

The more serious problem with Greene's analysis, however, is the assumption that the improvements in the test scores of the low-performing Florida schools can be attributed to vouchers per se, rather than to the high-stakes accountability system in which they are embedded. Vouchers represent only one (albeit very prominent) aspect of that accountability system; another important part is the grade itself, since a school that receives an F undoubtedly experiences considerable social and political pressure to improve, independent of the voucher threat. Because the grading system and the voucher threat were introduced in Florida as a package, there is no way to separate the impact of the grade from that of the voucher threat. The third paper responding to Greene, by Martin Carnoy of Stanford University, points to strong evidence that other high-stakes grading systems introduced by states—without using the threat of vouchers—have induced similar improvements in the test scores of low-performing public schools.[94]   The safest conclusion is that Florida's "F" schools improved their students' scores as a result of Florida's high-stakes accountability system, but that vouchers may or may not have contributed to that improvement.

---

[93]Neither of the two studies assesses the statistical significance of the residual (program-driven) outcomes for "F" schools in math or writing. Although both are highly critical of the Greene study, they suggest that the improvement in "F" schools in writing may be genuinely driven by the state's program. Moreover, neither study spends much time directly addressing Greene's "high F" vs. "low D" analysis. Both studies instead focus their criticism on a preliminary part of Greene's analysis that compares gains in "F" schools to gains in all other schools. They correctly point out that this preliminary analysis overestimates program effects by ignoring regression to the mean. But the same criticism may not apply to the "high F" vs. "low D" analysis. If the prior (1999) scores of "high F" schools are very similar to those of "low D" schools, then Greene's analysis is not biased by regression to the mean, because the two groups have similar starting points. Greene reports in a footnote that the average scores of "low D" and "high F" schools were similar in 1999; unfortunately, however, he does not provide the data, so it is difficult to assess the claim. (Greene, 2001, n. 16.)

[94]Carnoy, 2001.

The specific response of Florida's "F" schools—to focus on test skills—has more to do with the state's high-stakes accountability system than with vouchers per se. Nevertheless, the Florida story shows that public schools are capable of responding to external pressure. In addition, it shows that the specific nature of the response will follow directly from institutional incentives, perhaps with unintended consequences.

Even if the voucher threat contributed to the behavioral response of Florida's "F" schools—a possibility that must be considered speculative—it is important to recognize that the specific response may be contingent on the specific policy. Different voucher/charter policies might produce quite different competitive responses from the public schools. In Florida, "F" schools have a very clear incentive to raise test scores so that vouchers do not become available to their students.[95] In Milwaukee, by contrast, vouchers are available regardless of public-school performance, and the public schools must persuade parents of eligible students to stay. The strategies necessary to keep parents happy may be very different—in desirable or undesirable ways—from the strategies needed to raise test scores above a

---

[95]One concern about the Florida results relates to the specific methods by which "F" schools responded to the system and improved their students' test scores. A newspaper story in the *St. Petersburg Times* discussed the dramatic improvement in writing scores months before the Greene study was released, and looked into the changes in curriculum and instruction that produced the dramatic improvement (Hegarty, 2000). The reporter found that many schools had shifted their curricula to devote large amounts of time to practice in writing essays in exactly the format required by the FCAT writing exam. As the article declares, "Out of fear and necessity, Florida educators have figured out how the state's writing test works and are gearing instruction toward it—with constant writing and, in many cases, a shamelessly formulaic approach." Whether this approach yields a real improvement in writing skills or merely an improvement in test-taking skills is open to question. Similarly, a *New York Times* article found that, in the two Florida schools whose students had become eligible for vouchers, the curriculum had been narrowed dramatically to focus almost entirely on the fields included on the FCAT: math, reading, and writing. Those schools, like the other schools that received F grades in 1999, improved their performance on the FCAT substantially in 2000—enough to avoid another F grade. Despite this improvement, however, the principal of one of the schools said, "We're leaving out important parts of the education process. They're going to learn what's on a test. But are they going to learn to be able to cooperate with each other in the business world? Are they going to be creative thinkers?" (Principal Judith Ladner, as quoted in Wilgoren, 2000a.) Ironically, the *Times* found that the private (mostly Catholic) schools chosen by the students who used the vouchers apparently do not have narrow, test-focused curricula. For a more favorable view of the behavioral responses of Florida public schools threatened by vouchers, see Innerst, 2000.

minimum level. Unfortunately, no systematic studies of the competitive response of Milwaukee public schools are yet available.

Systemic effects in Chile. In Chile, Patrick McEwan and Martin Carnoy used a national longitudinal data set on student achievement to examine how the presence of competing voucher schools affects achievement in public schools.[96] Unlike the Florida studies, this one examined the effect of actual competition rather than the effect of threatened competition. Methodologically, this is difficult, because vouchers in Chile are available to anyone rather than being targeted to induce a response in a specifically defined group of low-performing public schools. Causation can run in both directions: the presence of voucher schools may cause nearby public schools to improve through competition, but the presence of low-performing public schools may induce voucher schools to enter the market. Disentangling these effects with a longitudinal research design, McEwan and Carnoy found that competition produced positive effects in the Santiago metropolitan area (of a magnitude of about 0.2 standard deviations in both math and Spanish achievement) but may have produced small negative effects (of about 0.05 standard deviations in math and Spanish) in the rest of the country (where three-fourths of the population resides). It is not clear why effects in Santiago differed from those elsewhere, but it is plausible that competition would work more effectively in an area of high population density.

Systemic Effects of Charter Schools

Eric Bettinger's study of academic achievement in Michigan charter schools also examined the effects of those charter schools on nearby public schools. He compared the performance of public schools located near charter schools with that of public schools not located near charter schools. He found, first of all, that charter schools in Michigan were not "skimming the cream"—i.e., drawing the best students from the public schools; in fact, charter-school students tended to be lower-performing than their public-school counterparts. He found no evidence, however, that nearby public schools benefited from the opening of charter schools nearby—public-

---

[96]McEwan and Carnoy, 1999.

school test scores showed "little or no effect" from the presence of neighboring charter schools.[97]

No other rigorous, quantitative studies of the effects of charter schools on conventional public schools are available to date. Two qualitative studies, however, cast doubt on the extent to which charter schools influence conventional public schools through competition or innovation. A recent study of five northeastern cities by Paul Teske and colleagues at SUNY Stony Brook found that "charter competition has not induced large changes in district-wide operations, despite the fact that a significant number of students have left district schools for charter schools."[98] The study suggests that district schools were insulated from competitive pressure by state and district policies as well as favorable demographic trends. Although charters were in fact taking away many of their students, the financial effects on the districts were muted. On the other hand, the study found some principals and superintendents who were more sensitive to the competitive threat of charter schools and were attempting to improve district schools in response.

Similarly, Amy Stuart Wells and her colleagues at UCLA, examining district responses to charter schools in California, found no mechanism for conventional public schools to learn from charters. Most district officials knew little about what was happening in charter schools and perceived little effect on district schools.[99] Indeed, often it appears that the general stance of public schools with regard to charters is to ignore them or deny their relevance to the conventional public schools.

Studies of Interdistrict and Public-Private Competition

Although the research literature that specifically examines the systemic effects of vouchers and charters is thin, there is a growing body of literature assessing more generally the effects of competition in

---

[97]Bettinger, 1999.

[98]Teske et al., 2000, p. 1.

[99]UCLA Charter School Study, 1998.

the K–12 education market.[100] As Patrick McEwan notes in a review paper, many of these studies employ a similar general strategy: they measure the level of competition using the proportion of students attending private schools in a locality, and they employ multiple regression to register the correlation between competition and outcomes, accounting for family background characteristics. As nonexperimental studies, they must deal with two potential sources of bias (noted by McEwan). First, communities are likely to have characteristics that influence both student outcomes and the number of private schools. If those characteristics are not adequately represented by observable factors such as socioeconomic status, then the competitive effects might be overstated, with the negative result that an effect appearing to be caused by competition might in fact be caused by some unobserved characteristic of the community. Second, the relationship between the quality of public schools and the number of private schools in a community surely flows in both directions. It is possible that competition improves public-school quality, but it is also likely that low public-school quality leads to the proliferation of private-school alternatives. A researcher who ignores this two-way relationship could easily underestimate any positive effects of competition on public schools.

Although most of the studies recognize these methodological hurdles, we agree with McEwan that the problems have not been fully resolved. The most prominent work that finds competition to have a positive effect on public-school quality is that of Carolyn Hoxby;[101] several others have also found positive effects.[102] In work more recent than these studies, however, Robert McMillan finds that the effect of private schools on public schools is zero at best and may be negative, because the reduction of parental pressure on public schools is as important as any positive effect of competition.[103] Regardless of whether the findings are positive, however, all of the

---

[100]For an excellent summary of this literature, see McEwan, 2000c. The literature includes, among others, McMillan, 1998; Arum, 1996; Hoxby, 1994a; Funkhouser and Colopy, 1994; Armor and Peiser, 1997; Dee, 1998.

[101]Hoxby, 1994a; see also Hoxby, 1994b, 1996.

[102]See, e.g., Arum, 1996; Dee, 1998.

[103]McMillan, 1998. Jepsen also generally finds no effect of private-school competition on public schools (Jepsen, 1999b).

studies have had difficulty identifying appropriate instrumental variables that can account for unobserved differences among communities.[104] In sum, this literature is highly disputed and has not yet produced definitive results.

WHAT IS NOT YET KNOWN ABOUT ACADEMIC OUTCOMES

Despite the proliferation of studies in recent years, there are significant gaps in what is known about the effects of vouchers and charter schools on academic achievement and attainment. First of all, academic outcomes have been narrowly defined, focusing on test scores. Future studies should include measures that reflect the richer set of academic outcomes that schools are expected to produce. At the very least, researchers should examine academic attainment (including continuation in school, graduation, and college attendance) in voucher and charter schools. More evidence on academic attainment measures will become available as the programs develop longer histories. Existing voucher and charter programs in the United States are all relatively new, and as yet all findings are but short-term results. It is regrettable that data are no longer being collected in Milwaukee, which has the nation's longest-running voucher program, now in operation for ten years. Intensive data collection in Milwaukee might quickly provide longer-term results on a wide variety of academic outcomes, particularly if the Wisconsin legislature amends the law to require testing of voucher students (as was required until 1995). Examination of a broader measure of academic outcomes is particularly important in places such as Florida, where narrowly defined test-score improvements are the specific target of the threat to impose vouchers.

Second, the best available evidence about the achievement effects of vouchers comes from black-box experimental studies, which do not explain why an achievement effect might occur. To predict whether the findings of the voucher experiments are generalizable, the mechanisms for the effects must be understood. More-extensive studies of the actual school and classroom conditions of voucher and control students would be extremely valuable.

---

[104]On this issue, see McEwan, 2000c.

A third weakness of the existing evidence is that academic outcomes in charter schools have received systematic attention only in a few states. To be sure, most charter schools are very new and just beginning to develop a record of achievement. Nevertheless, the nation has enough experience to support a substantial number of rigorous evaluations of charter-school achievement. Charter schools enroll far more students than voucher programs do, so they should merit at least as much assessment.

A final gap in the empirical record should be evident from the relative balance of the two major sections of this chapter: most studies have focused only on students in the choice schools, ignoring systemic effects (negative or positive) on students who remain in assigned public schools. The greatest uncertainties about the academic effects of vouchers and charters concern these systemic effects on nonchoosers. Overall, we can only conclude that the potential systemic effects of vouchers and charter schools are unclear. Given that, in terms of sheer magnitude, the effects on nonchoosers may dwarf those on students in the voucher/charter schools because most students are likely to remain in conventional public schools, it is critical that researchers find additional information to identify positive or negative systemic effects.

Chapter Four

CHOICE

One of the key characteristics that voucher and charter schools share is that they are schools of choice. Advocates of voucher and charter schools promote the model of family choice partly for instrumental reasons: they believe that the market incentives associated with a system of choice will produce more-effective schools and better academic outcomes for children. We address the available empirical evidence on this argument in Chapter Three. For many of the supporters of vouchers and charters, however, choice is a valued outcome in its own right. For a wide variety of reasons, parents may value the opportunity to take a more active role in directing their children's education. Indeed, the choice of a child's school is viewed by some as a basic parental liberty. Voucher and charter programs are intended to broaden the range of parental liberty in schooling.

This chapter begins by summarizing the theoretical arguments based on parental liberty. As in the rest of the book, however, our focus is empirical, and most of the chapter is therefore devoted to empirical evidence. To be sure, empirical measurements of choice are not as easily identified as empirical measurements of academic achievement. Nevertheless, the scope and significance of new choices created by vouchers and charters are subject to empirical measurement. To assess liberty empirically, we first consider evidence on the demand for vouchers and charters, examining information on applications to voucher and charter schools. Evidence about demand provides some indication of the magnitude of the potential choice benefit of vouchers and charters. The magnitude of a potential benefit to parental liberty is limited, however, by the supply of voucher and charter schools available; we therefore follow the discussion of parental demand by examining empirical evidence on the supply of schools. Finally, we attempt to gauge the subjective value of choice, using evidence on the satisfaction levels of parents who have chosen voucher and charter schools for their children.

THEORETICAL ARGUMENTS

Liberty arguments have been more prominent in the movement for vouchers than in the movement for charter schools. Indeed, the argument for a voucher system for the financing of public education can be traced back at least a century and a half to John Stuart Mill's classic essay *On Liberty*; and before Mill, Adam Smith and Thomas Paine had proposed voucher-like mechanisms.[1] Mill strongly endorsed compulsory education—a new idea at the time—but argued that a system of government-operated schools "is a mere contrivance for molding people to be exactly like one another." Although Mill believed that the government should require and subsidize education, he argued (in sharp opposition to early common-school advocates such as Horace Mann) that "the importance of individuality of character, and diversity in opinions and modes of conduct" demanded a system of multiple private providers of schooling.[2] The economist Milton Friedman brought the idea into the American public policy arena a century later when he argued that a voucher system would not only improve the efficiency of schools, but would also increase parental liberty, noting that he assumed "freedom of the individual, or more realistically the family" to be society's "ultimate objective."[3]

Although the association with Friedman has often identified vouchers with conservative or libertarian politics, their potential to expand the scope of choice for low-income families has also appealed to some thinkers on the political left. In 1970, the sociologist Christopher Jencks and a number of colleagues produced a report for the federal Office of Economic Opportunity that proposed a

---

[1]On the contributions of Smith and Paine, see Coons and Sugarman, 1978, pp. 18–19.

[2]Mill, 1859/1978, pp. 104–105. Mill assumed that government subsidies would be necessary only for low-income families and that most families would pay for the education of their own children.

[3]Friedman, 1955.

regulated voucher program designed to improve educational outcomes for disadvantaged children and "to give parents, and particularly disadvantaged parents, more control over the kind of education their children get."[4] Other advocates (notably John Coons and Stephen Sugarman) have advanced the same theme more extensively, supporting vouchers and charter schools specifically in order to promote access to choice for low-income and minority parents. We describe these arguments and the empirical evidence about access to voucher and charter schools in Chapter Five.

Opponents of vouchers and charters do not deny that parental choice is a legitimate goal of an educational system. Instead, they argue that any liberty benefit resulting from vouchers and charters is outweighed by significant harms on other dimensions, including equitable access, integration, and civic socialization; we explore these claims in subsequent chapters.

DEMAND FOR CHOICE

In terms of family choice, the first question to ask about charters and vouchers is whether parents want them. If parents are not interested in choosing schools or are satisfied with existing choices, then the benefit of vouchers or charters for parental liberty is only theoretical. Here we set the stage by discussing the extent of choice in the system today. We then examine direct measures of demand for voucher and charter schools, as well as the characteristics of the parents who are most interested in additional choice.

Extent of Choice in the Current System

The extent of choice exercised by families in the existing educational system varies widely. Many middle- and upper-income families currently exercise choice in schooling either by paying private-school tuition or, more commonly, by choosing a residence that puts their

---

[4]Center for the Study of Public Policy, 1970, p. 8. See also Areen and Jencks, 1971. The germ of the proposal can be found in a 1966 journal article by Jencks, in which he also suggests a contracting alternative that is a precursor to the charter school idea (Jencks, 1966).

children in a desired public school. Using national enrollment statistics and polling data, Jeffrey Henig and Stephen Sugarman estimate that, although only 10 percent of K–12 students in the United States are enrolled in private schools (and 2 percent more are home-schooled), the families of nearly three out of five American schoolchildren have exercised some kind of choice in selecting their schools (see Figure 4.1). Ten percent have exercised choice within their local school district through magnet programs, specialty schools, open-enrollment policies, or the use of false home addresses. About one percent are in charter schools, with another half of one percent participating in interdistrict choice programs. Henig and Sugarman tentatively estimate that the families of over a third of all schoolchildren have exercised school choice by deciding where to live.[5] For some families who already exercise choice, vouchers and charters may be perceived as unnecessary.

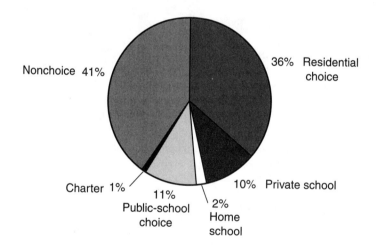

Figure 4.1—Choice in the Present System

---

[5]The estimate for residential selection is based on polling data from the 1993 National Household Education Survey, in which half of the parents of children assigned to a local public school (about 36 percent of all school-age children) said that school assignment influenced their residential decision. This figure and the others reported

Demand for Existing Voucher and Charter Programs

The demand for vouchers and charters can be estimated by examining the experience of existing programs and schools. The demand for existing voucher programs (both publicly and privately funded) that target low-income families is generally greater than the available supply of scholarships. In Cleveland's voucher program, over 6,000 students applied for 2,000 scholarships in the first year of operation, and demand far outpaced supply again in the second year.[6] In the early years of Milwaukee's publicly funded voucher program, applications exceeded the small number of available seats: 578 students applied for 406 seats in the first year, 1990–91; 1,046 students applied for 982 available seats in 1994–95.[7] Applications in the early years may have been limited by the program's exclusion of religious schools, which constituted the great majority of Milwaukee's private schools. When a privately funded scholarship program (Partners for Advancing Values in Education—PAVE) that included religious schools began operation in Milwaukee in 1993–94, it received over 4,000 applications—nearly double the program's available capacity—despite the fact that, unlike the publicly funded program, it required families to pay half of the applicable tuition.[8] In 1998–99, when the publicly funded program's restriction on sectarian schools was lifted, the program nearly quadrupled in size, growing in one year from 1,497 students to 5,758.[9]

---

in the paragraph can be found in Henig and Sugarman, 1999, Table 1-1, p. 29. Henig and Sugarman recognize that an estimate based on this kind of survey data is rough; their intention is not to provide a definitive number, but merely to point out that, in the aggregate, far more families exercise choice among public schools than private schools. The wide prevalence of residential school choice may help to explain why most respondents to the Phi Delta Kappa/Gallup poll gave much higher grades to the local public schools than to the public schools of the nation as a whole (see Rose and Gallup, 2000).

[6]Petro, 1998.

[7]Witte, 1998.

[8]Beales and Wahl, 1995.

[9]Wisconsin Legislative Audit Bureau, 2000. Today the program is operating at an estimated 88 percent of total capacity. Only 18 of 86 participating schools reported oversubscription, but this may understate true demand: application to the scholarship program typically is initiated at the school, and it is possible that schools near capacity may discourage applications.

Privately funded scholarship programs in other cities have generally received applications far in excess of their available spaces. New York's School Choice Scholarship Foundation received 20,000 applicants for 1,300 scholarships in its first year.[10] When the Washington Scholarship Fund offered 1,000 new scholarships to low-income students in 1998–99, it received over 7,500 applications.[11] Similarly, Dayton's program received 3,000 initial phone applications and 1,500 in-person follow-up applications for the award of 765 scholarships.[12] Edgewood, Texas, has one of the few voucher programs not oversubscribed: the Children's Educational Opportunity (CEO) Foundation offered scholarships to all 12,000 of Edgewood's low-income children, but only 837 children used them in the program's first year, 1998–99.[13] Meanwhile, even in the absence of voucher programs in most places, 40 percent of Catholic schools nationwide have waiting lists.[14]

Applications in many charter schools also exceed the supply of available spaces. In Massachusetts, demand for spaces in "Commonwealth" charter schools was twice as large as supply in 1995 and grew to five times as large as supply by 1999–2000.[15] In Michigan, 70 percent of charter schools have waiting lists, with an average length of nearly 200 students.[16] Similarly, a 1997 study found that 63 percent of surveyed charter schools in California had waiting lists.[17] In Arizona, by contrast, only 28 percent of a sample of charter schools had waiting lists in a recent survey.[18] But Arizona has the highest proportion of students in charter schools of any state,[19] which suggests that it may have managed to meet a larger proportion of the demand than other states have. A national survey of charter

---

[10]Peterson, 1998.

[11]Wolf, Howell and Peterson, 2000.

[12]Howell and Peterson, 2000.

[13]Peterson, Myers, and Howell, 1999.

[14]Egan, 2000.

[15]Pioneer Institute for Public Policy, 1999.

[16]Public Sector Consultants and MAXIMUS, 1999.

[17]SRI International, 1997.

[18]Mulholland, 1999.

[19]RPP International, 2000.

schools in 1998–99 found that Michigan and California were more representative of the national scene with seven of ten charter schools having waiting lists of applicants.[20]

In sum, vouchers and charters are both tapping a substantial demand for educational choice. The full extent of that demand may as yet be unclear, but the waiting lists for both voucher and charter schools suggest that, in most communities, it has not yet been met. The experiences of Edgewood (with widely available vouchers) and Arizona (with a large number of charter schools) suggest the possibility that total demand in most communities will amount to a relatively small share of the total student population.

The extent of the demand will depend in part on the characteristics of the supply. For some parents, for example, religion is a critical value in schooling; such parents may have little demand for nonsectarian charter schools. In addition, most parents like to send their children to schools close to home. Areas of high population density therefore present stronger potential markets for voucher and charter schools than do rural areas. (Indeed, the relatively low participation rates found in interdistrict choice plans surely result in part from the deterring effect of the need to travel to another school district.[21]) Programs that provide or subsidize transportation will achieve higher utilization than programs that do not. More generally, parents care about a variety of school characteristics, of which academic achievement is only one. In addition to caring about religion and convenience, parents may care about safety, athletics, arts programs, or the characteristics of the child's peer group. Different voucher and charter schools may choose to meet different parental demands. We address supply issues in more detail in the next section.

SUPPLY OF AUTONOMOUS SCHOOLS

The extent to which a voucher or charter program satisfies the demand for new choices, especially for families that now lack choice, depends to a great extent on the response of suppliers and prospec-

---

[20]RPP International, 2000. A large majority of surveyed charter schools in Colorado also reported waiting lists (Fitzgerald, 2000).

[21]See, e.g., Armor and Peiser, 1998; Tenbusch, 1993.

tive suppliers of autonomous schools. As Paul Hill points out, demand alone cannot guarantee equitable access to a wide range of high-quality schools. Moreover, problems of inequitable access (addressed in Chapter Five) may result in part from supply limitations: if options are limited, the available spaces may be taken by families with the most resources and best information.[22]

Proponents of vouchers and charters often devote little attention to how a large new supply of autonomous schools will be created.[23] It is very difficult to estimate how many new schools and new spaces will be created by a charter or voucher program. Most of the existing suppliers of autonomous schooling are not profit-seeking enterprises, and their response to additional public funding is not easy to predict. A number of key questions about the supply side must be asked. For example, how much will the Catholic school system— which today enrolls about half of all students in private schools—expand in response to vouchers? What is the size of the pool of educational entrepreneurs who are driven to establish charters? Will the profit-seeking sector largely fill the breach? If so, what kind of schools will they establish, and in what kinds of communities and neighborhoods? As should be clear, these questions are relevant not only to the total supply of spaces available in autonomous schools, but also to the qualitative characteristics of those schools.

Existing Empirical Evidence

America's current experience with voucher and charter programs provides some clues about supply response, but definitive answers are elusive. As noted in Chapter One, the charter-school sector has grown very rapidly in the last decade—a promising sign for advocates. Although the first charter school opened less than ten years ago, half a million students are now enrolled in over 2,000 charter schools across the country.[24] Moreover, the rate of growth remains rapid: the number of new charter schools opening in 2000–01 was larger than in any previous year, breaking the record set in 1999–

---

[22]Hill, 1999.

[23]One notable exception is Paul Hill, who has given considerable thought to the supply issue (see Hill, 1999).

[24]Wilgoren, 2000b.

2000.[25] Despite this rapid increase, however, it is not clear whether charter schools will ever enroll a large proportion of students in most communities. Nationally, charter schools enrolled about 1 percent of the total student population in 2000–01. In 1998–99, Arizona's charter schools enrolled a higher proportion of the public-school population than did charter schools in any other state, and still accounted for only 4 percent of the state's enrollment that year.[26] The charter schools of Washington DC have been especially successful in attracting students, and they now enroll over 10 percent of the city's public-school population.[27] As yet, it is not clear what level of charter-school operations will exhaust the pool of those with the desire and ability to open and operate new schools.

Milwaukee's voucher program provides perhaps the best evidence on the supply of voucher schools. Following its expansion to include parochial schools, the program grew rapidly, from only 1,500 students in 1997–98 to over 7,500 in 1999–2000—about 5 percent of the city's total student population.[28] Despite this increase, however, the 91 schools participating in the program reported that they had capacity for an additional 1,100 voucher students.[29]

A closer look at the private schools participating in the Milwaukee program in the 1998–99 school year shows that nearly a third had been founded since the program was inaugurated in 1990, including 22 percent founded since the state legislature decided to expand the program in 1995. The newer schools tend to focus specifically on voucher students: 60 percent of students in schools founded between 1990 and 1994 are voucher students, as are 79 percent of students in schools founded since 1995 (compared with 40 percent of students in schools that existed prior to 1990).[30] This suggests that the existence of the voucher program in Milwaukee has encouraged

---

[25]See Wilgoren, 2000b; RPP International, 2000.

[26]RPP International, 2000, p. 18.

[27]See Center for Education Reform, 2000a.

[28]See Wisconsin Legislative Audit Bureau, 2000, p. 11; Witte, 2000, p. 42.

[29]Wisconsin Legislative Audit Bureau, 2000.

[30]See Wisconsin Legislative Audit Bureau, 2000. Figures are from the 1998–99 academic year.

the creation of new schools, increasing the available supply of spaces.

In Cleveland, the program's first year saw the creation of two new schools designed to serve voucher students and the substantial expansion of at least two recently established schools.[31] Interestingly, the two Hope schools created for the program subsequently converted to charter status in order to take advantage of the larger funding offered to charter schools. In the third year of the program's operation, sufficient spaces were available to offer vouchers to approximately 3,700 students (equivalent to about 5 percent of the city's public-school enrollment) in over 50 schools.[32] A significant number of these students, however, had already been attending private schools.

Very little information is available about the schools attended by students using privately funded vouchers (in New York, Dayton, Washington DC, Charlotte, and elsewhere), but most of the programs are so small that they are unlikely to induce a substantial supply response.

Constraints on Supply

Despite considerable evidence of demand for both voucher and charter schools, they enroll only a very small share of students in most communities. This suggests that the supply of voucher and charter schools is limited. Supply limitations may result from both policy and market constraints.

Policy constraints. In many cases, voucher and charter policies restrain the supply of participating schools, intentionally or unintentionally, through a variety of mechanisms:

- *Charter caps*: Many states place limits on the total number of charter schools that may operate or on the number that may be authorized annually. Massachusetts, for example, permits only 50 charter schools; Connecticut permits only 24.

---

[31]Murphy, Nelson, and Rosenberg, 1997.

[32]Rees, 1999.

- *Limited operational funding*: Operating funds for voucher and charter schools vary widely. As Henry Levin points out, differences in the mix of services provided make it difficult to compare voucher and charter funding directly to per-pupil expenditures in conventional public schools.[33] Nevertheless, it is clear that funding is sometimes well short of costs. The privately funded voucher programs, for example, typically provide funding that is less than average tuition levels, which are themselves lower than true costs. Similarly, education tax subsidies usually produce very small benefit amounts. These kinds of programs are unlikely to induce substantial supply response. Even more-generous programs (such as most charter programs) produce subsidies that are less than average per-pupil expenditures. Although they may be sufficient to pay for relatively low-cost services (such as elementary education), they may not produce a supply of new providers of higher-cost services (such as secondary, vocational, and special education).[34]

- *Lack of startup and facilities funding*: Conventional public schools receive separate funding for facilities, in addition to funding for operational expenses. None of the existing voucher programs provide funding for facilities or for expenses associated with school startup. Charter laws vary, but many provide no startup or facility funding; those that do provide funding typically make available only modest amounts.[35]

- *Potentially burdensome regulations*: Some charter laws and chartering agencies impose regulations and accountability mechanisms that are as extensive as those required of conventional public schools, which may pose a daunting obstacle to

---

[33]Levin, 1998.

[34]For examples of subsidy levels in different voucher and charter programs, see Table 2.2 in Chapter Two. On the difficulties associated with inadequate funding of charter schools, see Hassel, 1999, ch. 5.

[35]Hill, 1999; see also Table 2.2 in Chapter Two. In the absence of substantial funding for facilities, Hill notes, the supply of charter schools may be "limited by the number of abandoned Catholic school buildings" (Hill, 1999, p. 155). See also Hassel, 1999, ch. 5.

educational mavericks who might like to start charter schools.[36] Similarly, some private schools may choose not to participate in voucher programs that impose regulations they dislike.

- *Chartering agencies with conflicts of interest:* In a number of states, local school districts have exclusive authority to issue charters. Many school districts have little desire to create new competition for themselves, particularly when the charter school will take resources that would otherwise go to the district.

- *Exclusion of existing private schools:* The single regulation likely to place the greatest constraint on supply is a prohibition on the participation of existing private schools. Starting a new school from scratch is substantially more difficult than bringing an existing school into a charter or voucher program.[37] Permitting private-school conversions but excluding religious schools (as do many charter laws) creates almost as much of a constraint on supply. Religious schools constitute the majority of existing private schools, and their importance to the supply of spaces available in a school-choice program can be seen in the dramatic expansion of the Milwaukee voucher program when the restriction was dropped.

Policymakers may have difficult tradeoffs to make in the design of voucher and charter programs: regulations intended to control the negative effects of the market, or to reduce costs, may have the unintended effect of reducing the supply of spaces in available autonomous schools. We explore these policy issues and tradeoffs in the concluding chapter.

Market constraints. Limits on the supply of voucher and charter schools are not only the result of policy constraints. Even a policy that actively seeks to encourage the growth of the supply of autonomous schools may encounter obstacles. First of all, as Paul Hill points out, most of the organizations that might operate new schools do not presently have the institutional capacity to start up large

---

[36]Hassel, 1999, ch. 4; Hill, 1999. Hassel notes that the charter law passed in Georgia was "so restrictive that charter schools had virtually no more autonomy than conventional public schools" (Hassel, 1999, p. 79).

[37]As Hassel points out, charter laws that exclude converted private schools "worsen the overall financial health of the charter-school sector" (Hassel, 1999, p. 125).

numbers of schools in a short period of time. If autonomous schools are to enroll a substantial proportion of all students, then the organizations that might operate the schools—whether they are churches, nonprofit community groups, educational design organizations such as Success For All, or profit-making companies—will have to make substantial investments in their institutional capacity to start and run schools.[38]

A second market uncertainty associated with the supply of autonomous schools derives from the fact that most existing private-school operators are not profit-seeking firms. In consequence, how they will respond to new market opportunities is unknown. Catholic schools, for example, typically receive substantial subsidies from the Catholic Church—tuition payments are not sufficient to cover the full cost of education.[39] If vouchers are sufficient to cover tuition but not the full cost of education, the Catholic Church and other nonprofits cannot be expected to open large numbers of new schools. Even in the absence of large-scale voucher programs today, many Catholic schools are not meeting demand: over 40 percent have waiting lists.[40] Generous vouchers that fund the full cost of education are more likely to create a substantial supply response, but organizations not motivated by profits may still not respond rapidly to market incentives. However, the fact that parochial and diocesan subsidies for Catholic schools are shrinking may put pressure on those schools to respond if vouchers are at a full-cost level of subsidy.[41]

While small-scale programs may be able to rely on existing private schools and other nonprofit startups, any program seeking to promote large numbers of autonomous schools (under vouchers or charters) will probably have to rely to a considerable extent on the for-profit sector. In Chile, which initiated a nationwide voucher program two decades ago, for-profit schools grew to become the largest segment of the voucher market.[42] For-profit firms that operate

---

[38]Hill, 1999.

[39]See Harris, 2000.

[40]Egan, 2000.

[41]See Harris, 2000.

[42]McEwan and Carnoy, 2000.

K–12 public schools are a new development in the United States, but they are proliferating in number and growing in size. Edison Schools, currently the largest for-profit operator of public schools, had about 57,000 students enrolled in over 100 schools around the country in the fall of 2000. This made Edison equivalent in size to the 60th largest school district in the United States, with approximately as many students as in the Atlanta public schools. Edison, however, is growing more rapidly than any comparably sized district—at a rate of nearly 50 percent per year. Nonprofit organizations are unlikely to match the rates of growth that profit-making firms can produce. Schools that exist under a large-scale market therefore may be quite different from the private-school sector today (or even the charter-school sector today). The character and effectiveness of for-profit schools, however, are as yet unknown.[43]

PARENTAL SATISFACTION IN AUTONOMOUS SCHOOLS

When parents have the opportunity to choose voucher or charter schools, are they happy with their choices? Measurements of parental satisfaction are useful for two reasons. First, they provide direct evidence about the subjective value of the choices created by vouchers and charters—how much choice really means to families. Second, they provide indirect evidence about a variety of school dimensions that are difficult to measure directly, such as discipline, safety, and opportunities for parental involvement. Here we examine general and specific measures of parental satisfaction in voucher and charter schools.

Parental Satisfaction in Voucher Schools

Most of the studies of both publicly and privately funded voucher programs have surveyed parents in an attempt to gauge their level of satisfaction with their children's new schools. Unlike the somewhat ambiguous findings on academic achievement, the findings on

---

[43]The long-term viability of for-profit EMOs is not yet clear. Edison, for example, has not yet made a profit. Edison hopes that, if it continues to grow rapidly, it will achieve profitability within a few years through economies of scale.

parental satisfaction in voucher programs have been strongly and uniformly positive.

The experimental evaluations of the privately funded voucher programs in Dayton, Washington DC, and New York compared the satisfaction of voucher parents with that of a control group. In Dayton, after one year of the program, 47 percent of parents whose children used vouchers gave their schools a grade of A, compared with only 8 percent of the control group. More specifically, voucher parents were far more satisfied than control parents on virtually every dimension of school quality, including academic program, teacher skills, safety, discipline, parental involvement, class size, school facility, moral values, and freedom to observe religious traditions.[44]

In Washington DC, parental satisfaction results after one year were very similar. Of parents using vouchers, 46 percent gave their children's schools an A, compared with 15 percent of the control group of parents who did not receive vouchers. Again, voucher parents had more favorable views of their children's schools on virtually every relevant dimension.[45]

Second-year results of New York's privately funded voucher program closely resemble the findings in Dayton and Washington DC. After two years, 38 percent of voucher parents deemed their children's schools worthy of A grades, compared to 9 percent of the control group.[46] Voucher parents were significantly more satisfied with their children's schools on all dimensions, from academic quality to discipline, safety, and sports programs.[47] The differences between voucher parents and the control group in the three cities remain large if A and B grades are aggregated.

---

[44]Howell and Peterson, 2000, Table 13b. All of these differences were statistically significant at .01.

[45]Wolf, Howell, and Peterson, 2000, Table 13. All of these differences were statistically significant at .01.

[46]Myers et al., 2000, Table 15.

[47]Myers et al., 2000, Table 15. Two studies of the publicly funded voucher program in Cleveland have found parental satisfaction results that resemble those in Dayton, Washington DC, and New York (Greene, Howell, and Peterson, 1997; Metcalf, 1999). We do not discuss these in detail because the control groups in both studies are problematic or not clearly defined. A third Cleveland study is discussed below.

It would be possible to overestimate the broader significance of the findings of the experimental studies. First of all, most of these are first-year findings, and first-year satisfaction may be influenced by a "Hawthorne effect," in which the result is driven by the mere fact of participation in an experiment. More specifically, parents may express higher levels of initial satisfaction merely as a result of having the opportunity to choose. If so, satisfaction of voucher parents would decline in subsequent years. New York is so far the only site where satisfaction data from the first two years can be compared. The proportion of voucher parents giving their children's schools A grades declined from 49 percent in the first year to 38 percent in the second year in New York. Nevertheless, the decline from first-year satisfaction levels is far less than the remaining advantage over the control group. Moreover, on the more specific dimensions of satisfaction, there were no significant changes for New York voucher parents from the first year to the second. In sum, these data suggest that, if a Hawthorne effect is operating, it does not explain most of the satisfaction advantage for voucher parents.

Second, in all three cities, both the treatment group and the control group consisted of parents who applied for vouchers—probably because they were dissatisfied with their children's existing public schools. Applicant parents whose children had to stay in the public schools were almost certainly more dissatisfied than typical public-school parents. The contrast between voucher users and those denied vouchers is therefore likely to be especially dramatic. In one sense, this comparison is entirely appropriate: it estimates the increase in satisfaction that vouchers may produce for a group of parents dissatisfied with their existing public-school options. Comparisons from the experimental studies should not, however, be viewed as general measures of parental satisfaction in public and private schools.[48]

---

[48]In Indianapolis, where one of the first privately funded voucher programs began operating in 1991, participating parents were asked to compare their children's new voucher schools with their previous public schools. The retrospective comparison by voucher parents is analytically similar to a comparison of accepted and rejected voucher applicants, though probably less reliable. Results were consistent with those found in the experimental studies. Parents reported being significantly happier with their new voucher schools than with their old public schools on a variety of dimensions, including overall performance, discipline, instruction, safety, parental input, and academic standards. (Weinschrott and Kilgore, 1998.)

Fortunately, several voucher studies have examined parental satisfaction using comparison groups other than rejected voucher applicants. The Dayton study compared the satisfaction level of voucher parents not only with that of rejected voucher applicants, but also with that of a general sample of public-school parents in Dayton. Although typical Dayton public-school parents were more satisfied than were public-school parents who had been denied vouchers, they were far less satisfied than parents who had used vouchers. Of the sample of public-school parents, 25 percent gave their schools A grades, compared to 47 percent of voucher parents. On every dimension compared—academic program, safety, parental involvement, and class size—the proportion of voucher parents who were "very satisfied" with their child's school was two to three times as high as the proportion of public-school parents who were "very satisfied."[49]

In Cleveland, two years after the initiation of the voucher program, voucher parents were significantly more likely than a sample of Cleveland public-school parents to be "very satisfied" with their school's academic program, discipline, parental involvement, moral values, and safety.[50] A multivariate analysis found that parents of voucher students in nearly all varieties of voucher schools had higher levels of satisfaction than did public-school parents. The highest levels of satisfaction were reported by parents of voucher students in Catholic schools and the newly created, nonsectarian Hope schools. Parents of voucher students in Lutheran and Muslim schools and in nonsectarian schools other than the Hope schools experienced somewhat lower levels of satisfaction, but the levels were still significantly higher than those of their public-school counterparts. Only the parents of students in other Christian (i.e., non-Catholic, non-Lutheran) schools reported satisfaction levels that were not significantly higher than those of public-school parents.[51]

In Milwaukee, a study of the publicly funded voucher program in its early years of operation (before it expanded to include parochial schools) compared satisfaction levels of voucher parents with those

---

[49]Howell and Peterson, 2000, Table 13a.

[50]Peterson, Howell, and Greene, 1999, Table 3c. All differences were significant at .05.

[51]Peterson, Howell, and Greene, 1999, Table 4.

of a sample of similarly low-income but public-school parents. In the program's third year, differences between voucher parents and public-school parents were less pronounced than those found in the experimental comparisons, but they favored the voucher program on every dimension measured. Thirty-five percent of voucher parents thought their children's schools earned an A, compared with 26 percent of the comparison group. Voucher parents were more satisfied than the comparison group with the school's program of instruction, the amount learned by their child, the performance of the child's teachers and principal, school discipline, and opportunities for their own involvement in school.[52]

In the early 1990s, a privately funded voucher program known as PAVE also operated in Milwaukee, offering smaller scholarships than the publicly funded program offered but permitting students to attend religiously affiliated schools. An evaluation of the PAVE program found parental satisfaction levels to be higher than those in both the Milwaukee public schools (low-income sample) and the publicly funded voucher program (which, at the time, excluded parochial schools). Fifty-six percent of the PAVE parents gave their children's schools A grades.[53] In 1998, the publicly funded voucher program in Milwaukee expanded to include parochial schools. Religious schools now dominate the program; they served 70 percent of voucher students in 1998–99.[54] Like many other outcomes, parental satisfaction in the Milwaukee program has not been directly measured since the program expanded to include parochial schools.

In Edgewood, Texas, where privately funded vouchers are available to all low-income children in the district, 39 percent of voucher parents give their schools A grades, compared with 28 percent of a sample of public-school parents. Voucher parents are more satisfied

---

[52]Witte, Bailey, and Thorn, 1993 (as reported in Beales and Wahl, 1995).

[53]Beales and Wahl, 1995.

[54]Wisconsin Legislative Audit Bureau, 2000. If the higher levels of satisfaction measured for PAVE parents are attributable to the religiously affiliated schools participating in the program, then the inclusion of such schools in the publicly funded program may have caused an additional increase in parental satisfaction in the last two years. Indeed, the largest part of the publicly funded program's growth in 1998–99 resulted from PAVE students switching to the more generously funded program. (Wisconsin Legislative Audit Bureau, 2000.)

than public-school parents on every one of 16 different dimensions surveyed, with the difference achieving statistical significance (.05) on 13 of the 16.[55]

Figure 4.2 summarizes the grades given to schools by parents in the six voucher programs discussed above and compares them with the

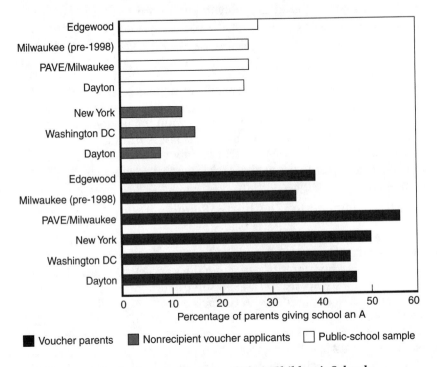

Figure 4.2—Parental Ratings of Their Children's Schools

---

[55]Peterson, Myers, and Howell, 1999, Table 1.16. Evaluating a privately funded voucher program in neighboring San Antonio, another study found that the proportion of voucher parents giving their schools A grades was only about equivalent to the proportion of a sample of public-school parents giving their schools A grades. Nevertheless, this represented a dramatic improvement in satisfaction for the voucher parents, who graded their children's previous public schools far more harshly. (Martinez, Godwin, and Kemerer, 1996.)

grades given to the public schools by the two groups: parents who applied to the voucher program but were denied, and a sample of local public-school parents. Regardless of which comparison group is used, it is clear that voucher schools have the advantage.

The story that unfolds when any one of five more-specific dimensions of parental satisfaction—academic quality/academic program, safety, discipline, parental involvement, and the teaching of moral values—is examined is similar to Figure 4.2's story. In each case, voucher parents rate their children's schools more highly than do comparison groups of parents in the local public schools. Caution is needed, however, in attributing objective differences to the differences in satisfaction levels on specific dimensions. It is possible that the favorable responses of voucher parents are somewhat inflated by psychological bolstering. Most parents want to feel good about their decisions and thus may view chosen schools through rose-colored glasses. Moreover, general satisfaction with a school may produce satisfaction on dimensions that lack objective advantages.

Parental Satisfaction in Charter Schools

Few studies of satisfaction levels of charter school parents are available as yet. The ones that do exist indicate that charter-school parents, like voucher parents, are generally happy with their children's schools. In Massachusetts, a 1998 survey compared the perceptions of charter-school parents with the perceptions of public-school parents in the communities where charter schools were operating. Charter-school parents were far more likely to give their children's schools A grades, by a margin of 60 percent to 37 percent. Sixty-seven percent of charter-school parents and 35 percent of public-school parents regarded the educational program of their child's school as "excellent." Sixty-eight percent of charter-school parents and 44 percent of public-school parents rated the teachers and staff of their child's school as "excellent."[56]

Polls of charter-school parents in Texas and Arizona lacked public-school comparison groups; they asked charter-school parents to compare their children's new charter schools with their previous

---

[56]Pioneer Institute, 1998.

schools. In Texas, 85 percent gave their children's schools A or B grades, and less then half of them viewed their previous schools as meriting a comparable grade.[57] In Arizona, 79 percent of charter-school parents reported that their children were doing better academically than they had been in their previous schools, including 55 percent who thought their children were doing "a lot better."[58] Short-run as they are, and without a public-school comparison group, these results are hardly definitive, but they do suggest that charter schools, like voucher schools, are desirable choices for some families.

In Michigan, two studies used the same questionnaire to survey charter-school parents in different parts of the state: one study examined charter schools in the urban and suburban areas in the state's southeastern section (including Detroit, Flint, and Ann Arbor), while the other examined the rest of the state (including Grand Rapids and rural areas).[59] Throughout the state, majorities of charter-school parents agreed that instructional quality was high, that school-to-family communication was good, and that their children's achievement was improving. Satisfaction with these dimensions was generally somewhat higher in southeastern Michigan charter schools than elsewhere. In those charter schools, but not in others, slight majorities of parents also agreed that support services (such as counseling and health care) were available to their children and that, as parents, they had influence over the school's "direction and activities." These studies did not survey public-school parents, but they did ask charter-school parents to compare their actual experience with their initial expectations for charter-school performance. In both parts of the state, some disappointment was evident. Initial expectations of charter-school parents in southeastern Michigan were 5 to 15 percent higher than actual experience on most dimensions. Charter schools in the rest of the state were having more difficulty meeting expectations; on most dimensions, the proportion of parents who had expected charter schools to meet

---

[57]Texas Education Agency, 2000.

[58]Mulholland, 1999.

[59]Results of the southeastern Michigan study can be found in Public Sector Consultants and MAXIMUS, 1999; results of the other study can be found in Horn and Miron, 1999.

a particular standard was 15 to 30 percent higher than the proportion who felt the standard was actually met. In Michigan, then, although most charter-school parents were generally happy, some were disappointed.

Unfortunately, we lack data to determine how many voucher parents are disappointed with their children's schools. It is possible that charter schools could engender more disappointment than voucher schools simply because they are so new. Voucher programs have largely made use of existing schools, whereas many charter schools are new startups. Starting a new school from scratch may produce challenges that lead to some parental disappointment. Charter-school parents should be surveyed again, several years after their schools begin operating, to determine whether levels of parental disappointment decline.

A Concluding Note on Parental Satisfaction

Despite evidence that some charter schools have not fully met parental expectations, the full body of evidence strongly indicates high levels of parental satisfaction in autonomous schools under both voucher and charter programs. Most parents of voucher and charter students are far happier with their child's chosen autonomous school than with their assigned public school. In experimental studies, voucher parents are much more satisfied than nonrecipient voucher applicants. And finally, some evidence from charter schools and considerable evidence from voucher programs suggest that parents of children in autonomous schools register higher levels of satisfaction than do similar parents of public-school students in the same communities.

The parental satisfaction data also suggest that academic achievement is only one outcome that parents care about. They also want their children's schools to promote discipline, to involve them in their children's education, to reinforce moral values, and to be safe environments. In fact, some studies have found safety to be one of the most important parental motivations for choosing a charter or voucher school.[60] The survey data suggest that parents strongly believe that their new voucher and charter schools are outperforming their previous public schools in terms of a wide range of non-academic outcomes. Again, however, direct measures of voucher and charter schools' success in these matters are unavailable.

SUMMARY

The evidence that both voucher and charter schools successfully meet a parental demand for educational options is substantial. Moreover, parents of children in voucher and charter schools are more satisfied, on a wide variety of dimensions, than are comparison groups of local public-school parents. The extent to which voucher and charter programs can create a large supply of high-quality options, however, is not clear and is likely to depend greatly on specific policy details (notably, the availability of funding and the inclusion of religious and for-profit providers).

---

[60]A study of the privately funded voucher program in Indianapolis, for example, found safety to be the most important reason for application to the program (Weinschrott and Kilgore, 1998). Among parents of pupils in Pennsylvania charter schools, safety was the second-most important reason for enrollment (Miron, 2000).

Chapter Five

ACCESS

Not surprisingly, the most common form of school choice—choosing a school district in which to live—is used more frequently by middle- and upper-income families than by low-income families.[1] Similarly, middle- and upper-income families are far more likely than low-income families to have the means to pay private-school tuition. Vouchers and charters have the potential to extend choice to low-income families that presently lack options. However, it is also possible that the options they created will, in practice, disproportionately benefit middle- and upper-income families.

Equity of choice for the poor is indeed the explicit goal of some voucher programs (such as those proposed by Jencks and by Coons and Sugarman).[2] Opponents of vouchers, by contrast, frequently argue that they will merely subsidize private education for the rich without providing meaningful options for the poor. Similarly, supporters and opponents disagree about whether choice will make meaningful options available to minorities or will be used primarily by white children. Moreover, a concern for access suggests that the availability of voucher and charter schools should be examined not only for low-income and minority students, but also for low-achieving students and students with disabilities (physical or learning).

---

[1]Henig and Sugarman, 1999, p. 16.

[2]See Jencks, 1966; Center for the Study of Public Policy, 1970; Areen and Jencks, 1971; Coons and Sugarman, 1978, 1999.

Access can be understood and interpreted in a number of ways. On one level, universal access would require only that eligibility rules be defined so that all students are technically allowed to draw program benefits. A $500 refundable income-tax credit for tuition expenses, for example, would meet this definition, while the Milwaukee voucher program—which cuts off eligibility for families above an income threshold—would not. In this book, access is understood to be one of the purposes of the educational system, so it requires a definition addressing actual access to schools rather than theoretical access to dollar benefits. Our empirical inquiry therefore examines who actually uses the choice policies to attend voucher and charter schools. Because choices are otherwise available to many students (through residential location or tuition payment), this inevitably involves a focus on those who have a disadvantage that might otherwise narrow their educational options.

This chapter does not address empirical evidence about how students are sorted across and within individual schools. Integration of students from different backgrounds is a separate question, which we address in depth in Chapter Six. For the purposes of this chapter, the key empirical questions are: Who uses vouchers? And who attends charter schools?

THEORETICAL ARGUMENTS

As noted in Chapter Four, some advocates hope that vouchers and charters will provide access to educational options for families that are especially disadvantaged in the existing system. Indeed, some voucher and charter programs specifically address issues of access by targeting or favoring at-risk populations or by constraining the admissions decisions of participating schools (as Chapter Two indicates). In 1970, Christopher Jencks and colleagues proposed a comprehensive voucher system specifically designed to favor low-income children.[3] Around the same time, John Coons and Stephen Sugarman proposed a voucher program motivated primarily by a concern for fairness to the poor. Coons and Sugarman argue that parental choice in schooling depends on having enough money to buy a

---

[3]Center for the Study of Public Policy, 1970.

house in the suburbs or pay private-school tuition.[4] In the 1978 volume that fully articulated their proposal and its rationale, they argue that a regulated voucher system favoring the poor is not only libertarian but "also egalitarian; it holds for one area of the child's life [education] the socialist ideal of an equal portion."[5] They contrast their vision with the existing system, which they say presumes "that only rich parents are the best judges of their child's educational interest."[6] In short, their "objective for education is an equality of freedom."[7]

More recently, some African-American education reformers have advocated vouchers as the next step in the civil rights movement. Howard Fuller, former superintendent of the Milwaukee public schools and a vocal advocate for choice, says the key question is this: "Should low-income, mostly African American parents receive vouchers that will empower them to make educational choices that a majority of Americans both cherish and take for granted?" In Fuller's view, "any answer but 'yes' is unacceptable." He argues that education reform must focus on "the urgent need to expand the educational power of low-income, African American parents."[8]

Charter schools, too, have been supported in part to promote choices for low-income parents. Joe Nathan, a prominent charter-school advocate, echoes the argument of Coons and Sugarman that the conventional system limits choice to those with means: "Middle and upper-income families can always move to exclusive suburbs, where the price of admission to 'public' schools is the ability to buy a home and pay real estate taxes." Charter schools, he argues, directly ad-

---

[4]Coons and Sugarman, 1971. Coons recently raised this point again, arguing that Americans labor under a misconception about conventional public schools: "What Americans still call the 'public' school is accessible only to its neighbors; to attend, one must first manage to live nearby. Stretching things one could, perhaps, say that the schools in poorer neighborhoods such as Watts are functionally 'public' because most of us could afford to move there. But Beverly Hills we cannot save, for it is a legislated scheme of private choice that in effect peddles school vouchers in the housing market. The rich buy autonomy; the rest get conscripted. 'Public?' To the contrary, the system is a balkanized plutocracy" (Coons, 2000).

[5]Coons and Sugarman, 1978, p. 2.

[6]Coons and Sugarman, 1978, p. 27.

[7]Coons and Sugarman, 1978, p. 2.

[8]Fuller, 2000.

dress this inequity in the distribution of liberty by creating "options for families who have the fewest options now."[9]

Opponents, by contrast, argue that school choice will not provide real options to low-income families. Vouchers, in particular, are singled out as an attempt to subsidize private schooling for the rich while neglecting the public schools, where most of the poor and nonwhite will remain. If so, vouchers may promote the liberty of some parents, but not of those who need it most. The ACLU of Southern California, for example, argued that California's Proposition 38 would be more likely to benefit high-income than low-income families, because private schools tend to be located in high-income neighborhoods and tend to select high-income children.[10] A report on Proposition 38 by Policy Analysis for California Education reached a similar conclusion.[11] The two national teachers' unions argue more generally that vouchers "tend to benefit more advantaged families."[12] Charter schools generally arouse less vocal opposition than vouchers, but they, too, are sometimes viewed as a means for highly educated, white, middle- and upper-income parents to remove their children from the conventional public schools. Amy Stuart Wells, a scholar at UCLA, expresses concern that some charter schools are escape routes for white families that wish to abandon more-diverse public schools.[13]

Critics worry that voucher and charter schools will leave behind not only low-income and minority students, but also low-achieving students and those with physical or learning disabilities, "skimming the cream" of high academic performers from the public schools. They point out that private schools today have no obligation to accept students with disabilities—who are often very expensive to educate—

---

[9]Nathan, 1998.

[10]American Civil Liberties Union of Southern California, 2000. Interestingly, Coons and Sugarman agreed with this position, arguing that Prop. 38, unlike their own voucher proposal, would benefit the rich more than the poor (Coons and Sugarman, 2000).

[11]Fuller, Huerta, and Ruenzel, 2000.

[12]National Education Association and American Federation of Teachers, 1999.

[13]As cited in Arsen, 2000.

and reasonably wonder whether such students would benefit from school choice programs.

Empirical evidence can address these disputes. In this chapter, we examine the evidence on the characteristics of the students and the families actually being served under different voucher and charter programs. We postpone examination of the separate question of how those children are sorted across individual schools until Chapter Six, which discusses integration in voucher and charter schools.

WHO USES VOUCHERS?

Opinion polls suggest that the greatest demand for vouchers comes from racial minorities and parents whose children are not doing well in public schools.[14] A 1999 poll conducted by the Joint Center for Political and Economic Studies, for example, found that 71 percent of African-American parents supported vouchers.[15] In general, the strongest supporters of vouchers are families whose children are currently in low-performing public schools and are most in need of educational alternatives. Whether those families are actually served by existing voucher programs is an important empirical question, which we examine below.

Family Income of Voucher Students

Demographic data on voucher users in Milwaukee and Cleveland and in various privately funded programs have been extensively examined by researchers. Most of the existing voucher programs, both publicly and privately funded, explicitly target low-income families. (The notable exceptions are the education tax subsidy programs,

---

[14]Rose and Gallup, 1999.

[15]Bositis, 1999. The same poll found that 63 percent of all parents supported vouchers. The overwhelming defeat of recent voucher initiatives in California and Michigan suggests that these figures may be overstated. When actually given an opportunity to create expensive new voucher programs, most voters have not responded favorably. The point here, however, is not to suggest that vouchers have majority support, but only to point out that substantial numbers of parents, especially among minorities, seem interested in using them.

which we discuss below.)[16] Income data from participants suggest that these programs have succeeded in attracting low-income families. In Milwaukee, average family income for students participating in the program in the early 1990s (when data were collected) was around $11,600.[17] In Cleveland in 1998–99, mean family income for voucher users was $18,750, and 70 percent of families were headed by single mothers.[18] Recipients of scholarships in New York's privately funded program in 1997–98 had average incomes of only $10,000.[19] In Dayton and Washington DC in 1998–99, mean family income of voucher recipients was closer to $18,000; over 75 percent of Washington DC voucher families were headed by single mothers.[20] Similarly, in Edgewood, Texas, in 1998–99, voucher families earned an average annual income of $16,000.[21] In short, it is clear that voucher programs can serve low-income families if they are explicitly designed to do so.

The distributional effects of voucher programs are likely to vary dramatically depending on specific policy details. Programs without income restrictions have prima facie equity because they are technically available to anyone. Nevertheless, it is possible that such programs will be disproportionately used by middle- and upper-income families. In particular, programs with small voucher amounts and no income restrictions are likely to be used primarily by middle- and upper-income families, because use of the voucher depends on the ability to pay additional tuition. Indeed, even in a targeted program, the number of low-income families that can use vouchers is limited

---

[16]Florida's voucher program targets students in low-performing public schools rather than low-income families, but the correlation between these two groups is likely to be high.

[17]Witte, 2000, p. 59. Regrettably, current data on the income levels of Milwaukee voucher participants are unavailable. Eligibility for the program, however, is restricted to families with incomes no greater than 1.75 times the federal poverty level.

[18]Metcalf, 1999. See also Peterson, Howell, and Greene, 1999, which in a 1998 survey of Cleveland voucher families found a mean income level that was $3,000 less than that reported in the Metcalf study.

[19]Peterson, 1998, Table 1.

[20]Howell and Peterson, 2000, Table 2; Wolf, Howell, and Peterson, 2000, Table 2.

[21]Peterson, Myers, and Howell, 1999, Table 1.3. This figure was equivalent to the average income of public-school students in Edgewood, which is a low-income district.

by the size of the voucher. Vouchers that fall short of tuition costs will have much lower take-up rates among low-income families than will more-generous vouchers.

Education tax subsidies are especially likely to have regressive distributional effects, disproportionately benefitting middle- and upper-income families. Benefit amounts of education tax subsidies are usually small, requiring families to pay the balance of tuition. In most cases, education tax subsidies are unavailable to families that have no tax liability (unless the subsidies are refundable credits). Moreover, if they operate in the form of deductions or exclusions (like federal education savings accounts—ESAs) rather than credits, they are worth more to families in higher tax brackets. The federal ESA has not yet taken effect, so empirical data on its use are unavailable.

Despite the absence of current data on the use of education tax subsidies, a limited amount of data from older tuition tax-credit programs supports the hypothesis that education tax subsidies are disproportionately used by families with above-average incomes.[22] We further address the significance of these and other issues related to the distributional consequences of specific voucher policies in the concluding chapter.

No data are available on the distributional consequences of the voucher tax credit in Arizona, because the vouchers themselves are distributed by private organizations that make their own decisions about student eligibility.[23] It is possible that the Arizona program is distributionally less regressive than other education tax incentives, because it does not provide a tax benefit for tuition payments for a family's own children. The new voucher credit in Pennsylvania is similar to Arizona's, but it caps student eligibility at an income level of $70,000 for a family with two children.

---

[22]Darling-Hammond, Kirby, and Schlegel, 1985. See also Catterall and Levin, 1982; Catterall, 1983.

[23]One study finds, not surprisingly, that families taking the Arizona tax credit have above-average income levels (Wilson, 2000). The study has no data, however, on the students receiving the vouchers.

Race and Ethnicity of Voucher Students

In most cities, minority racial/ethnic groups have been heavily represented in voucher programs—though the specific ethnic composition of voucher families varies substantially in different communities. In Washington DC, 95 percent of the mothers of voucher students were African-American.[24] In New York, 44 percent were African-American, an additional 47 percent were Latino, and only 5 percent were white.[25] In Milwaukee in 1998–99, 62 percent of surveyed voucher parents were African-American and 13 percent were Latino (these figures were nearly identical to those in the Milwaukee public schools).[26] Two-thirds of voucher recipients in Dayton were African-American, as were 60 percent of Cleveland voucher recipients.[27] Figure 5.1 shows the proportion of voucher recipients who were nonwhite in each of these cities. These figures undoubtedly reflect the fact that all of the voucher programs in question are targeted

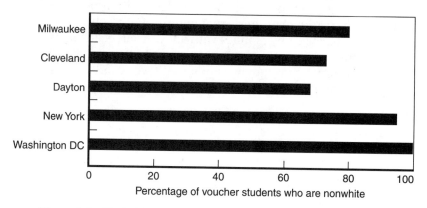

Figure 5.1—Nonwhite Representation Among Voucher Students

---

[24]Wolf, Howell, and Peterson, 2000, Table 2.

[25]Peterson, 1998, Table 1.

[26]Wisconsin Legislative Audit Bureau, 2000.

[27]Howell and Peterson, 2000, Table 2; Metcalf, 1999.

to low-income children in cities where the low-income population is disproportionately nonwhite. As with income distribution, different kinds of voucher programs are likely to produce different distributional effects in terms of race and ethnicity.

Prior Academic Achievement of Voucher Students

The bulk of the evidence indicates that students have quite low levels of achievement at the time they enroll in voucher schools. Several years of data from Milwaukee show that the prior test scores of students applying to the choice program between 1990 and 1994 were significantly below those for both average Milwaukee public school (MPS) students and a sample of low-income MPS students.[28] For voucher applicants, the mean normal curve equivalent (NCE) ranged from 35.5 to 39.8 over this four-year span, which represents a shortcoming of almost two-thirds of a standard deviation compared to the national average.[29]

Baseline data from privately funded voucher programs suggest that these programs are not "skimming the cream"—i.e., drawing high-achieving students away from the public schools. To the contrary, students entering voucher programs are performing rather poorly: at the time they enroll, their scores on standardized tests are generally far below the national average. In New York, for example, voucher students entered the program with average reading scores in the 23rd percentile and average math scores in the 17th percentile nationally.[30] In Dayton, reading and math scores of voucher students on entry were in the 25th percentile nationally.[31] Washington DC voucher students had similarly low scores when they entered the program: in the 33rd percentile nationally in reading and the 25th

---

[28]Witte, 2000, p. 69. The sole exception was in the first year of the program, when the differences between choice applicants and the low-income sample were not significant.

[29]As noted in Chapter Three, we have serious doubts about the reliability of the Cleveland data on achievement of voucher students.

[30]Myers et al., 2000.

[31]Howell and Peterson, 2000.

percentile nationally in math.[32] On national scales, students entering the voucher program in Edgewood, Texas, look similar to those in the other cities, with reading scores in the 35th percentile and math scores in the 37th percentile on entry. These scores were also relatively similar to those for a sample of Edgewood public-school students, whose math scores were not statistically distinguishable from those of Edgewood voucher students, but whose reading scores were slightly lower, in the 28th percentile.[33]

Again, nontargeted voucher programs may benefit a more advantaged group of students. Education tax subsidy programs, in particular, are likely to primarily benefit families already sending their children to private school. Students currently in private schools tend to have above-average achievement levels.

Education Level of Voucher Parents

In one respect, the families of voucher children tend to be less disadvantaged than other low-income children: their mothers usually have somewhat more education than other mothers at comparable income levels. In Dayton, for example, there was a small but statistically significant difference between the education level of voucher mothers and that of "decliners"—i.e., mothers whose children had applied for the program and won the lottery but ultimately failed to use the voucher. Voucher mothers averaged 13.6 years of schooling, versus 13.2 years for decliners; 20 percent of voucher mothers were college graduates, compared with only 6 percent of decliners.[34] In Washington DC, a similar comparison measured 12.9 years of edu-

---

[32]Wolf, Howell, and Peterson, 2000. All of these results are in striking contrast to those of the Assisted Places Scheme, a targeted private-school scholarship program in the United Kingdom. That program, begun in 1980 and phased out since 1998, awarded scholarships for private-school attendance to public-school students with high ability but low family income. Consistent with the selection criteria, evaluations found that participating students were from families with relatively low incomes; but they also found that relatively few parents of participating students were from the working class and that the majority had been educated in private or selective schools (Ambler, 1994; Edwards, Fitz, and Whitty, 1989).

[33]Peterson, Myers, and Howell, 1999, Table 1.2.

[34]Howell and Peterson, 2000, Table 2.

cation for the average voucher mother and 12.6 years for the average decliner.[35]

Similar differences in parental education have been seen in other cities. In New York, the study team compared the education level of voucher mothers with that of the eligible low-income population and found a more substantial difference. Only 46 percent of the mothers of the eligible population had graduated from high school, compared with 82 percent of the voucher mothers.[36] Voucher mothers in Edgewood had an average of 12 years of education, compared with 10.8 years for Edgewood public-school mothers; three-fourths were high-school graduates, versus half of public-school mothers.[37] In Cleveland, 92 percent of voucher mothers had completed a high-school degree, an education level reached by only 78 percent of public-school mothers.[38] In Milwaukee in the early 1990s, voucher parents in both the publicly funded program and PAVE were substantially more likely to have completed some college education than were a sample of low-income public-school parents.[39]

These differences may reflect a higher value placed on education by more-educated mothers, who were thus more willing to pay the additional tuition not covered by the voucher. Or more-educated mothers may have more success in navigating the admissions processes imposed by voucher schools. Indeed, both explanations may be true.

Vouchers and Students with Disabilities

As Chapter Two points out, the existing federal legal requirements defining the service that voucher schools must provide to students with disabilities are not entirely clear but are probably more limited than those defined for conventional public schools. Existing and proposed voucher programs can, of course, institute requirements

---

[35]Wolf, Howell, and Peterson, 2000, Table 2.

[36]Peterson, 1998, Table 1.

[37]Peterson, Myers, and Howell, 1999, Table 1.3.

[38]Metcalf, 1999..

[39]Beales and Wahl, 1995.

and funding support that go beyond the basic demands of federal law in encouraging voucher schools to serve disabled students. Florida, for example, has a voucher program, the McKay Scholarships Program, that is specifically designed for students with disabilities (and that operates independently of Florida's Opportunity Scholarship Program, which provides vouchers for students in low-performing public schools).[40]   Schools participating in the voucher programs in Milwaukee and Cleveland are not required to offer special services, however, and of 86 voucher schools in Milwaukee, only seven report offering special education.[41]   In consequence, many students with disabilities surely do not apply. Unfortunately, few data on students with disabilities are available for the publicly funded voucher programs in Milwaukee and Cleveland. As a general matter, private schools have no obligation to identify students with disabilities; unless voucher programs impose such a requirement, it will be difficult to determine the extent to which they include such students.[42]   In Cleveland, according to a 1998 parent survey, students with learning disabilities are underrepresented: 8 percent of voucher students had learning disabilities, compared to 15 percent of Cleveland public-school students.[43]

Some data are available on the proportion of voucher users with disabilities in the privately funded experimental programs in New York, Washington DC, and Charlotte. Given the small size of these programs, the total number of students with disabilities participating is small. In New York, 9 percent of voucher users had learning disabilities and 3 percent had physical disabilities.[44]   This is comparable to citywide figures indicating that 14 percent of public-school students were identified as having disabilities requiring Individual Education Plans (IEPs).[45]   In Washington DC, 11 percent of voucher users had

---

[40]For details, see http://www.opportunityschools.org/osas/spswd/.

[41]Wisconsin Legislative Audit Bureau, 2000.

[42]See Wisconsin Legislative Audit Bureau, 2000, p. 26, for a discussion of the lack of information on special-needs students and programs in Milwaukee's voucher schools.

[43]Peterson, Howell, and Greene, 1999, Table 2. Differences between voucher students and public-school students in terms of physical disabilities were not statistically significant.

[44]Myers et al., 2000, Table 7.

[45]Young, 2000, Table 3.

learning disabilities and 4 percent had physical disabilities;[46] districtwide, 11 percent of public-school students had IEPs.[47] In Charlotte, 4 percent of voucher users had learning disabilities and 3 percent had physical disabilities;[48] district figures indicate that 11 percent of Charlotte's public-school population had IEPs. Although none of these differences is large, interpretation requires caution because district data are reported by administrative sources and voucher-program data are reported by parents. Moreover, the data do not indicate the severity of the disabilities—indeed, we have seen no data that address the severity of disabilities for students in any voucher programs. Given the resource limitations, however, it seems unlikely that students with especially severe disabilities are being extensively served by existing voucher programs.[49]

The experimental studies also examine the extent to which parents of disabled children believe their children's needs are being served well by their schools. Unfortunately, the number of parents of students with disabilities involved in the voucher programs is so small that few statistically significant differences between voucher students and control students can be found.[50]

---

[46]Wolf, Howell, and Peterson, 2000, Table 7.

[47]Young, 2000, Table 3.

[48]Greene, 2000b, Table 2.

[49]It should be noted that school districts often contract with specialized private schools to serve some of their most-disabled students, at very high cost—though parental choice is typically not the intention of such contracts. Florida's new voucher program for students with disabilities, however, suggests that policymakers are aware of the possibility that special education funding can be converted to vouchers. We discuss this possibility further in Chapter Eight.

[50]In New York, parents of children with physical disabilities were more likely to report that their children's needs were being served "very well" in public schools, whereas parents of children with learning disabilities were more likely to report that their children were being served "very well" in voucher schools. Because of the small numbers involved, however, neither difference is statistically significant. (Myers et al., 2000, Table 7.) In Dayton, surveys register somewhat more satisfaction for public-school parents in both categories, but again there is no statistically significant difference (Howell and Peterson, 2000, Table 7). In Washington DC, evaluators found virtually no difference in satisfaction rates for parents of physically disabled children, but substantially and significantly (in statistical terms) greater satisfaction for voucher parents of learning-disabled students: 49 percent of voucher parents thought the schools were serving their learning-disabled children very well, versus 23 percent of the control group of public-school parents (Wolf, Howell, and Peterson, 2000, Table 7).

In sum, vouchers can be designed to favor the poor, and when they are, they will be extensively used by minorities (at least in communities with substantial minority populations). Among the poor, vouchers—like all programs of parental choice—are more likely to be used by parents with more education. Voucher programs not specifically designed to favor low-income families—including education tax subsidies, such as the federal ESA—may have very different distributional consequences. Although few data are available as yet on services for students with disabilities, it is clear that ensuring the participation of disabled students is a real challenge for voucher programs, and full access will require policymakers to make a substantial financial commitment to underwrite the costs of accommodations and special services in voucher schools.

WHO ATTENDS CHARTER SCHOOLS?

Unlike the existing voucher laws in Cleveland, Milwaukee, and Florida, charter-school laws are not typically designed specifically to focus on low-income or low-achieving students. In some states, however, charter-school authorizing laws make special provisions for schools designed to serve such at-risk students.[51] Moreover, even in states where authorizing legislation is not aimed specifically at at-risk students, some charter-school operators design their schools for an at-risk population. Nevertheless, because state laws typically permit charter schools to serve a general population, the student population in charter schools might be expected to be somewhat less disadvantaged than the population of students now using publicly and privately funded vouchers. In fact, the demographics of charter-school enrollments vary quite substantially across the country. While in some states charter schools serve predominantly disadvantaged students, in other states they serve a more advantaged population.

No data on the issue are reported for Charlotte. It would be interesting to see if a pattern emerges when the data across cities are aggregated.

[51]Texas is one example. Although the number of charter schools in Texas is limited, charters serving populations that include at least 75 percent at-risk students are not subject to the limit.

Charter Schools and Children in Poverty

Aggregated nationally, the proportion of charter-school students whose family income qualifies them for a free or reduced-price lunch is nearly identical to the proportion in conventional public schools: 39 percent of charter-school students were eligible in 1998–99, compared with 37 percent of public-school students.[52] This national average, however, obscures considerable variation across states. In 11 of 27 charter-school states in 1998–99, charter schools served a population that was substantially lower-income than the state's public-school population (i.e., the proportion of students eligible for a free or reduced-price lunch was at least 10 percent higher in charter schools than in public schools). Among states with large numbers of charter schools, Michigan and Texas were in this category. By contrast, charter schools in six states served a population that was substantially higher-income than the state's public-school population (i.e., the proportion of students eligible for a free or reduced-price lunch was at least 10 percent lower in charter schools than in public schools). Among states with large numbers of charter schools, California was in this category.[53]

Race and Ethnicity of Charter-School Students

Charter-school enrollments by race and ethnicity also present a variable picture in different states. Nationally, charter schools enrolled a somewhat higher proportion of nonwhite students (52 percent nonwhite) than did conventional public schools (41 percent nonwhite) in 1998–99. Among 13 states that had at least 20 charter schools, eight enrolled a charter-school student population that was at least 10 percentage points overrepresentative of nonwhites compared to the state's public-school average. And charter schools in six of these

---

[52]RPP International, 1999, p. 34.

[53]RPP International, 1999, p. 34. In the fall of 2000, five states each had at least 100 charter schools operating: Arizona, California, Florida, Michigan, and Texas (Center for Education Reform, 2000a). In the view of Amy Stuart Wells, who conducted an intensive study of charter schools in California, the substantial demands that charter schools place on parents "are more likely to discourage certain groups than others—single parents, parents working long hours or at more than one job, and those whose jobs do not permit them to take time off from work—in other words, a disproportionate number of poor, minority parents" (Wells, 1999, p. 24).

eight states, including Michigan and Texas, had minority representations at least 20 percentage points above their state's public-school average. Meanwhile, charter schools in two of the 13 states, including California, enrolled student populations that were under-representative of racial minorities, falling short of the state's public-school average by at least 10 percentage points.[54]

Prior Academic Achievement of Charter-School Students

Statewide information on the academic achievement levels of students attracted to charters comes from three studies that analyzed charter schools' academic achievement, as reported in Chapter Three. All three found that charter students have test scores below those of public-school comparison groups. In Arizona, statewide average scores of charter-school students are slightly lower than those of students in conventional public schools across the state.[55]   In Texas, the difference between charter students and conventional public-school students is greater: 81 percent of public-school students passed both the reading and math TAAS exams in 2000, compared with 51 percent of charter students.[56]

In Michigan, Bettinger compared test scores in charter schools with those of nearby public schools. He found that charter schools attract students with lower scores on the state assessment than do neighboring public schools. Among grade 4 students enrolling in new Michigan charter schools in 1996, 43 percent scored "low" on Michigan's state math assessment, compared with only 22 percent of students in nearby public schools. Similarly, 37 percent scored "low" on the reading assessment, compared with 24 percent of students in nearby public schools. The differences are virtually identical when all public schools in the state, rather than just nearby public schools, are used as the comparison group. [57]

---

[54]RPP International, 1999, pp. 30–33.

[55]Solmon, Paark, and Garcia, 2001, Table 1.

[56]Gronberg and Jansen, 2001, Table 8-d.

[57]Bettinger, 1999, Table 1a. Another study of Michigan charter schools found similar results (Horn and Miron, 2000).

Charter Schools and Students with Disabilities

Students with disabilities are slightly underrepresented in charter schools nationally. Although charter schools, like other public schools, are not permitted to deny admission to a student for reasons of disability, many of them lack the resources to provide special services and therefore might be less likely to be chosen by such students. In 1998–99, students with disabilities constituted 11 percent of conventional public-school enrollments and 8 percent of charter-school enrollments.[58] As with income and ethnicity, the proportion varied substantially across states—but in many states, because the total number of charter schools is small (and the proportion of students with disabilities is generally low), the proportion can change substantially from one year to the next. States with a relatively high proportion of disabled students in their charter-school enrollments tend to be those that have charter schools specifically aimed at special-needs students.[59] We have seen no data indicating the severity of the disabilities of students served in charter schools.

In sum, in many states, it appears that charter schools are, in fact, serving at-risk students. In some states, however—notably California—there is reason for concern that many (though certainly not all) charter schools may be serving primarily as a means for middle- and upper-income white students to opt out of more-diverse public schools.[60]

SUMMARY

In many cases, voucher and charter schools create new options for low-income and minority students who might otherwise lack a choice. Voucher programs specifically targeted at low-income families have been especially successful in this respect. Education tax subsidies, by contrast, are more likely to be used by middle- and

---

[58]RPP International, 1999, p. 36.

[59]RPP International, 1999, p. 36.

[60]The UCLA Charter School Study, led by Amy Stuart Wells, found in its sample a couple of charter schools where "the charter seemed to limit racial/ethnic diversity by using mechanisms such as admissions requirements or parent and student contracts to make demands of families that most regular public schools cannot legally enforce" (UCLA Charter School Study, 1998, p. 48).

upper-income families. The benefits of charter schools are distributed across the income scale. Some charter schools focus on urban, at-risk populations, while others (particularly in California and a few other states) cater to populations that are more middle-class, suburban, and white. In consequence, generalizing about the distributional effects of charter schools is difficult.

Most of the existing targeted voucher programs also serve relatively low-achieving students; there is no evidence that voucher schools are "creaming" high-achieving students from the public schools. The same can be said of charter schools, at least on average. In three prominent charter states where data are available, charter students have test scores below statewide averages.

The low-income parents of voucher students tend to have more education than do other low-income parents. Nevertheless, the absolute educational level of voucher parents in the targeted low-income programs is not high. Although we lack comparable data on charter parents, it is probable that they, too, would have somewhat more education than their peers. All programs of school choice are more likely to be used by better-informed families.

The one group of disadvantaged students clearly underrepresented in both voucher and charter schools is children with disabilities. This may be the result not only of school admissions policies, but also of resources: schools that are smaller and less generously funded are not likely to offer the special services needed by some students with physical or learning disabilities. Voucher and charter policies raise substantial questions about the participation of special-needs children. Only one state, Florida, has designed a voucher program specifically for students with disabilities.

Finally, it should be noted that all of the existing empirical evidence on charter and voucher schools comes from programs that so far enroll only a small proportion of all students. We do not know how these schools might look—and who would enroll in them—under larger-scale programs. In addition to scale, policy details related to funding levels and admissions requirements are likely to have a significant influence on access. We explore the importance of policy details in Chapter Eight.

Chapter Six

INTEGRATION

Historically, one purpose of the educational system has been to promote not only access for all students, but also integration of students by race, ethnicity, and socioeconomic status within schools.[1] As the long-discredited doctrine of "separate but equal" makes clear, access and integration are not necessarily synonymous. In educational systems using choice-based student assignment, the distinction is critical: even if voucher/charter programs enroll student populations that are fully representative of a community's demographic mix, whether they enroll those students together in integrated schools or separately in homogeneous schools is a key empirical question.

In the half-century since *Brown v. Board of Education*, the integrationist ideal has sometimes been challenged—even by members of the minority groups that are its primary intended beneficiaries. Frustration with "white flight," with unsuccessful busing schemes, and with poorly functioning urban schools has led some minority leaders to champion choice as a means of providing minority control over minority schools, even at the cost of integration. Despite these challenges, however, integration remains a widely held value.

---

[1] We do not directly address integration by academic ability in this chapter. In our view, integration by academic ability is primarily an instrumental goal, relevant to the extent that it affects academic achievement and attainment (which are addressed in Chapter Three) or is correlated with integration by race and socioeconomic status. Integration of children by race and socioeconomic status, by contrast, may be important social goals of an educational system in themselves.

We assume that integration remains a legitimate goal of the educational system, meriting recognition alongside academic achievement, choice, access, and civic socialization.[2] This book accepts the common view that, all else equal, schools should include students representing all elements of the larger community. Of course, all else is not always equal. We recognize that integration may be in tension with other goals, and we do not pretend that tradeoffs between integration and other goals can be value-neutral. At the end of the chapter, we explore some of the tradeoffs between integration and other goals. First, however, we examine the empirical evidence on integration in voucher and charter schools.

THE HISTORY OF CHOICE AND THE RACIAL POLITICS OF SCHOOLING

It is critical to begin this discussion of issues surrounding school integration by acknowledging the multiple forces that have created a school system in the United States that continues to this day to be highly stratified by race and socioeconomic status. Half a century after the legislated segregation imposed by many school districts was outlawed by the Supreme Court, by far the most important factor in creating stratification in our school system is residential segregation. Because school assignment is typically determined by residence, the differential residential patterns of white and minority families (as seen in the pattern of predominantly minority and poor central cities surrounded by predominantly white suburbs) have produced racially separate school districts.[3] As the decades following *Brown v. Board of Education* made clear, the end of de jure segregation did not necessarily lead to integrated schools. Persistent patterns of residential segregation—increasing with white flight in many cities—left many urban schools desegregated as a matter of law but racially homogeneous in fact.

---

[2]Of course, integration may not be entirely separable from other goals. The civil rights movement argued that integration was required to promote equal access. The work of psychologist Kenneth Clark, which suggested that integration was necessary to promote fundamental educational outcomes, was immortalized in *Brown v. Board of Education*. And it is often argued that integration promotes civic socialization.

[3]Farley et al., 1978; Orfield and Yun, 1999.

In the last half-century, school choice has been used both to undermine and to support efforts at integration. Immediately following the *Brown* ruling, some southern states responded by creating voucher-like programs to provide public support to private segregationist academies. White students used publicly funded tuition grants to escape public schools under desegregation orders in favor of a separate, entirely white "private" school system.[4] Although federal courts quickly invalidated such programs, the attempted use of school choice for the explicit purpose of maintaining segregation remains a powerful memory.

School choice was further tarnished by the "freedom of choice" plans that some school districts used in an attempt to achieve nominal desegregation while maintaining essentially separate schools for African-Americans and whites. Under this type of plan, any student assigned to a school where she was a member of the racial majority could transfer to a school where she would be in the minority. Districts claimed to have ended segregation, even if no whites chose to enroll in a school previously designated for African-Americans, and even if African-Americans were afraid to enroll in a "white" school. In 1968, in *Green v. County School Board of New Kent County*, the U.S. Supreme Court ruled that "freedom of choice" plans were not an adequate response in districts with a history of intentional segregation.

In the years following *Green*, however, the relationship between school choice and integration changed. During the late 1960s and early 1970s, the use of choice as a policy instrument made an about-face: rather than functioning as an escape route from desegregated schools, choice was adopted as a tool for achieving integration. Magnet schools and other forms of controlled-choice programs—which typically permit choices that increase integration but preclude choices that reduce integration—were offered as alternatives to mandatory busing, all of them designed to provide positive incentives for students to attend integrated schools.

Despite the efforts of earlier decades, however, integration remains an elusive goal for many public schools. In 1996–97, most of the

---

[4]See Orfield and Eaton, 1996; Henig, 1994.

largest city school districts enrolled more than 85 percent nonwhite students.[5] Schools that are racially stratified are extremely likely to be economically stratified as well: in schools with more than 90 percent African-American or Latino enrollments, 87 percent of students are poor.[6] National figures suggest that progress toward racial/ethnic integration in public schools came to a halt in the 1990s, even reversing slightly.[7]

Given this state of American schooling, some scholars have argued vociferously for or against school choice as a reform that could transform the integration of the education system. While most proponents of vouchers and charters today view them primarily as tools to improve academic achievement, the consequences of choice for school integration may be dramatic.

THEORETICAL ARGUMENTS

Opponents of school choice often object on the grounds that choice will lead to increased stratification along a variety of dimensions, including race, income, parental education, and academic ability. Some claim that choice will function as a sorting machine, redistributing students across schools in inequitable ways.[8] If the "cream skimming" argument in Chapter Five is correct, it will lead not only to inequities in access to choice schools, but also to stratification. If, as opponents of school choice sometimes argue, voucher/charter schools do seek out the "best and brightest" and avoid students who are difficult to educate, they will end up serving a population that is disproportionately white and middle-class, leaving the public schools full of nonwhite and low-income students.

The problem will be most severe in choice programs that give schools the discretion to set admissions standards and that permit

---

[5]Orfield and Yun, 1999.

[6]Orfield and Yun, 1999, Table 13.

[7]Between 1986 and 1998, the proportion of African-American students in schools that were at least 90 percent nonwhite increased from 32 to 37 percent; trends for Latinos were nearly identical (Orfield, 2001, Table 9).

[8]Moore and Davenport, 1990; Lee, Croninger, and Smith, 1994; Wells, 1993a; Levin, 1998.

schools to charge additional tuition above the level of public subsidy. But opponents argue that, even if schools are required to admit by lottery, and even if tuition add-ons are forbidden, choice will exacerbate stratification because of differences in parental information and motivation.[9] They worry that low-income parents with low levels of education who are living in segregated areas will be disadvantaged in the decisionmaking process. Social networks are a key method of obtaining information on educational options, and families living in segregated areas are closed off from many information channels and tend to belong to segregated social networks.[10]

Proponents of school choice, by contrast, point to the fact that the education system is already highly stratified. This stratification is evident not only at the level of schools and districts (as described above), but also at the classroom level, due to tracking and other forms of curricular differentiation. Advocates therefore argue that it is unlikely that choice would make matters worse; indeed, choice may even improve the situation by opening up traditionally white private schools to minority students (in the case of vouchers) and by promoting smaller, untracked schools.

The strongest argument for choice is that it bypasses the primary mechanism that creates stratified schools: residential segregation. By detaching school attendance from residence, choice may provide options for many families "trapped" in racially homogeneous central-city districts or attendance areas. These may include urban and suburban voucher or charter schools that also attract middle-class white students. Moreover, the most visionary advocates of choice hope that it will help to undermine residential segregation and reverse middle-class flight by giving families in all neighborhoods a number of high-quality educational options. If so, choice could improve integration throughout the educational system.

This chapter addresses these disputes by examining the evidence on integration in voucher and charter programs, as well as evidence from school choice in other contexts.

---

[9]Wells, 1993a; Levin, 1998.

[10]Schneider et al., 1997.

CONCEPTUAL AND MEASUREMENT ISSUES

Several thorny issues arise when attempting to evaluate how choice programs affect integration. First, as Douglas Archbald points out, stratification is not a one-dimensional phenomenon.[11] In evaluating the impact of choice on stratification, it is important to take into account the multidimensional student and family characteristics likely to play a role in school choice. It is possible, if not likely, that choice policies will increase stratification on one dimension while reducing it on another.

An additional issue critical to this discussion is how to define the appropriate comparison against which to measure the effects of school-choice programs. As many have argued, the issue is not whether schools within choice systems are stratified relative to some ideal, but whether they are stratified or integrated relative to the existing system.[12] Moreover, the varied history of school-choice policies suggests that it would be a mistake to assume that all choice policies will lead to the same results. Different voucher and charter policies may lead to different integration outcomes.

Methodologically, another key conceptual point concerns the distinction between access to voucher and charter programs (which we addressed in Chapter Five) and the integration of voucher/charter schools. Comparing the demographic characteristics of choosers to nonchoosers tells only part of the story: it does not explain how choosers and nonchoosers are distributed to individual schools. For example, across a state, charter schools might enroll an identical proportion of minority students as conventional public schools do, even while every individual charter school is racially homogeneous.[13] By the same token, a charter school could enroll a higher (or lower) proportion of minority students than the district average and still be

---

[11]Archbald, 2000.

[12]Moe, 1995; Levin, 1998; Archbald, 2000.

[13]An example illustrates this possibility. Assume that the state's school-age population is 60 percent white and 40 percent minority. Assume further that the state has ten charter schools and that, in the aggregate, their enrollment is also 60 percent white and 40 percent minority. Six of the charter schools could enroll all of the white students while the other four enroll all of the minority students. Enrollment data aggregated at the state level are insufficient to address integration in schools.

substantially more integrated than most or all of the conventional public schools in the district (if the public schools are concentrated at the extremes of demographic distribution). Demographic data that are averages at the city, state, or national level cannot distinguish these possibilities. Comparative, school-level data are essential to understanding how the integration of voucher/charter schools compares with that of conventional public schools.

Moreover, even school-level comparisons of integration levels of voucher/charter and local public schools are insufficient to explain how the introduction of vouchers or charters may *change* school integration levels, positively or negatively. Vouchers and charters may affect the sorting of students beyond the voucher/charter schools and the nearest public schools. As Henig and Sugarman point out (and as we discuss in Chapter Four), the alternative options available to voucher and charter students are not limited to the public school that happens to be nearby.[14] In the absence of vouchers/charters, some families will send their children to the neighborhood public school, some will pay tuition at a private school, some will relocate their residence to the enrollment district of a preferred public school, and some will school their children at home. The existence of voucher/charter options may affect all of these decisions, with resulting impacts on the integration of all of the schools in a metropolitan area—public and private, urban and suburban. Consider, for example, an urban charter school that is three-fourths white and located in an enrollment zone with a public school that is half white. Although it might be accurate to describe the charter school as less integrated than the public school, that does not necessarily mean that the opening of the charter school reduced integration. The effect of the charter school depends on where its students would otherwise be. If most of its white students would otherwise be in less-integrated environments (such as private schools, suburban public schools, or home schools), then the charter school may, paradoxically, improve integration. In sum, a complete assessment of the integration effects of vouchers and charters requires a dynamic model with data that can provide information about all of the alternative educational environments in which students might enroll.

---

[14]Henig and Sugarman, 1999.

A final conceptual problem concerns the interpretation of the distinction between stratification that is imposed by law and stratification that results from the choices of individual families. If inner-city African-American parents choose to pull their children out of a public school that is integrated through coerced busing and enroll them in a neighborhood charter school that has few white children (and perhaps an Afro-centric curriculum), is that objectionable? Such a charter school might be described as segregated, but it surely represents something quite different from the segregated schools that many African-Americans were required to attend in the years before *Brown*. This is a deep philosophical issue that we cannot pretend to resolve in this book. In the latter part of the chapter, however, we begin to address some of the tradeoffs that may be associated with integration.

Our exploration of the evidence is framed by several key questions about integration under voucher and charter programs. First, how does the integration of voucher and charter schools compare to that of local public schools? Second, how do vouchers and charters change levels of integration in all the schools that may be affected, public and private? Third, how do vouchers and charters affect integration at the classroom level? We seek evidence on these questions from existing U.S. voucher and charter programs, other forms of school choice in the United States, and choice programs in other countries. As the following pages show, evidence on all three questions is regrettably sparse, but more evidence is available on the first question than on the second or third.

INTEGRATION IN EXISTING VOUCHER AND CHARTER PROGRAMS

Existing evidence on the integration effects of operating voucher and charter programs is limited. This is partly because, as noted above, assessing effects on integration is far more complicated than simply identifying the demographic characteristics of voucher and charter users. Data must be available not only on the students, but also on the demographic characteristics of the voucher/charter schools and the schools that the students would otherwise attend. As seen in Chapter Five, many studies have collected demographic information on the students participating in voucher and charter programs. Far fewer have collected school-level data on the integration of voucher and charter schools (let alone classrooms), and fewer still permit a direct comparison with the integration of local public schools. We have not seen any studies that have the kind of linked student- and school-level data that would permit the rich, dynamic assessment of integration that is ideal. Nevertheless, some evidence is available to examine the integration of both voucher and charter schools on the dimensions of family income and race/ethnicity.

Integration in Voucher Schools

Income. By targeting low-income families, the existing voucher programs have likely increased the integration of voucher schools on the dimension of income. As demonstrated in Chapter Five, the evidence supports the claim that voucher programs have, in fact, successfully targeted low-income students. It is likely that most of their tuition-paying classmates come from somewhat higher-income families—although, unfortunately, we lack good information about the socioeconomic status levels of the classmates of voucher students that might confirm this.[15] Because the income levels of the voucher students are low, it is also unlikely that their departure has any negative effect on stratification by income in the public schools. Of course, outcomes under nontargeted programs, including education tax subsidies, might be quite different (no direct evidence is available).

Race and ethnicity. In Milwaukee, voucher schools are somewhat less stratified by race than are public schools. Examining data on 86 of the 91 private schools participating in the program in 1999–2000, Howard Fuller and George Mitchell found that 50 percent of Milwaukee public-school students attend schools with enrollments that are at least 90 percent minority or 90 percent white; the corresponding figure for students in voucher schools is slightly lower, at 43 per-

---

[15]The only evidence on the proportion of poor students in voucher schools comes from Cleveland, where Jay Greene finds that voucher students attend schools where on average 59 percent of students are below the poverty line, compared to 64 percent for the city (Greene, 1999a). Unfortunately, however, this does not tell us about school-level integration.

cent.[16] Among the voucher schools, those with religious affiliations are substantially more integrated: 30 percent of voucher students in religious schools are in schools that are over 90 percent minority or over 90 percent white, while 83 percent of voucher students attending secular schools are in schools serving populations that are over 90 percent minority.[17] Thirty percent of Milwaukee voucher students are in secular schools.[18]

The picture in Cleveland is mixed. Cleveland voucher students are slightly less likely than Cleveland public-school students to attend schools that are over 90 percent minority (36 versus 41 percent) but are more likely to attend schools that are over 90 percent white (14 versus 0 percent).[19] If the population of the Cleveland metropolitan area (including the suburbs) is used as a benchmark, voucher schools are somewhat more racially integrated than both Cleveland public schools and suburban public schools. Voucher students are more likely than public-school students to attend schools that are representative of the Cleveland metropolitan area, meaning that these schools have a proportion of minority students that is within 10 percent of the average for the metro area. Nineteen percent of voucher students attend a school that is racially representative of the Cleveland area, versus 10 percent of city public-school students (who are more likely to be in heavily nonwhite schools) and 3 percent of suburban public-school students (who are much more likely to be in heavily white schools).[20]

The evidence available on racial integration in the experimental voucher programs in New York City, Washington DC, and Dayton, Ohio, is limited and indirect, based on parent perceptions of classroom integration rather than actual enrollment data.[21] In New York (where 95 percent of voucher users were nonwhite), 30 percent of

---

[16]Fuller and Mitchell, 1999, 2000.

[17]Fuller and Mitchell, 1999, 2000.

[18]Wisconsin Legislative Audit Bureau, 2000.

[19]Greene, 1999a.

[20]Greene, 1999a.

[21]The evaluations of these programs use parental responses to gauge differences in segregation at the classroom level between public and participating private schools. Parents are asked, "What percentage of students in this child's class are minority?"

voucher parents reported that their children were in classrooms that were 100 percent minority, compared to 38 percent of the control group.[22] In Washington DC (where 100 percent of voucher users were nonwhite), 40 percent of both voucher parents and the control group reported that their children's classes were 100 percent minority.[23] In Dayton (where two-thirds of voucher users were nonwhite), voucher parents reported that their children were more likely to be in classrooms that were 100 percent minority (14 percent versus 5 percent of the control group) but that they were also more likely to be in classrooms where less than 50 percent of the students were minority (52 percent versus 30 percent of the control group).[24] In sum, the available data on the privately funded voucher experiments do not show a clear integration advantage for either voucher or public schools. Unfortunately, we do not know whether these inconsistencies stem from differences between the cities in terms of the racial makeup of public- and private-school populations, or are simply a result of inaccuracies associated with using parental responses to measure the racial composition of classrooms.

Concluding note on integration in voucher schools. While the limited evidence available to date suggests that existing voucher programs may move some low-income nonwhite students into more-integrated voucher schools, we are left with several unanswered questions. To appropriately gauge the impact on participating students, it is essential to have school-level data on the composition of the student body in both the voucher schools and the conventional public schools that voucher students would otherwise have attended, and these data would need to be matched with demographic data on individual students. We are aware of no evaluations of voucher programs that have collected all of this information and thus are unable to answer questions about how vouchers may have changed the integration of both sets of schools. For example, if an African-American voucher student moves from a public school that is 75 percent minority to a voucher school that is 90 percent white, it might be

---

[22]Myers et al., 2000. The first-year results were similar, with 28 percent of parents of choice students reporting that their children were in segregated classrooms, compared to 37 percent of the control group.

[23]Wolf, Howell, and Peterson, 2000.

[24]Howell and Peterson, 2000.

said that the student has moved from a more integrated to a less integrated school. Nevertheless, the student's move would have shifted the demographic mix of *both* schools in the direction of integration. Existing data provide some information about current levels of integration in the schools but little information about how vouchers affect those levels. Given the dominance of minority students in the enrollments of most voucher programs, however, it is unlikely that voucher programs have adversely affected racial integration in the public schools.

Finally, it is important to remember that most of the existing voucher programs are targeted to low-income students, most of whom are nonwhite (in the cities being discussed), and that they are small enough to be able to rely largely on existing private schools (although the largest program, in Milwaukee, includes a number of new schools as well). Wide-eligibility programs that are implemented on a larger scale could produce very different integration effects. We discuss the potential significance of such policy differences in the concluding chapter.

Integration in Charter Schools

Income. As noted in Chapter Five, at the national level of aggregation, charter schools and conventional public schools are serving comparable proportions of low-income students, as indicated by the proportion of their students eligible for a free or reduced-price lunch.[25] Unfortunately, we have seen no school-level data that demonstrate how charter schools compare to conventional public schools in terms of stratification by income.[26]

Race and ethnicity. At the national level of aggregation, charter schools appear to be serving populations similar to those served by traditional public schools with respect to student race and ethnicity.

---

[25]RPP International, 2000.

[26]One study at the national level attempted to compare the populations being served by charter schools to those of their host districts in the 1997–98 school year (Ascher and Wamba, 2000). Unfortunately, however, there is a strong possibility that low-income students were underreported in a substantial number of the charter schools. The authors of the study believe that this is due to the "bureaucratic obstacles to becoming part of the federal free and reduced-price lunch program."

The National Study of Charter Schools also provides data comparing the racial composition of charter schools with that of their local districts: as of 1998–99, 69 percent of charter schools had nonwhite enrollments within 20 percent of their district averages, 18 percent substantially overrepresented nonwhite students, and 14 percent substantially underrepresented nonwhite students.[27]

Unfortunately, these data are not definitive for comparing integration in charter and conventional public schools. Comparisons to district averages cannot indicate whether charter schools are more or less integrated than *individual* public schools. Consider a school district whose total enrollment is 50 percent African-American and 50 percent white and is divided among ten schools. If a local charter school enrolls a population that is 70 percent African-American and 30 percent white, it might be tempting to conclude that the charter school is less integrated than the conventional public schools. Without further information, however, such a conclusion would be unwarranted. The problem is that district-level demographic information does not tell us anything about the composition of individual schools. Each of this district's ten schools might be 50 percent white and 50 percent African-American—or the district might have five all-white and five all–African-American schools. Without knowing the racial composition of individual schools in the district, there is no way to know whether the charter school is more or less integrated than other local schools.

Nevertheless, the comparisons to district-level averages suggest that, nationally, a minority of charter schools are likely to have racial distributions outside the range of the conventional public schools of their local districts. In most districts of any substantial size, the range of racial distributions is likely to extend at least 20 percent above or below the district average.[28] The charter schools that fall within this range are therefore likely to resemble other district

---

[27]RPP International, 2000.

[28]We have not seen definitive national evidence of within-district variation to confirm this assumption, but we used publicly available Common Core Data from the National Center for Education Statistics to examine figures on a few districts for illustrative purposes. In 1996–97, the proportion of nonwhite students in individual schools ranged from 20 to 100 percent in Washington DC; from 57 to 100 percent in Kansas City, Missouri; and from 7 to 100 percent in Grand Rapids, Michigan.

schools in terms of racial distribution. Whether the remaining one-third of charter schools fall within the range of local public schools is less clear.

At the state and local level, only a few studies have gone beyond comparisons to district averages, directly comparing school-level data on charter and public-school integration. Three studies that have made these direct comparisons are described next; they serve to illustrate the fact that the comparative integration of charter schools may vary widely across different states.

In North Carolina, a substantial number of charter schools serve either very high or very low proportions of minority students. In 1997–98, only 18 of the state's 34 charter schools were within the range of local public-school demographic variation; ten had higher proportions of minority students than any of the conventional public schools in their districts, and five had lower proportions of minority students.[29] In other words, nearly half of the charter schools in North Carolina enrolled student populations that were more racially stratified than the populations at every conventional public school in their local district.

A similar analysis of Colorado charter schools in 1997 found that most charter schools looked similar to local public schools in terms of minority population. Twenty-four charter schools were operating in the state at the time; the proportion of minority students served by the charter school fell outside the range of variation in the local district schools in only one case out of those 24.[30]

A third study compared the ethnic composition of each of 55 charter schools in the Phoenix metropolitan area with that of its nearest public school. In 17 of the 55 matched pairs, white enrollment at the charter school exceeded that at the public school by 20 percent or more; one of the 55 charter schools had a white enrollment more than 20 percent below that of the nearest conventional public school.

---

[29]North Carolina Department of Public Instruction, 1998.

[30]Fitzgerald et al., 1998. Although more-recent studies in Colorado report racial and ethnic data on charter students, they compare charter schools only to district averages rather than to individual schools in districts (see Fitzgerald, 2000).

The remaining 37 pairs had white enrollment levels within 20 percent of each other.[31]

Interpretation of the Arizona data is complicated by the fact that about one in six charter schools in the state,[32] including a number of those in the matched analysis, were converted private schools.[33] Even if they were less integrated than local public schools, it is possible that they became more integrated when they changed to charters. Without longitudinal school- and student-level data, it is impossible to construct the dynamic model needed to determine how a private school's conversion to charter status may have changed its own demographic mix as well as the demographic mix of other local schools.

The variation in results from these three studies suggests the importance of examining state and local context. The relative stratification of North Carolina charter schools is particularly interesting given that the state's charter schools are subject to a legal requirement to "reasonably reflect" the demographics of local school enrollments.[34] Two studies have examined the relationship between charter-school demographics and racial-balance provisions; neither has found any consistent relationship between the racial composition of charter schools and charter-law provisions regarding admissions policies or racial balance.[35] Racial-balance provisions in charter laws may be largely symbolic. In California, for example, the law states that charter schools are to reflect the racial composition of the school district in which they are located, but Amy Stuart Wells

---

[31]Cobb and Glass, 1999, Table 11.

[32]RPP International, 2000, p. 15.

[33]Cobb and Glass, 1999.

[34]The law declares: "Within one year after the charter school begins operation, the population of the school shall reasonably reflect the racial and ethnic composition of the general population residing within the local school administrative unit in which the school is located or the racial and ethnic concentration of the special population that the school seeks to serve residing within the local school administrative unit in which the school is located. The school shall be subject to any court-ordered desegregation plan in effect for the local school administrative unit." (North Carolina General Statutes § 115C-238.29F.) It is not clear whether a "special population" might be defined in ethnic terms (e.g., for a charter school with an Afro-centric curriculum).

[35]Wells et al., 2000a; Ascher, Jacobowitz, and McBride, 1998, as cited in Ascher and Wamba, 2000.

and her colleagues found that this provision is not monitored or en-forced.[36] Overall, based on an analysis of more than 20 evaluations of charter schools, Wells and her colleagues conclude that the com-position of charter schools is strongly related to the local context and "the wide range of local reactions to racial inequality and the national confusion about race and educational policy."[37]

EVIDENCE FROM OTHER CONTEXTS

As the summary above indicates, the existing evidence on the inte-gration effects of voucher and charter programs is ambiguous and incomplete. Moreover, most of the programs are so new that student flows have not yet settled into long-term equilibria. Given these un-certainties, we also examine evidence from other contexts, including different varieties of school-choice programs in the United States and large-scale choice programs in other countries. Predictions of long-term integration outcomes from voucher and charter programs may be informed by evidence from these other contexts.

How Do Families Choose?

Evidence on school choice in other contexts is relevant to vouchers and charters partly because it can help in understanding parental preferences about schooling and integration. The arguments of both proponents and opponents of choice depend on assumptions about

---

[36]UCLA Charter School Study, 1998.

[37]Wells et al., 2000a, p. 218. Wells and her colleagues note that the states in which charter schools serve higher proportions of white students are located in the South, West, or Southwest, where districts tend to be larger (often countywide). In contrast, the states with higher proportions of students of color tend to be located in the North and East, where school districts tend to be smaller and more homogeneous. Wells and colleagues note that one possible explanation is that, in largely white northeastern areas with highly stratified and unequal school districts, dissatisfaction with public schools may be concentrated among poor and minority families; whereas in more southern and western states, dissatisfaction may be more dispersed. White and middle-class families in these latter areas may perceive that these more integrated school districts are not as good and may no longer see public schools as places "for people like them." Although this explanation is possible, it is also possible that charter schools in the South and West are drawing white students who would otherwise attend private school. Without further analysis involving all school sectors, explanations must be considered speculative.

how families will choose schools, given the opportunity to do so. Opponents assume that families will often choose racially homogeneous schools.

Several studies of private-school choice have found that families are sensitive to multiple school characteristics, including racial composition. Dan Goldhaber, for example, found that, along with being sensitive to differences in academic achievement, parents are highly sensitive to racial composition.[38] Similarly, an analysis of private-school choice in New York by Hamilton Lankford and James Wyckoff found that white families prefer to send their children to schools that lack substantial minority populations.[39] When the proportion of minority students in the public schools rises by one standard deviation, the likelihood of white, college-educated parents sending their children to private schools increases by one-third.[40] The authors conclude that "white families have a strong preference to avoid minorities and other socioeconomic attributes associated with minorities."[41] Robert Fairlie reached similar conclusions with nationally representative data, finding that a 10 percent increase in the proportion of African-American students in the local public school corresponds to a 19 percent increase in the likelihood of private-school attendance for whites in grade 8, and 26 percent in grade 10.[42] Both Fairlie and Lankford and Wyckoff conclude that these findings suggest that a voucher program widely available to white families will lead to increased stratification.

Other studies examining parental preferences within controlled-choice environments have yielded similar results. In Montgomery County, Maryland, which is a magnet-school district, white families were more likely to request transfers to schools with fewer minority students, whereas minority families tended to request transfers to

---

[38]Goldhaber, 1996.

[39]Lankford and Wyckoff, 2000.

[40]The likelihood of minority parents leaving, however, seems unrelated to the racial composition of the school (Lankford and Wyckoff, 2000).

[41]Lankford and Wyckoff, 2000, p. 16.

[42]Interestingly, there is no evidence that African-American families are responding to racial composition, whereas Latino families respond similarly to white families (Fairlie, 2000).

schools with higher proportions of minority students. Further, minority families were also more likely to seek transfers to neighborhoods with higher levels of poverty and lower incomes.[43]

Evidence from the controlled-choice plan in Minneapolis shows similar results.[44] Examining parents' first choice of schools for their kindergartners, Steven Glazerman found that African-American families are significantly more likely to choose a school having a higher proportion of African-American families, and the effect is even larger for Latino families. White families are not significantly more likely to choose schools with greater proportions of white students, but many white families may have already expressed their preference by leaving the city school system in favor of suburban and private schools having higher proportions of white students.

In sum, these findings about parental preferences suggest that unconstrained choice in a voucher or charter program could lead to higher levels of stratification.

Unrestricted-Choice and Open-Enrollment Plans

Evidence on integration in unrestricted-choice programs in the United States is ambiguous, but the findings of studies of large-scale choice programs in other countries are generally consistent with those on parental preferences, indicating that unrestricted choice often leads to increased stratification.

In Massachusetts and Michigan, choice programs allow students to attend public schools in any district in the state, provided the district has opted to accept students. Unfortunately, data from both states are insufficient for providing clear answers about the programs' effects on integration. In Massachusetts, white students were found to be overrepresented in the program, but the existing studies do not uncover any substantial effects on the racial balance of participating districts.[45] School-level results are unknown. In Michigan's case,

---

[43]Henig, 1996.

[44]Glazerman, 1997.

[45]Armor and Peiser, 1998. See also Fossey, 1994; Aud, 1999.

not only school-level information is lacking, but also information about the demographics of students participating in the program, making it impossible to gauge even district-level effects, let alone school-level effects.[46]

Although differences in institutional context require cautious interpretation, other countries' experimentation with school choice may provide useful information about potential impacts of vouchers and charters in the United States.[47] A few countries have enacted the kind of large-scale choice systems that have not yet been attempted in the United States; these countries therefore provide the only available empirical evidence on large-scale choice systems. The evidence most relevant to the American debate on vouchers and charters comes from Chile and New Zealand, which have large-scale choice systems that resemble (in some respects) those envisioned by ambitious reformers such as Milton Friedman, Christopher Jencks, and Hill/Pierce/Guthrie.[48]

Chile's large-scale voucher plan, strongly influenced by the ideas of Milton Friedman, has operated for two decades. Direct evidence on whether the plan has produced increased stratification is, unfortunately, unavailable as a result of data limitations. Nevertheless, an examination of existing choices suggests that vouchers may have reduced integration in Chile. Patrick McEwan and Martin Carnoy found that preferences for school attributes vary in relation to parental education. Less-educated parents choose schools with lower test scores and less-educated parents, whereas more-educated parents choose schools with higher test scores and parents like them. This suggests that vouchers may have encouraged stratification (on the dimension of socioeconomic status).[49]

---

[46]Arsen, Plank, and Sykes, 2000.

[47]We thank Patrick McEwan for informing us about the international evidence on school choice.

[48]In Chile and New Zealand, most of the data on segregation relates to socioeconomic status. Although New Zealand has an indigenous nonwhite Maori population, neither country has the kind of racial and ethnic diversity characteristic of the United States.

[49]McEwan and Carnoy, 1999.

New Zealand enacted a sweeping nationwide reform in 1991 that made local schools autonomous and allowed universal choice.[50] The system does not include a small number of strictly private schools, but it includes all public schools and the "integrated" schools that are government-funded but managed by institutions such as the Catholic Church. The reform therefore resembles (although not in all respects) the models of universal charters/vouchers promoted by Christopher Jencks and Hill/Pierce/Guthrie: all schools are autonomously operated schools of choice.

Parents in New Zealand are free to apply to schools, and schools are obligated by law to accept them—but only if space is available. If the number of applicants exceeds the number of available places, schools may enact an "enrollment scheme," giving them substantial discretion in determining which students they accept. In the late 1990s in major cities, a large percentage of schools were oversubscribed and had enrollment schemes in place. These schools tended to have more-privileged students.[51] Helen Ladd and Ted Fiske conclude that "enrollment schemes have effectively converted a system of 'parental choice' into a system of 'school choice.'"[52] One result is fairly substantial stratification by race, with Maori and Pacific Islander students disproportionately concentrated in schools that are not in high demand. Ladd and Fiske believe stratification in New Zealand may have been exacerbated by the policy permitting enrollment schemes, as well as by a policy permitting schools to charge "noncompulsory" fees.[53]

Scotland, too, has a large-scale choice program, although it merely makes choice an option rather than converting all schools to schools of choice. Researchers have examined characteristics of choosers, characteristics of chosen schools, and integration effects since the passage of the school-choice legislation in 1981.[54] Choosers were largely drawn from the ranks of the middle class during the initial years of the reform. Later, however, additional numbers of choosers

---

[50]Fiske and Ladd, 2000; Ladd and Fiske, 2001.

[51]Fiske and Ladd, 2000.

[52]Ladd and Fiske, 2001, p. 50.

[53]Ladd and Fiske, 2001.

[54]Willms and Echols, 1992; Willms, 1996.

came from working-class families.[55] Parents tended to choose schools that, compared to their children's designated schools, had higher average test scores and higher mean socioeconomic status.[56] Over time, stratification by socioeconomic status tended to increase most in communities with high levels of school choice.[57]

In sum, evidence from large-scale, uncontrolled-choice plans suggests a tendency toward increased stratification on the dimensions of race/ethnicity and socioeconomic status.

Controlled Choice and the Importance of Policy Details

Where choice has been used explicitly as a tool to promote integration, it has usually been constrained by racial-balance considerations. Under controlled-choice programs, typically, parents rank-order their preferences, and a centralized agency assigns students to schools in a way that ensures the racial balance of all schools in the district or geographic area. Controlled-choice programs sometimes include all schools in a district and are sometimes limited to designated magnet schools.[58] Districts such as Montclair, New Jersey, and Cambridge, Massachusetts, saw improvements in the racial balance of schools following the advent of controlled-choice programs.[59] A national study suggests that magnet programs have aided integration by increasing the representation of white students in predominantly minority districts and vice-versa.[60]

Despite the success of magnet schools and other varieties of controlled choice in promoting integration, these findings have little relevance to voucher and charter policies in which parental choices are

---

[55]Willms, 1996.

[56]Willms and Echols, 1992; Willms, 1996.

[57]Willms, 1996.

[58]See Wells and Crain, 2000; Lamdin and Mintrom, 1997.

[59]Henig, 1994.

[60]Blank, Levine, and Steel, 1996. Studies of magnet schools and other controlled-choice programs have also found that families that choose tend to be more advantaged than other families, which is consistent with the evidence presented in Chapter Five on voucher and charter families (Levin, 1999; Wells, 1993a). Evidence on the academic effectiveness of magnet schools is discussed briefly in Chapter Three.

unconstrained. As a few experts have pointed out, however, voucher and charter programs might be designed with provisions that explicitly promote integration. Even though the charter laws that currently require racial balance seem to be unenforced,[61] it is possible to imagine policies that more vigorously promote integration. For example, in the midst of a long battle to desegregate the Kansas City schools, in the early 1990s some African-Americans proposed (unsuccessfully) that a voucher program be created for African-American students, who could then move into more-integrated private schools.[62] Outside the context of desegregation litigation, policymakers more generally could tie voucher and charter funding to the demographic characteristics of a school, rewarding integration financially.[63] These kinds of proposals, however, have received little attention from policymakers.

UNRESOLVED COMPLEXITIES AND TENSIONS

As the pages above make clear, integration is a far more complex issue than access. The challenges of assessing integration involve not merely measurement issues, but also critical questions of interpretation. In some instances, school integration may be in tension with other important values. Here we summarize a few of the complexities associated with integration.

Between-School versus Within-School Integration

Although we have focused on evidence about the sorting of students across schools, sorting across classrooms within individual schools may be equally important. In public schools (especially large, comprehensive high schools), students are frequently tracked into separate groups based on their perceived academic abilities and ambitions.[64] Minority students are disproportionately likely to be found

---

[61]Wells et al., 2000a.

[62]Beck, 1993.

[63]In the context of vouchers, such a policy has been proposed by Epple and Romano (2000) and Hoxby (2000). Wells and colleagues have proposed that financial incentives could be provided to integrated charter schools (Wells et al., 2000a).

[64]Powell, Farrar, and Cohen, 1985; Oakes, Gamoran, and Page, 1992.

in lower academic tracks.[65] In consequence, schools that appear integrated from the outside may be quite stratified at the classroom level. Studies of Catholic schools have found that they are less likely than public schools to sort their students into separate academic tracks.[66] No studies have directly compared classroom-level integration in public, charter, and voucher schools (although, as we have seen, the experimental voucher studies attempted to do so indirectly through parental surveys, with mixed results). The mere fact that voucher and charter schools tend to have small enrollments, however, suggests that they will be less likely to sort their students into tracks than are conventional public schools, which are usually larger (as indicated in Chapter Two).

Integration in School versus Residential Integration

Now that de jure segregation of schools has ended, the most important source of stratification in schools is the segregation of housing. Even aggressive programs that bus students across neighborhood boundaries are limited by district boundaries, because suburban districts typically cannot be compelled to bus their students across district lines. Magnet schools have attempted to slow or reverse white flight by offering attractive educational options in public schools in the city. Similarly, a few advocates (including the mayor of Milwaukee) have argued that vouchers could be used to retain or attract middle-class and white parents. The effect of voucher and charter schools on residential segregation has not been examined empirically. Most existing programs, in any case, are too small to have had much of an effect, if any. Although some economic models predict a positive effect on residential integration resulting from a

---

[65]Oakes, 1985; Gamoran, 1987; Oakes, 1990; Braddock, 1990; Braddock and Dawkins, 1993.

[66]Bryk, Lee, and Holland, 1993; Coleman and Hoffer, 1987. A common core curriculum is an important part of the communal organization of Catholic schools, exerting "a strong integrating force on both students and adults, binding them together in a common round of school life that encourages each person's best efforts" (Bryk, Lee, and Holland, 1993, p. 125). Catholic schools may find it easier to avoid tracking because they serve populations that are more homogeneous in terms of student and family commitment to education.

large-scale voucher program,[67] in the absence of actual empirical data, the possibility of any such effect is only speculative.

Targeting versus Integration in Charter Schools

Targeting a choice program to low-income or other at-risk students is likely to have different effects on integration in voucher programs (which include existing private and parochial schools) than in charter programs (which exclude existing private and parochial schools). As we have seen, targeted voucher programs tend to serve a high proportion of low-income minority students, but they also may improve integration by placing those students in existing private schools alongside tuition-paying students, who are more likely to be middle-class and white. Charter schools focused on at-risk students, by contrast, are likely to be highly stratified because their enrollments do not include white middle-class students. Consider the Texas charter law that gives favorable treatment to charter schools serving at least 75 percent at-risk students: such schools may serve their students well, but they are likely to be stratified by class and race. Charter laws that favor schools for at-risk students will tend to create a system in which those students are served in separate schools.

Quality of Integration

A simple count of the number of students of different racial/ethnic groups in a school tells us nothing about how those students interact in school. Limited evidence on the quality of schools' racial climate suggests that, in some instances, relationships among ethnic/racial groups may be happier in chosen schools than in assigned schools. Voucher parents in the experimental privately funded voucher programs in New York, Dayton, and Charlotte were significantly less likely than the control group of public-school parents to report that racial conflict is a serious problem in their child's school.[68] Similarly, Cleveland voucher parents were less likely than a sample of

---

[67]See, e.g., Nechyba, 1996.

[68]Myers et al., 2000; Howell and Peterson, 2000; Greene, 2000b.

Cleveland public-school parents to report racial conflict.[69] In Edgewood, Texas, and Washington DC, by contrast, voucher parents were no less likely than public-school parents to report racial conflict.[70]

If vouchers and charters could produce healthier social interactions among students of different racial/ethnic groups, this might be a more significant outcome than any change in the raw numbers of students attending school together. Unfortunately, too little evidence is available to provide solid empirical guidance on this point.

Choice, Integration, and Social Trust

A related issue concerns the potential effect of vouchers and charters on building social trust among inner-city minority parents. As we have seen, although small-scale, targeted voucher programs may marginally improve integration, unrestricted-choice programs may increase racial stratification. Increases in stratification may result both from a parental desire to keep children close to home (in schools likely to reflect segregated residential patterns) and from the development of schools that cater to specific racial/ethnic groups (e.g., schools with Afrocentric curricula). Some inner-city minority leaders view charters and vouchers as a means of taking control of their own schools. This leads to a difficult policy question: Is stratification that results from the voluntary choices of minority parents acceptable? Inner-city minority parents may not appreciate busing plans that send their children to distant schools in support of desegregation, and they are the strongest supporters of vouchers. Is desegregation worth the cost of denying choice to the minorities who are intended to benefit from integration? If charter schools are willing to take on students that have been poorly served by traditional public schools, who might have dropped out altogether, are they worth the price of stratification? John Coons argues that choice for low-income, minority families will increase their trust in government and society and lead to the creation of social capital.[71]

---

[69]Peterson, Howell, and Greene, 1999.

[70]Wolf, Howell, and Peterson, 2000; Peterson, Myers, and Howell, 1999.

[71]Coons, 1992.

Unfortunately, we know of no evidence on this issue, and it is not clear how such evidence could be gathered. For now, these questions cannot be resolved empirically.

SUMMARY

Evidence on the integration effects of voucher and charter programs is regrettably weak. Although quite a lot is known about the extent to which voucher and charter schools provide access to children of various ethnic, racial, income, and ability groups (as shown in Chapter Five), far less is known about how students are distributed across individual schools, and how that distribution is affected by voucher or charter programs. No studies have yet attempted the longitudinal analysis of the dynamic effects of vouchers and charters that would be required for a comprehensive assessment of integration. Still, enough evidence on integration is available to make a few tentative conclusions:

- A number of the existing voucher programs (publicly and privately funded) have helped low-income minority children move into voucher schools that may be less stratified (by socio-economic status and race/ethnicity) than local public schools because the voucher schools include middle-class and white students who are paying tuition. Overall, these programs may have led to a small increase in the integration of the city's private schools. (Education tax subsidies, which are more likely to be used by middle- and upper-income families, are unlikely to have similar effects.)

- The impact of existing voucher programs on integration in local public schools is less clear. Given the demographics of voucher users, however, it is unlikely that existing programs have caused any substantial increase in the stratification of local public schools.

- In charter schools, the picture is also murky. Nationally, most charter schools probably have racial distributions within the range of local public schools. In some states, however, most charter schools serve populations that are either largely white or largely minority, with few being highly integrated.

- Charter policies, unlike voucher policies, create a tension between goals for at-risk students and those for integration. In the case of vouchers, targeting at-risk students may increase integration by putting such students in private schools alongside tuition-paying students. In the case of charters, targeting at-risk students encourages the creation of schools focused entirely on those students and thus more likely to be highly stratified.

- Other evidence on school choice, both in the United States and abroad, suggests that unrestricted-choice programs are likely to lead to increased stratification by race/ethnicity and socioeconomic status, especially if schools are permitted to choose students.

- When explicitly designed to do so, choice plans can improve the racial balance of schools.

- Voucher and charter programs have the potential to improve *within-school* integration because they rely on smaller schools, which are less likely to track students (most clearly demonstrated in the case of Catholic schools). Moreover, there is limited, suggestive evidence that they may also improve the quality of integration in schools, as suggested by survey responses about schools' racial climate.

In sum, evidence on how vouchers and charters affect the sorting of students across schools is incomplete and so far yields mixed results. Future studies should aim to remedy this evidentiary weakness not only by providing better school-level data on integration, but also by exploring what integration actually means in terms of the social climate of voucher, charter, and conventional public schools.

Chapter Seven

CIVIC SOCIALIZATION

Both proponents and opponents of voucher and charter schools maintain that the well-socialized, democratically active citizen is an essential outcome of schooling, as important as any other outcome save, perhaps, having basic reading and math skills. In this conviction, they echo two centuries of American educational discourse and are strongly supported by today's students, teachers, parents, and administrators. Predictably, though, each side in the debate maintains that the schooling system championed by the other side does not and will not produce such outcomes and, in fact, undermines traditional democratic purposes.

This chapter begins with a brief review of the historical antecedents of this issue in American education so as to demonstrate both its enduring significance and the inherent difficulties of defining meaningful goals and of moving beyond normative declarations to operational definitions of practice and outcome. We then review the theoretical arguments of those who propose and oppose voucher and charter schools as they bear on the civic socialization of students. Finally, we review the empirical literature on the issue—literature created and applied mostly on behalf of the advocates of choice, suggestive in its implications but, all in all, sparse and inconclusive.

HISTORICAL PERSPECTIVE

No issue has been more prominently developed and argued in American educational history than the role of schools in a democratic society. At the same time, the issue has never been fully settled. It has contained, moreover, profound complexities and tensions in both political and educational theory, such as the balance between participating in the state and keeping it in check, between individual and societal interests, between economic and political objectives, and between old and new interests. Such complexities and tensions resonate strongly in today's arguments about choice, as they have throughout American educational history.

Historic Roots of the Democratic Purposes of Public Schools

The democratic imperative was first spelled out by Thomas Jefferson and his colleagues as a lesson drawn from their study of the fate of earlier republics: citizens must be educated for a free nation to persist and prosper. They located the development of democratic citizens in the study of history, politics, and rhetoric, and they believed in the local control of schools, which should be encouraged and supported by leadership in the states.[1]

In the mid-19th century, Horace Mann and the founders of the public school movement developed the notion of the "school common to all people" with the explicit purpose, beyond intellectual development, of creating a common value system and a sense of community and harnessing the growing diversity of the citizenry. In the pan-Protestant values they actually espoused, however, these schoolmen alienated Catholics and disparate others, who reacted by founding parochial and other private schools—which have persisted until the present as largely separate educational venues.[2]

Over the next hundred years, the schools were assigned a variety of social and democratic missions: to contribute to economic progress through agricultural and manual trades programs, to spearhead the Americanization of immigrants, and to help counteract the effects of industrialization on children and communities.[3] More recently, the schools were given particular responsibility for overcoming the educational ill-effects of poverty and discrimination—providing equal educational opportunity and targeted instructional assistance but

---

[1]Pangle and Pangle, 2000; Gilreath, 1999.

[2]Cremin, 1961; Tyack and Hansot, 1982.

[3]Cremin, 1961; Tyack and Hansot, 1982.

also preparing all students more effectively in terms of social development and the exercise of citizenship.

As a consequence of this amalgamation of missions, public schools have had, for most of the last century, several broad, ill-defined, and contentious responsibilities:

- Impart the knowledge and skills of citizenship in an increasingly complicated polity.

- Inculcate a set of civic values—such as mutual respect and tolerance, fairness, honesty, generosity, and helpfulness—where there is no substantial consensus on their meaning and appropriate application in society.

- Prepare students for the practical dimensions of adult life and work through a "hidden curriculum" concerned with adaptation to economic life, orderliness, punctuality, persistence, and, more recently, teamwork.

The relative significance of these expectations is fiercely argued by persons with different value perspectives. And any or all of these outcomes are comprehended by various definitions of the social and democratic purposes of schooling embedded in current discussions of educational choice.

Civic Socialization in the 21st Century

Caught in the cross fire of values that characterize these matters, educators have become increasingly loathe to express value-laden positions about the exact nature of the expected "democratic" outcomes.[4] It is thus not surprising that the issue of civic socialization has been mostly off the table throughout the course of the modern school-reform movement, beginning with *A Nation at Risk*.[5] Academic achievement in reading and math (seen to be in the service of economic prosperity) have been the dominant outcomes sought; these are the desired outcomes in the voucher and charter discussions, too.

---

[4]Grant, 1988.

[5]National Commission on Excellence in Education, 1983.

Nevertheless, the issues remain highly significant to students, educators, and the general public. A series of recent reports from Public Agenda show that large majorities of each group (typically between 60 and 90 percent) rate such attributes as honesty, tolerance, responsibility, hard work, and the habits of good citizenship as extremely important outcomes of schooling—more important than all subject-matter learning; in fact, more important than anything except basic skills in reading and mathematics.[6]

THEORETICAL ARGUMENTS CONCERNING CIVIC SOCIALIZATION AND CHOICE

Arguments in Favor of Vouchers and Charters

Although civic socialization has not played a leading role in the movement for vouchers and charters, supporters have developed theoretical arguments that voucher and charter schools will be more effective than existing public schools in the advancement of democratic purposes. Among the advocates of vouchers, this view has perhaps been most prominent in the work of John Coons and Stephen Sugarman. They argue that the modern instruments of democratic control have produced a public-school curriculum that avoids or shortchanges consideration of such essential public values as tolerance and civic responsibility. They also argue that autonomous, chosen voucher schools can acknowledge and build on legitimate differences in values that characterize America's pluralistic society without abetting abhorrent ideologies, particularism, or civic fragmentation.[7] Chester Finn, Bruno Manno, and Gregg Vanourek, meanwhile, predict that charter schools will recreate local democratic governance and thus help rebuild civil society around schools.[8]

Over the past two decades, in studies focusing mostly on Catholic schools, other scholars have developed an elaborate theory of the ways in which such schools' graduates should be well prepared for

---

[6]See, e.g., Johnson and Immerwahr, 1994; Johnson and Farkas, 1997; Farkas and Johnson, 1996.

[7]Coons and Sugarman, 1978. See also Coons, 1998.

[8]Finn, Manno, and Vanourek, 2000.

democratic citizenship. This theory has been most fully set forth by Anthony Bryk, Valerie Lee, and Peter Holland in *Catholic Schools and the Common Good*.[9] Building on the earlier work of James Coleman, Andrew Greeley, and others, and on their own field studies and analyses of national data sets, Bryk and colleagues argue that character formation of each student as a "person-in-community is the central educational aim" of Catholic schools. They go on to say:

> From this perspective, schooling involves more than conveying the acquired knowledge of civilization to students and developing in them the intellectual skills they need to create knowledge. Education also entails forming the basic disposition for citizenship in a democratic and pluralistic society. A commitment to the pursuit of truth, human compassion, and social justice is essential to society's well-being. Fostering such a commitment makes serious demands on schools. If they are to teach children how they should live in common, they must themselves be communities. The school must be a microcosm of society—not as it is but as it *should be*.[10]

Taken together, the theories of those sympathetic to or advocating choice seek to turn the conventional wisdom about the importance of the common school on its head: they suggest that choice schools would enhance rather than diminish the preparation of students for a democratic society.[11]

Arguments in Favor of Conventional Public Schools

Theories that are more skeptical of choice and supportive of the common school model of public education reach precisely the opposite conclusions. There have not been many formal theoretical defenses of the democratic value of public education; its defenders have relied largely on rhetorical recapitulations and refinements of traditional common school notions, as well as lamentations about the insidious effects of individualistic market-oriented philosophies. By far, the most important theoretician among those apprehensive

---

[9]Bryk, Lee, and Holland, 1993.

[10]Bryk, Lee, and Holland, 1993, p. 289.

[11]See, e.g., Bryk, Lee, and Holland, 1993; Greene, 1998; Sikkink, 1999; Smith and Sikkink, 1999; Guerra, Donahue, and Benson, 1990.

about choice has been Amy Gutmann, in *Democratic Education* and subsequent writings.[12] Her view proceeds from a theoretical analysis of the requirements for a "democratic state of education," as distinguished from an education determined predominately by the state or by the preferences of families.[13] For Gutmann, the public interest in schooling manifestly involves education in citizenship, especially now, when political issues are complex and require citizens to have extensive knowledge and capacity for deliberation. Given the pluralism and diversity of society, she argues, the decision of which democratic values to teach can be made only through continual deliberations among diverse parties and perspectives. In her view, public control is the only way that this public interest may be fully expressed and protected.

For Gutmann, vouchers are inimical because they short-circuit democratic deliberation and undervalue the community's public interest in promoting citizenship. She argues that voucher programs place the vital decisions about appropriate democratic values beyond the influence of the community, creating an undemocratic "state of families," in which parents have excessive influence over the education of their children.[14] (Most of Gutmann's theorizing on this issue occurred prior to the invention of charter schools, so it is not clear what her theory implies about them. In more recent work, she suggests that charter schools might represent a healthy kind of decentralized, yet democratic governance.[15])

---

[12]Guttman, 1987, 2000.

[13]Gutmann also talks about a state of individuals, a sort of paragon of liberal neutrality, but it has little real relevance to the actual choice debate (Guttman, 1987).

[14]Other contemporary commentaries from perspectives similar to Gutmann's raise additional related concerns. Stephen Macedo argues that the impact of religious beliefs on public education is especially worrisome in the contemporary case of Christian fundamentalist influences (Macedo, 2000). In *The Demands of Liberal Education*, Meira Levinson shares Macedo's concerns about religious influences. In her view, an educational system aimed at promoting autonomy must constrain religious and parental views that are illiberal. (Levinson, 1999.) Both Macedo and Levinson show some willingness to permit school choice and even vouchers—but Macedo would exclude "pervasively sectarian" schools, and Levinson would require all participating schools to promote a common, liberal curriculum.

[15]Guttman, 2000.

Moreover, in counterpoint to Bryk, Lee, and Holland, other scholars have cautioned that the community values promoted in some religious schools may be incompatible with larger social goals. Law professor James Dwyer argues that religious schools promote narrow, authoritarian ideologies that are hostile not only to the healthy social and psychological development of their students, but also to tolerance and pluralism in a democratic society.[16] Similarly, Alan Peshkin suggests, in the context of a case study, that a fundamentalist Christian school's orthodoxy in values seems incompatible with teaching students that "dissent and compromise are critical attributes of healthy democracies."[17]

Our aim in this chapter is to attempt to sort out these competing claims by examining the empirical evidence that demonstrates the relative effectiveness of voucher, charter, and conventional public schools in socializing students to become effective citizens in a democracy. Unfortunately, as we will see, the evidence on this point is thin indeed.

EMPIRICAL FINDINGS

What Is Civic Socialization?

The democratic performance of schools—whether public or private, choice or not—has not been much studied empirically.[18] The first challenge associated with studying civic socialization involves finding measures that can achieve consensus endorsement. As the historical and theoretical discussion in the preceding pages suggests, Americans have long agreed on the importance of civic socialization in the schools but not on the specific content of that socialization. We do not intend to settle debates about the content of the civic and democratic values that should be promoted in publicly funded schools. Nevertheless, we believe that there is sufficient consensus on these issues to describe, in general terms, the kinds of empirical outcomes that might be examined to assess school performance in

---

[16]Dwyer, 1998.

[17]Peshkin, 1986, p.296.

[18]See Niemi and Chapman, 1998, pp. 3–7, for a concise review of this literature.

promoting civic values. For example, most Americans would agree that all students (or graduates) should demonstrate

- *Civic knowledge* about the formal operations of government, American history, and competing points of view on important political and policy issues.

- *Civic attitudes* that include tolerance and respect for diversity.

- *Civic behavior* that includes voting and community participation, as well as the avoidance of criminal behavior.

Policymakers need to know whether voucher and charter schools are more or less effective than conventional public schools at promoting these kinds of civic knowledge, attitudes, and behavior, which are surely necessary aspects of healthy citizenship in a democracy. In fact, however, few reliable measures or benchmarks exist for any of these outcomes, nor have scholars developed substantial theories of what would constitute appropriate levels of performance. Still, we attempt here to sift through the little evidence that is available.

Evidence from Existing Voucher and Charter Schools

Most of the existing voucher and charter evaluations have collected no data on student learning in the realm of civic socialization, nor have they examined the democratic attitudes and behavior of voucher and charter students. We are aware of only two exceptions, both involving privately funded voucher programs and both carried out by Paul Peterson and colleagues. The first of these, which examined a voucher program in the San Francisco Bay Area, used a telephone survey of a small number of students to assess their attitudes regarding tolerance of opposing views.[19] The study found that voucher students in San Francisco were as tolerant as students who had applied for but not used vouchers. As the authors recognize, however, these data are purely descriptive and cannot be used to make any kind of causal claim about the effectiveness of voucher

---

[19]Peterson, Campbell, and West, 2001. The study also compared San Francisco voucher students with a national sample. We do not believe that a national sample of students is a good comparison group for students in the San Francisco Bay Area, which is a famously liberal community.

schools in socializing citizens. Students were not randomly assigned to receive vouchers, so the comparison of voucher students and voucher applicants who remained in the public schools is likely to be plagued by selection bias. In short, this study may say more about the prior political beliefs of voucher students than it says about the effectiveness of voucher schools in promoting tolerance.

The second evaluation, carried out by Peterson and David Campbell (both of Harvard), assessed the effects of a voucher program initiated by the Children's Scholarship Fund (CSF) on a nationwide scale in 1999. This evaluation also relied on a telephone survey (one year following the award of vouchers), but it had the advantage of random assignment: scholarships were awarded by lottery, creating a more appropriate control group of nonrecipients.[20] Among a variety of other topics, the study examined, in five brief questions, students' political knowledge and tolerance. On the tolerance measure, scores of the voucher students and the control group were very similar, and no significant differences were found.[21] Voucher students answered the two civic knowledge questions correctly more often than their public-school counterparts did, but the differences were not statistically significant.[22] Although these results do not support the fears of voucher opponents, we hesitate to give them much weight, because the measures are very thin and the results are very short-term, based on only a single year of voucher experience.

In sum, as of today, researchers and policymakers have very little convincing empirical evidence on civic socialization outcomes in existing voucher and charter schools. We hope future studies will address the issue (which could be examined, for example, in the randomized voucher studies in New York, Dayton, Washington DC, and Charlotte).

---

[20]Peterson and Campbell, 2001. It should be noted, however, that this study, like many of the other experimental evaluations, had a low response rate: 46 percent. Response rates were similar for lottery winners and losers.

[21]Scores of private-school students were slightly higher on all three measures of tolerance (Peterson and Campbell, 2001, Table 19).

[22]Peterson and Campbell, 2001, Table 20. The questions about civic knowledge asked the name of the current vice president and the name of the U.S. president during the civil war.

Civic Socialization in Public and Private Schools

Lacking adequate socialization data from voucher and charter programs, we turn to studies that examine civic socialization in existing public and private schools. Most of the available empirical studies have sought to measure the civic performance of public or private schools and their students in relatively specific ways, using survey or interview techniques that cannot measure deep or long-term effects, and they have not been conducted in schools affected by voucher/ charter policies. Still, these studies may begin to provide suggestive information for the debate over vouchers and charters.

Using large-scale national data sets, recent studies of public- and private-school students found limited suggestions of an advantage for private-school students on some aspects of civic socialization— or, as choice proponents emphasize, some reassurance that private schools do not foster the civic ignorance or undemocratic attitudes that many critics of charters and vouchers fear.

A study by Jay Greene that used data from the National Education Longitudinal Survey (NELS) found that, compared to their public-school counterparts, private-school students, teachers, and administrators report greater levels of racial tolerance, less racial conflict, more volunteering (though not greater commitment to its importance), and a higher level of commitment and success in promoting good citizenship.[23] This study controlled for differences in the socioeconomic status and race of public- and private-school populations, but did not adjust for unobserved prior differences in the values and attitudes of public- and private-school families, which may be substantial. In consequence, it would be a mistake to conclude definitively that the measured differences are caused by private-school attendance.

Another study examined the civic activity and political participation of the parents of public- and private-school children. Controlling for a variety of background variables, it found that the parents of students in church-related private schools are more civically and politi-

---

[23]Greene, 1998.

cally active than other parents.[24] Again, however, an attribution that the schools caused higher civic involvement is undermined by an inability to account for unobserved prior differences in values and attitudes.

To date, the best study of the relationship between school sector and civic socialization is David Campbell's multivariate analysis of the 1996 Household Education Survey.[25] Using several aspects of civic socialization—including community service, civic skills, political knowledge, and political tolerance—Campbell compared students in conventional (nonchoice) public schools with students in public schools of choice (i.e., magnets et al., but not charters), Catholic schools, non-Catholic religious schools, and secular private schools. Because the Household Education Survey includes data on parents as well as students, Campbell's analyses were able to control not only for standard background variables including socioeconomic status and parental education, but also for measures of the civic participation and attitudes of parents. Although selection bias remains a concern—the data are neither experimental nor longitudinal—the usual problem of unobserved differences should be less serious than in most studies, because many of the potentially important differences are "observed" in this data set and controlled in the analyses.[26] Campbell also controlled for a number of school characteristics, including racial composition, school size, and the existence of a student government. Campbell's findings, comparing schools in each of the other sectors to conventional public schools, are as follows:

- Controlling for student, parent, and school variables (including the level of parental volunteering and whether the school requires community service), levels of *community service* are higher among students in Catholic schools by a statistically sig-

---

[24]Smith and Sikkink, 1999. As in the Niemi study, data are from the 1996 National Household Education Survey.

[25]Campbell, 2001b; an abridged version is available elsewhere: Campbell, 2001a. An earlier study using the same data set reached results that are generally consistent with those of Campbell (Niemi and Chapman, 1998).

[26]The data set nevertheless might be a good candidate for an analysis using instrumental variables, if appropriate instruments can be identified. Campbell does not attempt an IV analysis.

nificant margin. Also, there are no statistically significant differences among the other school sectors.[27]

- For *civic skills*—controlling for student, parent, and school variables (including the civic skills and political participation of parents)—there is a small but statistically significant advantage for students in Catholic schools; other sectors have results comparable to those of conventional public schools.[28]

- For *political knowledge*—controlling for student, parent, and school variables (including the political knowledge and participation of parents)—Catholic-school students have a statistically significant advantage and there are no statistically significant differences for other sectors.[29]

- For *political tolerance*—controlling for student, parent, and school variables (including the political tolerance of parents)—there is a statistically significant advantage for students in non-religious private schools, a statistically significant disadvantage for students in non-Catholic religious schools, and no statistically significant differences among the other sectors.[30]

Summarizing these findings across sectors, then, Campbell found

- No significant difference along any aspect of civic socialization between conventional public schools and public schools of choice (e.g., magnets).

- Advantages for Catholic schools in community service, civic skills, and political knowledge, and no significant difference between Catholic schools and conventional public schools in political tolerance.

---

[27]Campbell, 2001b, Table 1. Note that he finds that the Catholic school advantage holds even among schools that do not require community service.

[28]Campbell, 2001b, Table 2.

[29]Campbell, 2001b, Table 4.

[30]Campbell, 2001b, Table 5. For Catholic schools, Campbell finds a small tolerance advantage that is significant at .1 but not .05. The tolerance test used here is especially challenging for religious schools, because one of the two tolerance questions relates to tolerance of an antireligious speech.

- An advantage for secular private schools in political tolerance, and no significant differences between these schools and conventional public schools in community service, civic skills, or political knowledge.

- Less political tolerance among students in non-Catholic religious schools, though no statistically significant differences between these schools and conventional public schools in community service, civic skills, or political knowledge.

It would be a mistake to make too much of these findings. In the absence of an experimental manipulation or longitudinal data, attributing causation to the measured school-sector effects is problematic. But even if the positive findings for Catholic and secular private schools are discounted, opponents of choice will find little here to support their concerns—with the notable exception of the finding of lower tolerance in non-Catholic religious schools.

In sum, although several studies find that private-school students (or their parents) score relatively well in terms of some measures of civic participation, knowledge, and attitudes, existing research is far short of being able to provide a causal attribution of those outcomes to attendance in private schools. Unfortunately, data on civic socialization outcomes have not received nearly as much sophisticated methodological attention as data on student achievement in public and private schools.[31]

Civic Socialization in Catholic Schools

It is worth considering the effectiveness of Catholic schools in particular in promoting civic socialization, for more than one reason. First, as we have seen, Catholic schools play a prominent role in all of the existing voucher programs. Second, Campbell's findings suggest

---

[31]Additional evidence, including richer measures of civic socialization, may become available from the International IEA Civic Education Study, which surveyed public- and private-school students in the United States and many other countries in 1999. Descriptive statistics comparing American public- and private-school students' civic knowledge and civic skills were reported in April 2001, but analyses controlling for student background characteristics have not yet been conducted. In the absence of controls, private-school students slightly outscored public-school students in both knowledge and skills. (Baldi et al., 2001, pp. 29–30.)

the possibility that Catholic schools may have unique advantages in terms of promoting civic socialization. Third, intensive case study research has led some scholars (notably Bryk, Lee, and Holland) to conclude that Catholic schools exhibit a communal organization promoting a strong focus on socializing students into communal values.[32]

A 1990 report published by the National Catholic Education Association examined "values, beliefs, and behaviors" of Catholic high school students in both Catholic and public high schools.[33] It found evidence that Catholic students in Catholic high schools were somewhat more likely than their co-religionists in public high schools to express concern for others and support for distributive justice. It found no difference between these two groups in their acceptance of members of other races, attitude toward equal opportunity, or community involvement. As in the more general private-school studies, unobserved differences were not factored out.

The empirical work of Bryk, Lee, and Holland suggests that Catholic schools manifest (vis-à-vis public schools) several characteristics that promote a communal environment that might contribute toward effective civic socialization:[34]

- They demonstrate a positive school climate and a shared school culture.

- As a matter of strong conviction, they avoid bureaucratization and seek to build a local school community.

- They are safer and more disciplined.

- They develop high orders of identity and self-esteem in their students, attributes shown to promote tolerance.

- They afford more-frequent and more-intensive opportunities for student service.

- In their efforts at character formation, they see themselves as "bridges" to adult life in society with an emphasis on the virtues

---

[32]See Bryk, Lee, and Holland, 1993.

[33]Guerra, Donahue, and Benson, 1990.

[34]Bryk, Lee, and Holland, 1993.

of mutual obligation and trust—key ingredients in the formation of social capital.

Although these characteristics might plausibly be related to civic socialization, Bryk and colleagues have been primarily interested in their influence on outcomes such as teacher commitment (e.g., efficacy, morale, absenteeism) and student engagement (reduced class cutting, disorder, absenteeism, and dropping out).[35] Their direct influence on civic attitudes, values, and knowledge remains, for now, only speculative.

SUMMARY

The relative brevity of this chapter should be taken as an indication of the scarcity of evidence rather than the importance of the topic. The empirical results consist of a small handful of surveys or case studies of a few schools, without experimental or longitudinal character. They are inherently insufficient to the task methodologically and tell very little about the relative performance of public and private schools in producing students who will function well in the American democracy. Moreover, they shed almost no empirical light on the performance of schools participating in voucher or charter programs. Indeed, we have seen no evidence of any kind on civic socialization in charter schools.

The absence of evidence on civic socialization in voucher, charter, and public schools is not inevitable. Civic socialization has been neglected by most researchers, but the neglect could be remedied fairly quickly. First of all, existing national data sets should be mined more carefully, using the same sophisticated methodologies that have improved the understanding of student achievement differences between public and private schools.[36] Second, more effort should be devoted to developing an array of empirical measures by which to gauge civic socialization. Third, existing and future studies of voucher and charter schools should explicitly incorporate such mea-

---

[35]See Bryk and Driscoll, 1988; Bryk, Lee, and Holland, 1993.

[36]In particular, instrumental variables (IV) approaches might be used to analyze the data from both the National Household Education Survey and the International IEA Civics Study.

sures into their research designs; in the case of the randomized voucher experiments, this might provide, in the near future, valuable information with the possibility of making causal attributions. Finally, the most important aspects of civic socialization are evident only in the long term, after students reach adulthood; in consequence, future studies should make efforts to examine long-term outcomes including voting, community involvement, and (as evidence of minimal socialization) the avoidance of criminal behavior.

The importance of understanding the effects of voucher and charter schools on civic socialization should not be underestimated. For nearly two centuries, the common school model has assumed that the promotion of well-socialized citizens requires schools that are operated by government under democratic control. Voucher and charter advocates explicitly or implicitly assume that this assumption is false. Policymakers need to know which assumption is correct.

Chapter Eight

CONCLUSIONS AND POLICY IMPLICATIONS

ASSESSING THE CHALLENGE

Conceptually and structurally, vouchers and charters represent a departure from the common school model that has been the basis for the American system of public education for a century and a half. Voucher and charter laws assume that it is not necessary to have all children in the same public schools that offer the same educational program under the control of government institutions. Instead, vouchers and charters assume that pluralism in the provision of education is acceptable (or even preferable) and that a system based on family choice and nongovernment operation of schools will produce better outcomes for students.

Whether the conceptual and structural shift associated with vouchers and charters yields differences in empirical effects is the key question of this book. Our task has been to understand the empirical effects of vouchers and charters in terms of student outcomes. We have not assumed that empirical effects follow directly from the theoretical arguments of the supporters and opponents of vouchers and charters; we have instead attempted to maintain a rigorous empirical perspective on all arguments. The fact that vouchers and charters challenge the conventional structure of public education does not necessarily mean that they will inevitably undermine the values associated with the conventional structure. Whether a system based on family choice undermines the values associated with the common school is an empirical question.

Moreover, our empirical examination aims to compare likely outcomes under vouchers and charters with outcomes under the existing system. The common school model may be intended to promote values such as integration and civic socialization, but the extent to which it succeeds in doing so is an empirical question. By the same token, even though vouchers and charters are intended to promote parental choice, the extent to which they succeed is also an empirical question. On both sides, we keep the comparison as close as possible to empirical realities: effects (and likely effects) of actual voucher and charter schools should be compared with effects of actual public schools.

Because vouchers and charters represent potentially fundamental change, it is critical to consider the empirical effects on all of the key outcome dimensions that American society seeks from its schools. These include

- Academic achievement, measured both directly—for students in voucher and charter schools—and systemically—for students remaining in conventional public schools.

- Choice, representing the value of parental liberty in choosing schools.

- Access to voucher and charter schools, particularly for traditionally underserved populations.

- Integration of students from varied racial, ethnic, and socioeconomic backgrounds.

- Civic socialization, representing the public interest in the promotion of effective citizenship in American democracy.

Chapters Three through Seven address the empirical evidence on these dimensions in sequence. Below, we summarize that evidence.

SUMMARIZING THE EVIDENCE

What Is Known

As the previous five chapters demonstrate, many of the important empirical questions about vouchers and charters have not yet been answered. Indeed, it would be fair to say that none of the important empirical questions have been answered definitively. Even the strongest evidence is based on programs that have been operating for only a short time with a small number of participants; serious questions about generalizability remain. Nevertheless, the evidence is converging in some areas. In particular:

Academic Achievement

- Small-scale, experimental privately funded voucher programs targeted to low-income students suggest a possible (but as yet uncertain) modest achievement benefit for African-American students after one to two years in voucher schools (as compared with local public schools).

- For children of other racial/ethnic groups, attendance at voucher schools has not provided consistent evidence of either benefit or harm in academic achievement.

- Achievement results in charter schools are mixed, but they suggest that charter-school performance improves after the first year of operation. None of the studies suggests that charter-school achievement outcomes are dramatically better or worse on average than those of conventional public schools.

Choice

- Parental satisfaction levels are high in virtually all voucher and charter programs studied, indicating that parents are happy with the school choices made available by the programs. In the experimental voucher programs that have been studied for two successive years, levels of parental satisfaction declined somewhat in the second year but remained substantially higher than those of public-school comparison groups.

Access

- Programs explicitly designed with income qualifications have succeeded in placing low-income, low-achieving, and minority students in voucher schools.

- However, in most choice programs (whether voucher or charter), students with disabilities and students with poorly educated parents are somewhat underrepresented.

- Education tax subsidy programs are disproportionately used by middle- and upper-income families.

Integration

- In communities where public schools are highly stratified, targeted voucher programs may modestly improve racial integration in that they put minority children into voucher schools that are less uniformly minority without reducing integration in the public schools.

- Limited evidence suggests that, across the nation, most charter schools have racial/ethnic distributions that probably fall within the range of distributions of local public schools. In some states, however, many charter schools serve racially homogeneous populations.

- Evidence from other school-choice contexts, both in the United States and abroad, suggests that large-scale unregulated-choice programs are likely to lead to some increase in stratification.

Civic socialization

- Virtually nothing is yet known empirically about the civic socialization effects of voucher and charter schools.

What Is Not Known

The brevity of our list of findings should send a note of caution to policymakers and to supporters and opponents of choice. For most of the key questions, direct evaluations of vouchers and charter schools have not yet provided clear answers, and the list of unknowns remains substantially longer than the list of knowns. In particular:

Academic Achievement. Unknowns in the realm of academic achievement include, first of all, an explanation for the (possible) voucher advantage for African-American students. In addition, the academic effectiveness of charter schools must be examined in a larger number of states over a longer period of time. Long-term effects on achievement in both voucher and charter programs are as yet unexamined. Moreover, there is little information that would permit the effectiveness of vouchers and charters to be compared with other, more conventional reforms, such as class-size reduction, professional development, high-stakes accountability, and district-level interventions. Finally, the systemic effects—positive or negative—of both voucher and charter programs have yet to be clearly identified. Whether the introduction of vouchers/charters will help or harm the achievement of students who stay in conventional public schools remains for the moment entirely unknown. This is perhaps the most important achievement issue, because most students are likely to be "nonchoosers" and remain in conventional public schools.

Choice. The most important unknown related to parental liberty concerns the quality and quantity of the schools made available by voucher and charter programs. The number of high-quality alternatives that different varieties of voucher and charter programs will produce is for the moment highly speculative.

Access. Critical unanswered questions about access to voucher and charter schools relate to the variability that would result from different kinds of programs. As we have seen, the characteristics of voucher students in existing programs differ from those of charter students, and the characteristics of charter students vary across states. Other programs might differ further still in the access they provide to different groups of students. In particular, many types of vouchers may be disproportionately used by middle- and upper-income families.

Integration. The effects of voucher and charter programs on the sorting of students across schools have not been well explored. Studies have produced extensive amounts of demographic data on the students participating in voucher and charter programs, but very few of them provide school-level information—on both voucher/charter schools and local public schools—that is linked to information on individual students, which is essential to understanding dynamic integration effects. Even a direct comparison of school-level integration in voucher/charter schools and conventional public schools does not explain how the introduction of a voucher/charter policy changes levels of integration across schools. A full understanding of integration effects requires a clear assessment of all possible counterfactuals. Where would students of different racial/ethnic groups be in the absence of vouchers/charters? Different answers to this question imply very different effects for vouchers and charters. Would these students attend local public schools? Would they pay tuition at racially homogeneous private schools? Would their families move to the suburbs to enable them to attend racially homogeneous public schools? Would they be schooled at home? Unfortunately, no studies of vouchers or charters have undertaken the kind of dynamic analysis needed to provide clear answers.

Civic socialization. Despite the fact that civic socialization is commonly recognized as a critical public purpose of the educational system, next to nothing is known about the relative effectiveness of voucher, charter, and conventional public schools in socializing students to become responsible citizens. The best evidence available is far short of that available for assessing each of the other outcome dimensions, for two reasons: existing measures of civic socialization are thin, and they have been applied only to broad comparisons of public and private schools, rather than to schools actually participating in voucher and charter programs. This slim evidence provides little support for the view that existing private schools are on average any worse than public schools at socializing citizens.

What Could Be Known

Knowledge about the empirical effects of vouchers and charters could be expanded dramatically through additional study of existing programs. Several lines of inquiry that might be particularly fruitful are worth mentioning:

Getting inside the black box. Although some of the best existing evidence on achievement effects is from experimental voucher studies that suggest a possible benefit for low-income African-American children, these studies have not (as yet) explained *why* such an effect might exist. Considerable progress toward understanding the mechanism behind the apparent effect could be made by collecting school-level information on the backgrounds and demographics of choice and nonchoice students as well as their peers (i.e., tuition-paying students in voucher schools). In addition, studies might intensively examine the schools attended by voucher and nonvoucher students to illuminate differences in actual educational experience that could explain the difference in achievement outcomes.

Similarly, the newest and best studies on achievement in charter schools (from Texas and Arizona) do little to explain the sources of any differences in school performance. The Texas study is particularly intriguing in that it suggests that charters focusing on at-risk students may be performing slightly better than conventional public schools while other charters may be performing slightly worse. Even the Arizona study, which shows a performance advantage for charters on average, surely obscures wide variations in the performance of individual charter schools. The next step should be to assess why some charters do well (and others do not).

Returning to Milwaukee. Milwaukee's publicly funded voucher program has now been operating for a decade. Data on student achievement during the first five years of the program have been extensively examined by at least three different teams of researchers. Unfortunately, however, the data collection effort in Milwaukee stopped in 1995, when the Wisconsin legislature chose to end the requirement that voucher students be tested. And since then, the program has expanded its enrollment dramatically and opened its eligibility to religiously affiliated schools—two changes that could have had major effects on student outcomes. Despite the substantial number of evaluations of the original Milwaukee voucher program, virtually nothing is known about the effects of the existing program (apart from demographic data on the participating students). More data from Milwaukee would be especially useful because the program differs substantially from the experimental privately funded voucher programs: it involves a larger proportion of the local school population; the voucher amount is relatively generous, and it requires participating schools to admit all voucher applicants. All of these factors are especially relevant to policymakers considering the establishment of other publicly funded programs. Extensive additional research in Milwaukee should examine short- and long-term achievement outcomes of voucher students, systemic effects on students remaining in the Milwaukee public schools, and effects on student integration and socialization.

More systematic charter research. We were surprised to discover only a few rigorous studies of academic achievement effects in the vast and growing literature on charter schools. Longer-term and multistate evaluations should be able to go a step beyond existing studies in examining both charter-school effectiveness and systemic

effects on students remaining in conventional public schools. Moreover, the outcomes studied should go beyond test scores to include
all empirical issues critical to assessing school-choice programs.

Attention to civic socialization. Civic socialization is the least studied of all the important outcomes associated with vouchers and
charters. The dearth of information is surprising, because civic socialization has been regarded as a fundamental public purpose of
schooling since the establishment of the first American public
schools. Although it has been considered a bedrock justification for
the common school model, there is no substantial empirical data to
demonstrate how well schools—whether they are conventional public schools, private schools, voucher schools, or charter schools—
perform this function. This is a key point of contention between opponents and supporters of autonomous schooling, and future studies of charter and voucher schools should examine it explicitly. To be
sure, it will be a challenge to construct reliable, agreed-upon measures of civic socialization; nevertheless, the near-total absence of
information on this key outcome is disappointing.

What Might Be Learned Through a Grand Experiment

A recent report of the National Research Council proposed that some
of the gaps in the existing knowledge could be remedied by a new,
large-scale publicly funded voucher experiment.[1] Small-scale experiments of privately funded voucher programs have produced useful
evidence on some important questions already, and social experiments have produced critical information for policymakers in a variety of policy domains.[2] A grand school-choice experiment might
answer a number of additional questions that are difficult or impossible to address in existing programs (including both large-scale
publicly funded programs and small-scale privately funded voucher
experiments). In particular, a public experiment might help to determine how demand, supply, and academic achievement are af-

---

[1]Ladd and Hansen, 1999.

[2]See, e.g., Brook et al., 1984, and Manning et al., 1988, on the results of the RAND
health care experiment; Buddin, 1991, on a U.S. Army experiment in recruiting;
Ellickson, Bell, and McGuigan, 1993, on an experimental evaluation of a drug-abuse
prevention program.

fected by levels of funding substantially higher than those available in the existing private experiments. Such an experiment might require participating schools to be open to research, thereby permitting researchers to get inside the "black box" to attempt to determine the specific reasons for any observed effects. This could, for example, help to determine important differences in effectiveness based on, for example, a school's age and its religiosity.

Even a carefully designed experiment will be subject to a number of methodological concerns, however. First of all, an experimental design requires an artificial restriction on the number of students participating in the program. Because the experiment requires a comparison group of those who lose the voucher lottery, it inevitably must operate on a scale that is smaller than full implementation. In the case of school choice, many of the alleged benefits and harms—for nonparticipating students, in particular—depend on the number of students participating. The systemic effects of vouchers/charters on nonchoosing students may become apparent only when a program is fully scaled up—i.e., no longer experimental.

This problem is especially acute in the context of proposals involving complete restructuring of the whole system of school governance, finance, and assignment. Hill, Pierce, and Guthrie, for example, advocate a system in which all schools are schools of choice. The effects of such a system cannot be estimated with an experiment that assigns some students to a nonchoice condition.

However, if an experiment is large enough to create systemic effects, students who remain in the conventional public schools will cease to be an appropriate control group to compare with voucher/charter students. That is, if the introduction of choice affects the conventional public schools—whether positively through competitive pressure or negatively through "cream skimming"—students in the public schools will be affected by the program and therefore should not be used for baseline comparisons. As a result, interpretation of differences in outcomes for students in autonomous schools and students in conventional public schools will be extremely problematic. If choice students are found to do better than nonchoice students, it may be because they have moved to better schools, or it may be because the public schools have deteriorated. If choice students are not found to do better than nonchoice students, it may be because the program has failed to increase achievement, or it may be because both autonomous schools and conventional public schools have improved.[3]

Finally, regardless of scale, a voucher/charter experiment may not produce the same supply response that would follow an institution-alized voucher/charter program. The impact of a choice program depends to a great extent on the supply of seats available in au-tonomous schools. The supply of autonomous schools, in turn, may depend on the extent to which the program is believed to be perma-nent. Although a mere experiment may induce some existing au-tonomous schools to admit additional students, the high costs of startup make it unlikely that many new schools will open unless their operators believe that the program will be permanent.

In sum, even a large-scale publicly funded experiment that is well designed is unlikely to provide definitive answers to all of the impor-tant empirical questions about vouchers and charters. Nevertheless, we agree with the National Research Council that a generously funded public experiment could substantially improve the state of knowledge about the empirical effects of voucher/charter programs.

A Note on Cost

Another empirical dimension of voucher and charter policies—one that we have not systematically addressed in this book—is their cost. Like virtually all of the other empirical issues connected to school choice, cost is hotly disputed by the opposing sides in the debate. Choice opponents argue that voucher and charter programs will break the public budget by imposing the cost of a large number of additional schools on the treasury. Advocates, by contrast, argue that school choice can actually reduce educational costs because children will move from inefficient, high-cost conventional public schools into more-efficient, lower-cost autonomous schools.

---

[3]Theoretically, both of these problems could be solved with an experiment conducted across multiple communities. Rather than randomly assigning individual students, such an experiment would randomly assign communities to choice and nonchoice conditions. David Myers recently proposed such an experiment (see Glenn, 2001b). The political feasibility of conducting such an experiment—which would have to involve at least one entire state—is doubtful, however.

A complete assessment of the costs of vouchers/charters is not easy, because not all costs are captured in the direct fiscal cost of operating the program. From the cost-benefit perspective of economics, calculation of cost depends on recognizing the difference between fiscal cost—represented by direct outlays from government funds—and economic cost—represented by the full burden of the program, as borne by government and private parties.[4] In the case of vouchers and charters, fiscal cost may actually overestimate true economic cost, because operating the program may lead to a cost reduction for the conventional public schools (which will no longer have to educate the voucher/charter students) or the families (which save tuition payments).[5]

As Henry Levin points out, however, some aspects of voucher and charter programs almost inevitably create costs that are beyond what the current system requires and that may not be reflected in fiscal program costs.[6] A vigorous system of school choice requires not only the dissemination of information about school choices to parents, but also a complex system for transporting students to schools that may be far from their homes. These costs may be borne privately, but they must be borne by someone.

In short, sorting out economic cost from fiscal cost is a thorny problem. Policymakers should expect, however, that the cost of voucher and charter programs will vary dramatically depending on both the details of program design and the number of students who enroll. It is possible to design a voucher/charter program that would actually lower the total cost of the educational system. Privately funded voucher programs provide very small scholarships (typically around $1,500 or less), and a publicly funded program designed along the same lines (such as, for example, Cleveland's voucher program)

---

[4]See Levin, 1983. For a sophisticated example of a cost-benefit analysis in the narrower context of school-based drug prevention programs, see Caulkins et al., 1999.

[5]For example, a voucher student who formerly attended the same school at the expense of her family represents additional fiscal cost to the program but no additional economic cost (because she is getting the same education in the same school but with a different source of funding). Eligibility rules may therefore have a substantial effect on fiscal cost, if not economic cost. And some programs with zero or even negative economic cost may have a large fiscal cost.

[6]Levin and Driver, 1997; Levin, 1998.

would be relatively inexpensive. Indeed, if a program were to be funded at a level substantially below per-pupil expenditures in conventional public schools, and substantial numbers of students were to transfer to voucher/charter schools, then the total cost of the educational system might decline. Although policymakers may view this possibility as enticing, they should recognize that a low-cost voucher/charter policy may require sacrifices in one or more of the key outcome dimensions. Later in this chapter, we suggest a number of specific policy provisions likely to improve outcomes in terms of achievement, choice, access, integration, and civic socialization; few of these provisions come cheaply.

More generally, any large-scale system requires a major supply response that will not be induced by a funding level below the actual cost of educating students. No one should expect a dramatic expansion of voucher/charter schools at funding levels of 50 percent (for example) of the current per-pupil expenditures in conventional public schools. Existing private-school tuition rates can be deceptive. Even though tuition for most private schools is substantially lower than public per-pupil expenditures, the overwhelming majority of low-tuition private K–12 schools are religiously affiliated nonprofits that charge less than they spend on each student.[7] They are subsidized by their denominations, and they cannot afford to accept large numbers of additional students at existing tuition levels. A better guide to the subsidy levels necessary to induce a large-scale supply can be found in the new for-profit firms that operate public schools. Edison Schools, for example, the nation's largest for-profit provider, expects the full amount of the local district's per-pupil expenditures to operate a contract school, and it does not operate in communities where expenditures are not high enough to support its educational program.

In sum, policymakers should not expect that voucher/charter programs will provide substantial savings to the public purse if they are to provide high-quality choices to a substantial number of children. Policymakers should expect that most carefully designed voucher/charter programs will cost about as much per pupil as do current public schools.

---

[7]See Henig, 1999; Levin and Driver, 1997.

Costs may be especially relevant as policymakers consider vouchers and charters along with alternative methods of reforming existing public schools. Class-size reduction in the early grades of elementary school, for example, is on the table in many districts and states. It has well-documented achievement benefits, similar in order of magnitude to those found (tentatively) for African-American students in the experimental voucher programs.[8] Reducing class size, however, is an unusually expensive educational intervention.[9] More complete information about both the costs and benefits of voucher/ charter programs and their alternatives—including not only class-size reduction, but also high-stakes accountability, district-based initiatives, and comprehensive school reform, among others—will be needed if policymakers are to clearly assess tradeoffs.

IMPLICATIONS FOR LARGE-SCALE CHOICE PROGRAMS

Specific variations in the details of voucher/charter policies (on a number of the policy-design dimensions described in Chapter Two) are likely to make a big difference in many of the empirical outcomes. Program scale is one variable likely to be especially important.

Nearly all of the existing empirical evidence on the effects of vouchers and charters comes from relatively small-scale programs. In the case of the targeted "escape-valve" voucher programs, most of the existing evidence is neutral or somewhat favorable: they provide valued new choices to low-income families and may provide achievement benefits to African-American students. Although little is known about empirical effects in dimensions other than achievement— including integration, civic socialization, and cost—it seems unlikely that escape-valve programs would result in major harms to any of them. In brief: in some contexts—such as high-poverty cities with substantial African-American populations, or communities that have underperforming public schools—targeted voucher programs may produce discrete benefits. Such programs will not be the silver bullet

---

[8]Krueger and Whitmore, 2001; Stecher and Bohrnstedt, 2000.

[9]Brewer et al., 1999.

that will rescue urban education, but they are unlikely to produce the negative consequences that voucher opponents fear.

Evidence on existing charter laws is harder to summarize, because variation across states is dramatic in terms of both the provisions of the laws and the observed empirical effects. Existing charter schools frequently satisfy a parental demand and are producing mixed but promising academic results. Other effects are ambiguous or unknown.

As for what the existing findings imply for larger-scale choice programs, that is unclear. The experimental privately funded voucher programs, which provide much of the evidence about academic performance and other outcome dimensions, enroll only a tiny proportion of students in the cities where they operate. Publicly funded voucher programs in Cleveland and Florida also enroll only a small number, and the Milwaukee program, which is larger, still includes no more than 10 percent of the city's student population. The maximum size of all of these programs is constrained by built-in restrictions that limit eligibility to specific students (typically defined by family income). Charter schools typically have no such eligibility requirements; nevertheless, as a result of supply limitations and the newness of the sector, they currently enroll no more than 5 percent of all students in any state.

More-ambitious proposals and programs seek to provide autonomous schools that are widely available to a large number of students. Such programs include California's Proposition 38, Arizona's voucher tax credit, and the federal education savings account (ESA). Charter programs in states where the constraints on charter supply are minimal (such as Arizona) may also ultimately achieve much larger scale (though how much larger is not yet clear). Universal-choice systems of autonomous schools are the most ambitious of all. Unfortunately, for all of these large-scale programs, the available empirical evidence is very limited. The weaker research base here has at least two sources. First, fewer large-scale programs have been passed. Proposition 38, for example, failed by a wide margin, and the federal ESA passed Congress only very recently. Moreover, no universal-choice systems of autonomous schools have ever been implemented in the United States. Second, many of the proposals are difficult to study. The beneficiaries of programs that work through the income-tax system, for example, are a very diffuse group that is difficult to find and study.

Using evidence from small voucher/charter programs to infer the outcomes of large-scale choice programs is not easy, for several reasons. First of all, the voucher experiments providing some of the best evidence on achievement effects are black boxes and thus do not explain the mechanisms that produced the apparent achievement advantage for low-income African-American students who use vouchers. As we describe in Chapter Three, the possible explanations for the observed achievement difference are wide ranging, and different explanations have profoundly different implications for whether the effect is reproducible in a larger-scale program. If, for example, these voucher students benefited only because the program put them in classrooms with high-achieving peers, then the effect might disappear in a larger-scale program that puts large numbers of low-achieving students in voucher classrooms together. Similarly, if the experimental advantage is attributable to a context of underperforming public schools, then a universally available alternative might show no advantage when compared to a broader range of higher-performing public schools. Other mechanisms that could explain the experimental findings may be more easily duplicated on a larger scale. Until the source of the experimental findings is understood, however, there is no way to know whether they apply to larger-scale programs.

Similar issues arise with respect to achievement in charter schools. The existing charter studies show mixed results but some agreement that academic performance is lowest in the first year of a charter school's existence. Programs that seek to open large numbers of new charters should not expect high achievement in the short term.

The empirical effects on the dimensions of access and integration will almost certainly differ for large-scale programs. Most existing voucher programs are escape valves that serve low-income or other at-risk students because they are explicitly designed to do so, with eligibility tied to family income or to the performance of the local public school. Universally available voucher programs, by contrast, may disproportionately benefit highly educated and upper-income families that have the means to take advantage of them, particularly if the programs are funded at low levels and permit supplemental tuition payments. (Universal-choice systems, in contrast, try to avoid inequitable access by ensuring that all students are choosers; whether they can succeed in this ambition is as yet unknown.) Similarly, large-scale choice programs (whether voucher or charter) are more likely to undermine school-level integration than are escape-valve vouchers that put low-income students in existing private schools.

The economic costs of large-scale voucher/charter programs are also highly unpredictable. They depend not only on the program's policy design details, but also on the "take-up rate"—i.e., the number of students who switch schools to participate in the program. Costs will go up if students switch into higher-cost schools, but costs could actually decline if students switch from higher- to lower-cost schools. The existing escape-valve programs provide little guidance on what the take-up rate of universally available programs would be.

Even if the findings of small-scale programs are theoretically generalizable, moreover, programs in the process of scaling up may encounter unexpected difficulties. Class-size reduction is a case in point. A carefully designed experiment in Tennessee in the 1980s has provided powerful evidence that, when other factors are held equal, primary-grade students learn more in small classes (13 to 17 students) than in larger classes (22 to 25 students).[10] The state legislature in California took this message to heart, creating a statewide incentive program to reduce class size in grades K–3. Although the California program succeeded in achieving the immediate goal of shrinking classes, it encountered an array of unexpected problems that insured other factors were not equal. Most notably, the rapid simultaneous reduction of class size in nearly all districts in the state created a massive boom in teacher hiring. The available supply of highly qualified teachers was quickly exhausted, and the number of uncredentialed and inexperienced teachers entering California's classrooms rose dramatically—with the largest increases in high-poverty schools.[11] The general point is that scaleup often results in a distortion of the original conditions that made treatment effective.

---

[10]See Krueger, 1999.

[11]Stecher and Bohrnstedt, 2000.

More directly analogous to vouchers and charters is the "comprehensive school reform" movement that has sought to create and disseminate whole-school designs for adoption by schools across the country. Many design teams (promoting designs such as Roots & Wings, Modern Red Schoolhouse, ATLAS, and Co-NECT) have had great difficulty moving their designs from a few pilot schools to a large number of schools.[12] Problems in scaleup result in part from a variation in local conditions and needs. Whereas class-size reduction is less effective in the absence of qualified teachers and suitable classroom space, comprehensive school reform is less effective when school staff are not fully informed and supportive of the design.

Scaling up voucher and charter programs could lead to similar problems. Just as a large-scale class-size reduction program strains the supply of high-quality teachers, a large-scale choice program may strain the supply of high-quality schools. Newly established voucher/charter schools may or may not be as effective as pre-existing private schools. High-quality nonprofit providers (including religious institutions) may lack the capacity and incentive to expand, and the supply may be filled largely by for-profit school operators, whose effectiveness is as yet unknown.

However, vouchers and charters may in some respects be relatively easy to scale up because they are not programmatic and can be uniquely sensitive to local needs and desires. They are fully compatible with all programmatic reforms that are chosen and implemented at the school level rather than imposed from above. In consequence, they may bypass at least a few of the implementation and scaleup problems that have undermined a wide variety of educational reforms over the past 30 years. Whether they will succeed in doing so—and in producing the achievement, access, choice, integration, and civic socialization outcomes desired from America's schools— remains to be seen.

A note on universal-choice systems. The most ambitious voucher/ charter programs would replace the existing system of educational governance and finance with an entirely new system in which all

---

[12]See Bodilly, 1998; Berends et al., 2001.

schools are autonomous and every family must choose a school. Christopher Jencks's 30-year-old proposal to create a comprehensive, regulated voucher system fits this category, as does the more recent proposal of Paul Hill, Lawrence Pierce, and James Guthrie to turn all public schools into independently operated contract schools. Similarly, Hugh Price of the National Urban League has proposed that all urban schools be converted to autonomous charter schools.[13] A governance commission sponsored by the Education Commission of the States has also suggested, as a promising alternative governance arrangement, universal choice among schools that are independently operated by contractors.[14]

Not surprisingly, direct evidence on these highly ambitious proposals is very limited, because they have never been fully implemented in the United States. In the early 1970s, the federal government tried to find communities willing to try the Jencks plan. The program ultimately implemented in the one community willing to accept it (Alum Rock, California), however, bore little resemblance to what Jencks had proposed: schools were operated by the district rather than by independent organizations.[15] A few urban districts (notably New York City's District 4, in East Harlem, at the middle-school level) have established universal-choice plans, but these include only public schools that are operated by the district.

Universal-choice programs would, of course, encounter many of the implementation challenges described above. In addition, because they would directly change the entire educational system, they have the potential to create larger effects—both positive and negative— than other varieties of programs do. Systemic effects would not merely result indirectly from competition or cream skimming, but would follow directly from the changes to all public schools. These proposals therefore could create either the greatest benefits or the greatest harms.

One advantage of universal-choice programs over those that run alongside the existing system is that they turn all students into

---

[13]Price, 1999.

[14]National Commission on Governing America's Schools, 1999.

[15]See Levinson, 1976.

choosers. This might reduce the likelihood that cream skimming would occur: if all students choose, then none are "left behind" in an assigned school. Cream skimming remains a possibility, however, if schools are permitted to admit students selectively. If a universal-choice system means that schools choose students rather than vice versa, then a high degree of stratification may result. To reduce the likelihood of cream skimming and other negative effects, regulation of some form is almost certainly necessary. Jencks and colleagues recognized this 30 years ago, when they proposed a system with regulated admissions, higher funding levels for low-income students, a prohibition on tuition charges above the voucher amount, and a system for public dissemination of information about schools.

In sum, care in the details of design might permit the construction of a universal-choice program that could avoid negative consequences and perhaps produce substantial benefits. But predicting such benefits depends for now on theory rather than existing evidence.

CONSIDERATIONS IN POLICY DESIGN

Despite the large number of remaining uncertainties about the empirical effects of vouchers and charters, it is possible to provide some guidance on how to intelligently design the details of voucher/charter programs. Policymakers considering voucher or charter laws can maximize program benefits and mitigate harms through thoughtful policy design. Here we consider a series of questions that address the relationship between policy details and empirical effects in the five key outcome dimensions that were discussed separately in Chapters Three through Seven. In some instances (as indicated below), a policy that promotes a favorable result for one outcome may be antithetical to another outcome. In such instances, a tradeoff among desired outcomes becomes necessary. The ideal policy design therefore depends to some extent on how policymakers value the various outcomes promoted by the educational system. Nevertheless, the relationship among outcomes is often complementary rather than competing: a few of the same policy prescriptions can serve multiple purposes.

The prescriptions below should be considered tentative rather than definitive. They are promising policy options based on plausible inference from the available evidence.

How Might Policymakers Maximize the Likelihood That Voucher/Charter Schools Will Be Academically Effective?

Include existing private and parochial schools. Evidence demonstrating the academic effectiveness of voucher and charter schools is thin. Some of the most favorable evidence available, however, comes from experimental voucher programs that include existing private and parochial schools. This evidence is consistent with some non-experimental study findings of academic benefits for African-American children in Catholic schools. Moreover, the best evidence on achievement in charter schools suggests that school performance is worse in the first year of operation. Given the challenges associated with starting a new school, these findings are not surprising. Although we do not believe policymakers should discourage new schools (charter or voucher) from starting, positive academic results may be seen more quickly if existing schools are allowed to participate.

Enforce requirements for testing and information dissemination The efficient operation of markets requires that consumers have good information about product quality. School choice is more likely to produce academically effective schools if student achievement is regularly evaluated and reported publicly, and information about curriculum, instructional methods, and staff is provided so that families can make informed choices.

Do not skimp on resources. The fact that parochial-school tuition is typically far less than per-pupil expenditures in public schools sometimes misleads policymakers into believing that they can get great results from voucher/charter programs on the cheap. As we have already noted, however, tuition at religious schools substantially understates the true cost of education because both operating and facilities costs are subsidized by churches and charitable contributions (including in-kind contributions from parents and teachers). The experimental voucher studies suggest that it is possible to benefit a small number of students with very limited funding. Any program that aims to improve achievement for a substantial number of students, however, will need to provide funding substantial enough to ensure a supply of spaces in high-quality autonomous schools.

How Might Policymakers Maximize the Likelihood That Systemic Effects on Nonchoosers Will Be Positive Rather than Negative?

Establish communication among schools. At the most mundane level, if conventional public schools are to learn from voucher/charter schools, a mechanism for communication must be in place. Public and private schools have historically operated in almost entirely separate worlds, and there are disturbing signs that this separation is too often replicated in the case of charter schools—despite the fact that one of the avowed purposes of charter laws is to create "laboratories" for innovation.[16] Public-school officials should have formal lines of communication to autonomous schools (charter and voucher). More generally, however, the culture of the education profession should change so that teachers think of themselves as part of a single professional community rather than as occupying separate sectors.

Impose consequences on schools that do not perform at acceptable levels. If competitive pressures are to improve the conventional public schools, it may be necessary to have consequences for competitive failure. Florida's high-stakes accountability system seems to have produced improvement in the test scores of low-performing schools (although whether that improvement is attributable to vouchers is unknowable). A voucher/charter program that does not impose costs on public schools that fail to keep their students may not induce improvement. The loss of per-pupil funding will undoubtedly arouse considerable political resistance from the public schools. Indeed, some voucher opponents seem to think of systemic effects in terms of financial costs imposed on public schools. Reduced funding to the public system, however, is important only if it has detrimental effects on students—and the loss of a voucher or charter student does not reduce *per-pupil* funding in the conventional public schools. Economic theory suggests that the imposition

---

[16]The extent to which most charter schools are actually innovative is a matter of some doubt. Studies in California and Michigan found that most charter schools are using educational programs used in conventional public schools (UCLA Charter School Study, 1998; Arsen, Plank, and Sykes, 2000). Nevertheless, charter schools may be offering programs not available in their nearby public schools (see Finn, Manno, and Vanourek, 2000).

of financial costs may be necessary to produce academic benefits. Public schools rarely feel threatened by private schools that take students without taking resources.

Give public schools the autonomy to act competitively. Effective competition also suggests, however, that conventional public schools should be empowered to respond to market pressures. Public-school advocates often complain—with some justification—that their competition with voucher and charter schools does not take place on a level playing field. Autonomous schools may have considerable competitive advantages over conventional public schools burdened with extensive regulatory structures. Some deregulation of conventional public schools should accompany any large-scale choice program if competition is to be effective. In the extreme case, this would involve creating a universal-choice system (à la Hill, Pierce, and Guthrie) that turns all schools into autonomous schools of choice.[17]

Require open admissions. Opponents of choice are concerned that voucher/charter schools will "skim the cream" from the public schools, taking the students who are high-achieving, highly motivated, and otherwise advantaged compared to those left behind in the public schools. To the extent that academic achievement is partly the result of peer effects, removing high-achieving students will reduce the achievement of those left behind. As Chapter Five demonstrates, there is little evidence that existing voucher and charter schools are skimming the cream. Nevertheless, the concern is legitimate—particularly for larger-scale programs that do not specifically target at-risk students. One solution is to require participating voucher/charter schools to admit all applicants (or to admit by lottery if they are oversubscribed). Stratification of students by academic ability and consequent negative peer effects on academic achievement are likely to be greater in a system that permits schools to choose their students. Open admissions have been proposed by Jencks and by Coons and Sugarman and are an explicit requirement

---

[17]See Hill, Pierce, and Guthrie, 1997; Center for the Study of Public Policy, 1970.

of the voucher program in Milwaukee and Cleveland; some states' charter laws also require open admissions.[18]

Require all students to choose. Grand plans for systemic reform, such as those of Jencks and Hill/Pierce/Guthrie, attempt to elegantly make the problem of nonchoosers disappear by eliminating the category: under their proposals, every child's family must choose a school, and every school must compete for students. Such a policy is not wholly fanciful: New York City's Community School District 4, in the low-income neighborhood of East Harlem, has made choice a requirement for all middle-school students for many years.[19] Establishing a system of universal choice is the most dramatic solution for policymakers willing to throw out the traditional system of residential assignment to schools. It should be noted, however, that there will always be differences among parents in terms of access to information permitting a well-informed choice;[20] even universal-choice systems cannot entirely solve that problem.

How Can Policymakers Ensure That a Substantial Number of Autonomous Schools Will Be Available?

Permit existing private and parochial schools to participate. The surest way to constrain the supply of autonomous schools is to exclude existing providers. Charter legislation always excludes religious schools and often excludes all private schools, dramatically reducing the potential supply of spaces (and imposing a constraint on the range of parental choice). As compared with charter laws, voucher programs provide families with more options among well-established autonomous schools, at least in the near term.

---

[18]As noted in Chapter Two, Jencks and Coons and Sugarman have also proposed a variation on this policy that would permit schools to select half of their students and admit the other half by lottery (Center for the Study of Public Policy, 1970; Areen and Jencks, 1971; Coons and Sugarman, 1978). Similarly, some charter schools make exceptions for the children of founders and for siblings of current students. These kinds of variations might be as effective as completely open admissions.

[19]See Meier, 1995; Wells, 1993b; Teske et al., 1998.

[20]See Schneider, Teske, and Marschall, 2000, on information disparities related to schooling options.

Provide generous funding. Perhaps the single most important determinant of the supply of spaces in autonomous schools is the amount of funding provided. Policymakers who are serious about creating a supply of spaces for a substantial number of students should be prepared to fund voucher/charter programs at levels comparable to spending in conventional public schools—including funding for facilities, transportation, and special-needs students, as well as for operating expenses.

As we note in Chapter Two, in practice—although not in principle—charters often receive more-generous public funding than do vouchers. This may be the result of different comparison points. When setting scholarship amounts for voucher programs, policymakers tend to look at tuition rates for existing private schools.[21] For charter schools, by contrast, the baseline for comparison is typically existing per-pupil expenditures in conventional public schools—though many states allocate less than 100 percent of that baseline to charter schools. Moreover, both charter schools and voucher schools are often denied the facilities funding routinely given to conventional public schools.[22] Inducing a substantial supply response will require a substantial investment of resources.

Avoid overregulation. Excessive regulation constrains supply by reducing the number of schools (and educational entrepreneurs) who wish to participate in the program. Existing private schools, for example, may balk at participating in voucher systems involving extensive regulation of curriculum and hiring practices. Prospective charter-school operators, too, may be discouraged if red tape prevents them from pursuing their educational vision.

This is the clearest instance in which one desirable outcome (choice) may conflict with other desirable outcomes. Some regulation (of admissions policies, for example) may be important to ensure equitable access and other public goals of the system, but it may also re-

---

[21]Data from 1997–98 indicate that median tuition was $1,500 in Catholic elementary schools and $4,100 in Catholic high schools (Youniss and McLellan, 1999). Tuition at other religiously affiliated schools tends to be somewhat higher but is still far lower than that at elite independent private schools (Choy, 1997).

[22]For a recent report on variations in charter-school financing, see Nelson, Muir, and Drown, 2000.

duce the supply of providers willing to participate. The possibility of overregulation is a particular concern of those who want to maximize parental freedom of choice. Those who prefer to preclude all regulation on private schools are likely to favor education tax subsidies over charters or vouchers. Such subsidies typically impose few, if any, regulations on private schools. (This means, of course, that it is difficult under an education tax subsidy program to impose regulations that might promote other desired outcomes.)

More generally, policymakers who value both choice and other outcomes will need to undertake a balancing act. Some regulation may be necessary, but too much regulation will defeat the purpose of a system whose goal is to promote autonomy in schools. One possible compromise, implicit in some charter agreements, is to focus regulation on outcomes, permitting the school to determine the inputs necessary to achieve those outcomes.

Create multiple chartering authorities, including but not limited to the local school board. The charter-school sector has grown fastest in states such as Arizona and Michigan, where the charter law permits bodies other than school districts (such as state universities or a state charter board) to authorize charter schools. Local districts are frequently reluctant to authorize their own competition. Indeed, they may be more willing to create options of their own if other options are present (as has happened in Milwaukee, for example, where the Milwaukee public schools have created a number of options within the district). If policymakers want to see a sector of publicly funded autonomous schools grow substantially, they should not make the size of that sector entirely contingent on the authority of local school boards.

How Can Policymakers Ensure That Autonomous Schools Will Serve Low-Income and Special-Needs Children?

Actively disseminate information about schools. Parents must be able to distinguish among schools based on differences that are relevant to desired educational outcomes. Studies of the school-choice experiment in Alum Rock, California, in the 1970s found that, in the early years of its operation, low-income families had less information about their options than did middle- and upper-income families.

Reducing that information gap may require active efforts to provide information to low-income parents. Parent information centers have been shown to make a difference in providing information about educational options in Massachusetts.[23]

Target specific children. Among supporters of vouchers, there is considerable disagreement about whether voucheres should be universally available or targeted. While California's Proposition 38 would have made vouchers available to all students, existing voucher programs in Cleveland, Milwaukee, and Florida target low-income families or students in low-performing public schools. A second voucher program in Florida is designed specifically for students with disabilities. Charter laws and education tax subsidies, by contrast, typically have no explicit mechanism to favor low-income students; they are open to families of all income levels (though a few states, such as Texas, favor the charter applications of schools serving at-risk students). The evidence presented in Chapter Five clearly demonstrates that targeted voucher programs do serve low-income students. Charter schools, lacking income requirements, normally serve a population with a wider range of incomes. Policymakers who want to focus on low-income and disabled children can easily design voucher/charter programs to target those children.[24]

Forbid tuition add-ons. If a voucher or charter program does not include a provision for means testing, then policymakers might, alternatively, choose to forbid participating schools from charging tuition to subsidized students. Additional tuition is forbidden in Milwaukee's voucher program but permitted in Cleveland's. Tuition charges are universally forbidden in charter schools (though an in-kind family commitment may be required, in the form of volunteer work at the school). If additional tuition charges are permitted, many schools may be priced out of reach for low-income families.

---

[23]Glenn, McLaughlin, and Salganik, 1993, as reported in Archbald, 2000. But note that benefits may accrue generally even if not all parents are informed. Schneider et al. argue that a minority of well-informed parents can serve as "marginal consumers" who induce the market to operate efficiently, so that even uninformed parents benefit from improved schooling (Schneider et al., 1998).

[24]It should be noted, however, that targeted programs carry some risk that their beneficiaries will be subject to a degree of social stigma (as associated, for example, with food stamps and welfare payments).

Provide generous funding. Means testing and a prohibition on additional tuition are less critical if autonomous schools are funded at a high level. Without means testing or a prohibition on add-ons, a small voucher will benefit only those who can afford to pay the additional tuition. Real choice for the poor requires generous funding; some programs (such as the Jencks voucher proposal and charter laws in Michigan and Minnesota) make a special effort to reach at-risk children by providing supplemental funding for them.[25] To the extent that they are inadequately funded, voucher/charter schools in wealthy communities with access to external resources will have an advantage.[26] From the perspective of access for the poor, the worst case is a universal voucher (or tax subsidy, such as the federal ESA) in a small amount. Such a program would largely represent a redistribution of tax funding from the poor to the rich. An effective, equitable choice system should not be expected to be substantially less expensive than the current system of public education.

Use a direct funding method. In distributional terms, vouchers provided as direct scholarships and charter schools are more likely than education tax subsidies to be used by low-income families. Even if a tax credit is fully refundable, many low-income families may not be able to pay tuition up front and then wait several months for a refund check from the state. A tax deduction/exclusion (such as the federal ESA) is skewed even more strongly in favor of upper-income families, because its value is greater for those in higher tax brackets. Tax subsidies for private-school tuition payments are far more likely to benefit middle- and upper-income families than low-income families.[27]

---

[25]See Nelson, Muir, and Drown, 2000, Table 7.

[26]The importance of access to external resources for underfunded charter schools has been documented by Amy Stuart Wells and colleagues (UCLA Charter School Study, 1998).

[27]Tax credits for charitable donations to private voucher programs (as exist in Arizona and Pennsylvania) have the potential to be less regressive than tax subsidies for a family's own tuition payments, because the private voucher programs may choose to target low-income families. Indeed, under Pennsylvania's law, families with two children are ineligible for vouchers if their income exceeds $70,000—which excludes upper-income families. Participating private voucher programs may choose to set an income cutoff that is lower still.

Provide supplemental funding for students with special needs. If they are to be served by voucher/charter schools, students with disabilities should receive additional funding to defray the additional cost of their education. In principle, this should not be difficult to do: it is an implicit part of the current system, which requires Individual Education Plans (IEPs) for students with disabilities. On average, students in need of special education cost 2.3 times as much to educate as other students do; those with more-serious disabilities cost more still.[28] Florida's McKay Scholarships Program is aimed specifically at students with disabilities; it sets the voucher amount at a variable level depending on the student's needs.[29] In practice, students with disabilities are expensive to educate, and any program of autonomous schools that seeks to serve them will have to include some provision for subsidizing the additional costs. Today, this happens rarely in voucher programs and only to a limited extent in many charter laws, surely explaining why disabled students are often underrepresented in voucher and charter schools. To encourage voucher and charter schools to serve students with disabilities, programs should provide supplemental funding that recognizes not only the existence of disabilities, but also their severity.[30]

Require open admissions. As noted above, one condition often imposed on both voucher and charter schools is a constraint on their ability to select students. The voucher programs in Milwaukee and Cleveland and most charter laws do not permit schools to discriminate on the basis of academic performance. Some programs, however—including the federal ESA and other education tax subsidies—impose no limits on schools' selection processes. And charter laws in a number of states permit schools to impose geographic restrictions on enrollment. Choice policies that permit schools to select their

---

[28]See Moore et al., 1988.

[29]For details, see http://www.opportunityschools.org/osas/spswd/.

[30]As a recent report on charter-school financing points out, a number of charter laws provide special-needs funding in amounts that are insensitive to the specific needs of the student; this provides an incentive to serve students with relatively minor disabilities and to avoid those with major disabilities. A few laws provide special-needs funding that does not even account for the number of special-needs students served in the school, instead assuming that each school serves the same proportion of special-needs students as is served by district schools. This creates an incentive to avoid disabled students entirely. (Nelson, Muir, and Drown, 2000.)

students by academic performance encourage cream skimming and may provide few high-quality options for at-risk students. Choice policies that permit schools to restrict access to those living in a particular neighborhood or school district duplicate one of the notable flaws of the existing public system, which denies urban students access to suburban schools. A policy that aims to provide choices to low-income families should provide open access to a variety of autonomous schools. The idea should be to ensure that the critical choices are made by families rather than by schools.

It may not be necessary to deprive schools of all discretion in admitting students in order to ensure access to low-income parents and at-risk students. As Jencks and as Coons and Sugarman have proposed, a voucher/charter policy might permit schools to select half of their student body (to promote the school's particular mission) while requiring that the other half be admitted by lottery. Thus, for example, a school that focuses on musical instruction would be ensured that it could select up to half of its students on the basis of musical talent. This sort of limited selection might control the cream-skimming problem and leave schools with enough discretion to be willing to participate in the program.[31]

Admittedly, enforcement of admissions regulations for large numbers of autonomous schools may not be easy. Several voucher schools in Milwaukee have been accused of violating program regulations by giving admissions tests to voucher applicants.[32] In most voucher and charter schools, admissions decisions are made informally; interview requirements make it possible to discourage undesired applicants even if they are not formally rejected. Nevertheless, it should be possible to require a formal lottery in schools that are oversubscribed. Despite the enforcement challenges, policymakers concerned about ensuring wide participation by at-risk students should seriously consider imposing such a requirement.[33] In

---

[31]Coons and Sugarman suggest a variety of alternative admissions policies aimed at ensuring fair access while permitting schools to maintain their desired character (Coons and Sugarman, 1978, pp. 135–145).

[32]See Borsuk, 2000.

[33]Schools' authority to suspend and expel students may be a concern as well. Jencks and colleagues propose that participating schools be required to adhere to standard procedures for suspending and expelling students (Center for the Study of Public

the absence of some regulation of admissions, many of the "best" schools may choose to become academically selective (as seems to have happened in New Zealand under a large-scale choice system[34]).

How Can Policymakers Promote Integration in Programs of Autonomous Schooling?

Require open admissions. Regulation of admissions might help to control stratification in programs of school choice. Requiring open access (and admission by lottery) would prevent the supply side from imposing segregation. The stratification by student ability and socioeconomic status that has been evident in school-choice systems in Chile, New Zealand, and the United Kingdom might be avoided if schools are precluded from selecting their students. Regulation of admissions would not, however, address stratification that results from parental preferences (regardless of whether those preferences are explicitly for same-race schools or for other characteristics, such as geographic proximity or curriculum content, that might be correlated with race).

Target communities with racially homogeneous public schools. Many existing voucher programs operate in cities where public schools are highly stratified and white students are extremely rare. In such communities, voucher/charter programs may serve to improve integration by permitting minority children to attend schools having larger numbers of white children.

Policy, 1970; Areen and Jencks, 1971). To date, little systematic evidence exists about suspensions and expulsions in voucher and charter schools. A survey of Cleveland voucher users after one year found that less than half of one percent had been expelled from their voucher schools (Greene, Howell, and Peterson, 1998, 1997). The experimental voucher studies in New York, Dayton, and Washington DC found no statistically significant differences in expulsion rates between voucher users and the control group (Myers et al., 2000; Howell and Peterson, 2000; Wolf, Howell, and Peterson, 2000). Suspension rates were also comparable for voucher users and the control group, except in the case of older students (grades 6–8) in Washington DC, who were suspended at substantially higher rates in voucher schools, suggesting that adjustment to the voucher school may have been more difficult for older students (Wolf, Howell, and Peterson, 2000). We are aware of no studies that have examined suspension and expulsion in charter schools.

[34]Fiske and Ladd, 2000.

Include existing private and parochial schools. Programs that permit the participation of existing private schools have the potential for improving integration, because such schools may already enroll substantial numbers of white and middle-class children. This is particularly important in programs that are targeted to minority or low-income children: if targeting is coupled with the exclusion of existing private schools (as in some charter laws), newly created autonomous schools are almost guaranteed to be highly stratified. When targeting is coupled with the inclusion of existing private schools (as in most voucher programs), there is at least the possibility of reducing stratification.

Reward integration financially. Imposed assignment to specific schools is not the only way to encourage racial integration. Most urban magnet schools were established with the intention of stemming white flight in order to maintain integration. Choice programs specifically designed with this purpose in mind have been able to promote integration.[35] Moreover, as Carolyn Hoxby points out, policymakers who value integration can design the financial rewards of a voucher/charter system to encourage it.[36] Dennis Epple and Richard Romano also note this possibility, suggesting that the amount of funding provided to a school for each student could vary depending on whether the student improves the school's integration.[37] Such a proposal has never been tried, but it might be a promising, noncoercive way to promote integration (though we cannot attest to its political viability).

How Can Policymakers Ensure That Voucher/Charter Schools Will Effectively Socialize Their Students to Become Responsible Citizens of the American Democracy?

Disseminate information about mission, values, curriculum, and outcomes. Because there is so little information about schools' success in civic socialization, it is difficult to make policy recommendations. One possibility is that policymakers could require a specific

---

[35]See Blank, Levine, and Steel, 1996; Wells and Crain, 2000.

[36]Hoxby, 2000.

[37]See Epple and Romano, 2000.

curriculum in civic education. Given the complete absence of empirical evidence about the effectiveness of any particular program, however, we think such a prescription would be a mistake. An examination of outcomes might be more appropriate. For example, a required assessment system might include a component related to civic knowledge. At a minimum, schools should be required to make public statements of their mission, values, and curriculum in order to ensure that parents are fully informed about the socialization that each school aims to inculcate.

FINAL THOUGHTS

Our review of the evidence leaves us without a crisp, bottom-line judgment of the wisdom of voucher and charter programs. To be sure, those in favor of autonomous schools can point to strong demand and parental satisfaction, especially among minority parents, and (particularly in targeted programs) to a demonstrated ability to focus on disadvantaged students. They can also point to promising indications of modest, short-run achievement gains, as evident for students in Arizona charter schools, students in at-risk charters in Texas, and African-American students participating in privately funded voucher programs. And they can point to the absence of evidence of rampant cream skimming and repugnant educational purposes.

Those opposed to vouchers and charters can point to the existing studies of the performance of autonomous schools, describing how those studies are uneven in quality and how the results are both early and inconclusive. They can point as well to a growing number of studies of other sorts of interventions—state policy reforms, urban reform efforts, class-size reductions, and innovative curricula—that demonstrate outcomes similar in scale and significance without the trauma of major changes in governance.[38] And they can point out that there is both domestic and international evidence not only that social stratification is likely to increase in large-scale choice programs, but also that effective policy control of choice schools may

---

[38]On differences in the performance of public schools across states, and the potential importance of state policies, see Grissmer et al., 2000.

often be part of the design of public authorizing agencies but rarely is part of their practice.

Prudent observers will note that, at the current scale of things, many important questions cannot be answered at all, notably those concerning total demand, supply response of educational providers, and school characteristics and performance at scale—or final impact on public schools in the new equilibrium. Moreover, in important respects—notably civic socialization—the effects of current or proposed autonomous schools are virtually unknown. And design is crucial: autonomous school policy can be targeted or not, regulated or not, generously funded or not, inclusive of existing providers or not. Each of these policy levers has important implications for student outcomes.

A program of vigorous research and experimentation is called for, but not one confined to choice programs. Better information on the performance of conventional public schools and alternative reform models is needed as well. In the meantime, political decisions will undoubtedly be made, for and against vouchers and charter schools. They will be informed by good evidence, one hopes, but they will not be fully justified by it for many years to come.

REFERENCES

Altonji, Joseph G., Todd E. Elder, and Christopher R. Taber. 2000. "Selection on Observed and Unobserved Variables: Assessing the Effectiveness of Catholic Schools." Cambridge, MA: National Bureau of Economic Research. Available at http://papers.nber.org/papers/W7831.

Ambler, John S. 1994. "Who Benefits from Educational Choice? Some Evidence from Europe." *Journal of Policy Analysis and Management* 13:454–476.

American Civil Liberties Union of Florida. 1999. "Summary of the Florida School Voucher Program." Available at http://www.aclufl.org/voucherssummary.html.

American Civil Liberties Union of Southern California. 2000. *Bridging the Difference or Widening the Gap? Proposition 38 and Equal Access.* Available at http://www.aclu-sc.org/docs/report_prop38.pdf.

American Federation of Teachers. 1998. *Student Achievement in Edison Schools: Mixed Results in an Ongoing Enterprise.* Washington DC: American Federation of Teachers.

Angrist, Joshua, Eric Bettinger, Erik Bloom, Elizabeth King, and Michael Kremer. 2001. "Vouchers for Private Schooling in Colombia: Evidence from a Randomized Natural Experiment." Cambridge, MA: National Bureau of Economic Research. Available at http://papers.nber.org/papers/W8343.

Angus, M. 2000. "Choice of Schooling and the Future of Public Education in Australia." Paper given at the School Choice and Educational Change Conference. Michigan State University. 15–17 March.

Archbald, Douglas A. 2000. "School Choice and School Stratification: Shortcomings of the Stratification Critique and Recommendations for Theory and Research." *Educational Policy* 14:214–240.

Archer, Jeff. 1999. "Two Cleveland Voucher Schools Plan Rebirth with Charter Status." *Education Week* (14 July).

Areen, Judith, and Christopher Jencks. 1971. "Education Vouchers: A Proposal for Diversity and Choice." *Teachers College Record* 72:327–336.

Argys, L.M., D.I. Rees, and Dominic J. Brewer. 1996. "Detracking America's Schools: Equity at Zero Cost?" *Journal of Policy Analysis and Management* 15:623–645.

Armor, David, and Brett Peiser. 1997. *Competition in Education: Interdistrict Choice in Massachusetts*: Cambridge, MA: Harvard University.

Armor, David L., and Brett M. Peiser. 1998. "Interdistrict Choice in Massachusetts." In *Learning from School Choice*, edited by Paul E. Peterson and Bryan C. Hassel. Washington DC: Brookings Institution.

Arsen, David. 2000. "Does Choice Enhance the Educational Opportunities Available to Poor Children?" Pp. 15–22 in *The School Choice Debate: Framing the Issues*, edited by David N. Plank and Gary Sykes. Lansing, MI: The Education Policy Center at Michigan State University.

Arsen, David, David Plank, and Gary Sykes. 2000. *School Choice Policies in Michigan: The Rules Matter*. East Lansing, MI: School Choice and School Change, Michigan State University.

Arum, Richard. 1996. "Do Private Schools Force Public Schools to Compete." *American Sociological Review* 61:29–46.

Ascher, C., R. Jacobowitz, and Y. McBride. 1998. *Charter School Access: A Preliminary Analysis of Charter School Legislation and Charter School Students.* New York: New York University, Institute for Education and Social Policy.

Ascher, Carol, and Nathalis Wamba. 2000. "Charter Schools: An Emerging Market for a New Model of Equity?" Paper given at the School Choice and Racial Diversity Conference. Teachers College, Columbia University. 22 May.

Aud, Susan L. 1999. *Competition in Education: A 1999 Update of School Choice in Massachusetts.* Boston, MA: Pioneer Institute for Public Policy Research.

Baldi, Stephanie, Marianne Perie, Dan Skidmore, Elizabeth Greenberg, and Carole Hahn. 2001. *What Democracy Means to Ninth-Graders: U.S. Results from the International IEA Civic Education Study.* Washington DC: National Center for Education Statistics.

Bashir, S. 1997. "The Cost Effectiveness of Public and Private Schools: Knowledge Gaps, New Research Methodologies, and an Application in India." Pp. 124–164 in *Marketizing Education and Health in Developing Countries: Miracle or Mirage?* edited by C. Colclough. Oxford: Clarendon Press.

Beales, Janet R., and Maureen Wahl. 1995. "Private Vouchers in Milwaukee: The PAVE Program." In *Private Vouchers*, edited by Terry M. Moe. Stanford, CA: Hoover Institution Press, Stanford University.

Beck, Deborah E. 1993. "Jenkins v. Missouri: School Choice as a Method for Desegregating an Inner-City School District." *California Law Review* 81:1029.

Bedi, A.S., and A. Garg. 2000. "The Effectiveness of Private Versus Public Schools: The Case of Indonesia." *Journal of Development Economics* 61:463–494.

Bellah, Robert N., Richard Madsen, William M. Sullivan, Ann Swidler, and Steven M Tipton. 1985. *Habits of the Heart: Individualism and Commitment in American Life.* Berkeley, CA: University of California Press.

Berends, Mark, Sheila N. Kirby, Scott Naftel, and Christopher McKelvey. 2001. *Implementation and Performance in New American Schools: Three Years into Scale-Up*. Santa Monica, CA: RAND.

Berman, Paul, and Milbrey W. McLaughlin. 1978. *Federal Programs Supporting Educational Change: Vol. VIII, Implementing and Sustaining Innovations*. Santa Monica, CA: RAND.

Bettinger, Eric. 1999. "The Effect of Charter Schools on Charter Students and Public Schools." New York: National Center for the Study of Privatization in Education. Available at http://www.tc.columbia.edu/ncspe.

Bickel, Robert, and Craig Howley. 2000. "The Influence of Scale on School Performance: A Multi-Level Extension of the Matthew Principle." *Education Policy Analysis Archives* 8.

Bland, Karina. 2000. "School Tax Credits Wide Open to Abuse: Millions Are Diverted from Needy Students." *The Arizona Republic* (9 April).

Blank, Rolf K., Roger E. Levine, and Lauri Steel. 1996. "After 15 Years: Magnet Schools in Urban Education." In *Who Chooses? Who Loses? Culture, Institutions, and the Unequal Effects of School Choice*, edited by Bruce Fuller, Richard F. Elmore, and Gary Orfield. New York: Teachers College Press.

Bloom, Alan David. 1987. *The Closing of the American Mind: How Higher Education Has Failed Democracy and Impoverished the Souls of Today's Students*. New York: Simon and Schuster.

Bodilly, Susan J. 1998. *Lessons from New American Schools' Scale-Up Phase: Prospects for Bringing Designs to Multiple Schools*. Santa Monica, CA: RAND.

Borsuk, Alan J. 2000. "School, State OK Settlement on Choice." *Milwaukee Journal Sentinel* (24 August).

Bositis, David A. 1999. *1999 National Opinion Poll*. Washington DC: The Joint Center for Political and Economic Studies.

Bowles, Samuel, and Herbert Gintis. 1976. *Schooling in Capitalist America: Educational Reform and the Contradictions of Economic Life*. New York: Basic Books.

Braddock, Jomills H. 1990. *Tracking: Implications for Race-Ethnic Subgroups*. Baltimore, MD: Center for Research on Effective Education for Disadvantaged Students, Johns Hopkins University.

Braddock, Jomills H., and Marvin Dawkins. 1993. "Ability Grouping, Aspirations, and Achievement: Evidence from the National Educational Longitudinal Study of 1988." *Journal of Negro Education* 62:324–336.

Brewer, Dominic J., Cathy Krop, Brian Gill, and Robert Reichardt. 1999. "Estimating the Cost of National Class Size Reductions Under Different Policy Alternatives." *Educational Evaluation and Policy Analysis* 21:179–192.

Brook, Robert H., John E. Ware, William H. Rogers, Emmett B. Keeler, Allyson Ross Davies, Cathy Donald Sherbourne, George A. Goldberg, Kathleen N. Lohr, Patti Camp, and Joseph P. Newhouse. 1984. *The Effect of Coinsurance on the Health of Adults: Results from the RAND Health Insurance Experiment*. Santa Monica, CA: RAND.

Bryk, Anthony S., and Mary Erina Driscoll. 1988. "The High School as Community: Contextual Influences, and Consequences for Students and Teachers." Madison, WI: National Center for Effective Secondary Schools.

Bryk, Anthony S., Valerie E. Lee, and Peter B. Holland. 1993. *Catholic Schools and the Common Good*. Cambridge, MA: Harvard University Press.

Buddin, Richard J. 1991. *The Enlistment Effects of the 2+2+4 Recruiting Experiment*. Santa Monica, CA: RAND.

Burtless, Gary. 1995. "The Case for Randomized Field Trials in Economic and Policy Research." *The Journal of Economic Perspectives* 9:63–84.

Calderon, Alberto. 1996. "Voucher Program for Secondary Schools: The Colombian Experience." Washington DC: World Bank.

Human Capital Working Paper 16232, May 1. Available at http://www-wds.worldbank.org.

Camilli, Gregory, and Katrina Bulkley. 2001. "Critique of 'An Evaluation of the Florida A-Plus Accountability and School Choice Program.'" *Education Policy Analysis Archives* 9.

Campbell, David E. 2001a. "Bowling Together: Private Schools, Serving Public Ends." *Education Next* (Fall).

Campbell, David E. 2001b. "Making Democratic Education Work." In *Charters, Vouchers, and Public Education*, edited by Paul E. Peterson and David E. Campbell. Washington DC: Brookings Institution.

Capell, Frank J. 1981. *A Study of Alternatives in American Education.* Santa Monica, CA: Rand Corporation.

Carnoy, Martin. 2001. *Do School Vouchers Improve Student Performance?* Washington DC: Economic Policy Institute.

Catterall, James S. 1983. "Tuition Tax Credits: Issues of Equity." Pp. 130–150 in *Public Dollars for Private Schools: The Case of Tuition Tax Credits*, edited by Thomas James and Henry M. Levin. Philadelphia: Temple University Press.

Catterall, James S., and Henry M. Levin. 1982. "Public and Private Schools: Evidence on Tuition Tax Credits." *Sociology of Education* 55:144–151.

Caulkins, Jonathan P., C. Peter Rydell, Susan M. Sohler Everingham, James R. Chiesa, and Shawn Bushway. 1999. *An Ounce of Prevention, a Pound of Uncertainty: The Cost-Effectiveness of School-Based Drug Prevention Programs.* Santa Monica, CA: RAND.

Center for Education Reform. 2000a. "Charter School Highlights and Statistics." Washington DC: Center for Education Reform. Available at http://www.edreform.com.

Center for Education Reform. 2000b. "Charter School Laws Across the States 2000: Ranking Score Card and Legislative Profiles." Washington DC: Center for Education Reform. Available at http://www.edreform.com.

Center for the Study of Public Policy. 1970. *A Report on Financing Elementary Education by Grants to Parents*. Cambridge, MA: Center for the Study of Public Policy.

Choper, Jesse. 1999. "Federal Constitutional Issues." Pp. 235–265 in *School Choice and Social Controversy*, edited by Stephen D. Sugarman and Frank R. Kemerer. Washington DC: Brookings Institution.

Choy, Susan P. 1997. *Public and Private Schools: How Do They Differ?* Washington DC: National Center for Education Statistics, U.S. Department of Education.

Chubb, John E., and Terry M. Moe. 1990. *Politics, Markets, and America's Schools*. Washington DC: Brookings Institution.

Cobb, Casey D., and Gene V. Glass. 1999. "Ethnic Segregation in Arizona Charter Schools." *Education Policy Analysis Archives* 7.

Coleman, James S. 1966. *Equality of Educational Opportunity*. Washington DC: U.S. Department of Health, Education, and Welfare.

Coleman, James S., and Thomas Hoffer. 1987. *Public and Private High Schools: The Impact of Communities*. New York: Basic Books.

Coleman, James S., Thomas Hoffer, and Sally Kilgore. 1982. *High School Achievement: Public, Catholic, and Private Schools Compared*. New York: Basic Books.

Coons, John E. 1992. "School Choice as Simple Justice." *First Things* 22 (February):193–200.

Coons, John E. 1998. "Education: Nature, Nurture, and Gnosis." Pp. 55–78 in *Natural Law and Contemporary Public Policy*, edited by David F. Forte. Washington DC: Georgetown University Press.

Coons, John E. 2000. "Populism and Parental Choice." *First Things* 107 (November):1622.

Coons, John E., and Stephen D. Sugarman. 1971. "Family Choice in Education: A Model State System for Vouchers." *California Law Review* 59:321–438.

Coons, John E., and Stephen D. Sugarman. 1978. *Education by Choice: The Case for Family Control.* Berkeley, CA: University of California Press.

Coons, John E., and Stephen D. Sugarman. 1992. *Scholarships for Children.* Berkeley, CA: Institute of Governmental Studies Press, University of California, Berkeley.

Coons, John E., and Stephen D. Sugarman. 1999. *Making School Choice Work for All Families.* San Francisco, CA: Pacific Research Institute for Public Policy.

Coons, John E., and Stephen D. Sugarman. 2000. "It's Not a Good Choice for Our Poor Families." *Los Angeles Times* (27 July).

Cox, D., and E. Jimenez. 1991. "The Relative Effectiveness of Private and Public Schools: Evidence from Two Developing Countries." *Journal of Development Economics* 34:99–121.

Cremin, Lawrence. 1961. *The Transformation of the School: Progressivism in American Education, 1876–1957.* New York: Knopf.

Cuban, Larry. 1993. *How Teachers Taught: Constancy and Change in American Classrooms, 1890–1990.* New York: Teachers College Press.

Darling-Hammond, Linda, Sheila Nataraj Kirby, and Priscilla M. Schlegel. 1985. *Tuition Tax Deductions and Parent School Choice: A Case Study of Minnesota.* Santa Monica, CA: RAND.

Daun, H. 2000. "Market Forces and Decentralization in Sweden: A Threat to Comprehensiveness and Equity and an Impetus to School Development?" Paper given at the School Choice and Educational Change Conference. Michigan State University. 15–17 March.

Dee, T.S. 1998. "Competition and the Quality of Public Schools." *Economics of Education Review* 17:419–427.

Dwyer, James. 1998. *Religious Schools v. Children's Rights.* Ithaca, NY: Cornell University Press.

Education Commission of the States. 1999. "Vouchers, Tax Credits and Tax Deductions." ECS Online. Available at http://www.ecs.org.

Edwards, T., J. Fitz, and G. Whitty. 1989. *The State and Private Education: An Evaluation of the Assisted Places Scheme.* London: The Falmer Press.

Egan, Timothy. 2000. "The Changing Face of Catholic Education." *New York Times* (6 August).

Ellickson, Phyllis L., Robert M. Bell, and Kimberly A. McGuigan. 1993. "Preventing Adolescent Drug Use: Long-Term Results of a Junior High Program." *American Journal of Public Health* 83:856–861.

Epple, Dennis, and Richard Romano. 2000. *Neighborhood Schools, Choice, and the Distribution of Educational Benefits.* Cambridge, MA: National Bureau of Economic Research. Available at http://papers.nber.org/papers/W7956.

Evans, William N., and Robert M. Schwab. 1995. "Finishing High School and Starting College: Do Catholic Schools Make a Difference?" *The Quarterly Journal of Economics* 110:941–974.

Fairlie, Robert. 2000. "Racial Segregation and the Private/Public School Choice." Paper given at the School Choice and Racial Diversity Conference. Teachers College, Columbia University. 22 May.

Farkas, Steve, and Jean Johnson. 1996. *Given the Circumstances: Teachers Talk About Public Education Policy.* New York: Public Agenda.

Farley, Reynolds, Howard Schuman, Suzanne Bianchi, Diane Colasanto, and Shirley Hatchett. 1978. "Chocolate City, Vanilla Suburbs: Will the Trend Toward Racially Separate Communities Continue?" *Social Science Research* 7:319–344.

Figlio, David N., and Joe A. Stone. 1999. "Are Private Schools Really Better?" *Research in Labor Economics*:115–140.

Fine, Lisa. 2001. "Florida's 'Other' Voucher Program Taking Off." *Education Week* (8 August).

Finn, Chester E., Bruno V. Manno, and Gregg Vanourek. 2000. *Charter Schools in Action: Renewing Public Education*. Princeton, NJ: Princeton University Press.

Fiske, Edward B., and Helen F. Ladd. 2000. *When Schools Compete: A Cautionary Tale*. Washington DC: Brookings Institution Press.

Fitzgerald, Joy. 2000. *1998–99 Colorado Charter Schools Evaluation Study: The Characteristics, Status and Performance Record of Colorado Charter Schools*. Denver, CO: Colorado Department of Education.

Fitzgerald, Joy, Pam Harris, Peter Huidekoper, and Meera Mani. 1998. *1997 Colorado Charter Schools Evaluation Study: The Characteristics, Status and Student Achievement Data of Colorado Charter Schools*. Denver, CO: The Clayton Foundation.

Fletcher, Michael A. 2001. "Milwaukee Will Vouch for Vouchers: Parochial, Private Schools Draw Pupils—and Questions About Success." *Washington Post* (20 March).

Fossey, Richard. 1994. "Open Enrollment in Massachusetts: Why Families Choose." *Educational Evaluation and Policy Analysis* 16:320–334.

Fowler, W. 1995. "School Size and Student Outcomes." *Advances in Educational Productivity* 5:3–26.

Friedman, Milton. 1955. "The Role of Government in Education." In *Economics and the Public Interest*, edited by Robert A. Solo. Piscataway, NJ: Rutgers University Press.

Friedman, Milton. 1962/1982. *Capitalism and Freedom*. Chicago, IL: University of Chicago Press.

Fuller, Bruce, Elizabeth Burr, Luis Huerta, Susan Puryear, and Edward Wexler. 1999. *School Choice: Abundant Hopes, Scarce Evidence of Results*. Berkeley, CA: Policy Analysis for California Education.

Fuller, B., and P. Clarke. 1994. "Raising School Effects While Ignoring Culture?" *Review of Educational Research* 64:119–157.

Fuller, Bruce, Luis Huerta, and David Ruenzel. 2000. *A Costly Gamble or Serious Reform? California's School Voucher Initiative—Proposition 38*. Berkeley, CA: Policy Analysis for California Education.

Fuller, Howard. 2000. "The Continuing Struggle of African Americans for the Power to Make Real Educational Choices." Paper given at the Second Annual Symposium on Educational Options for African Americans. Milwaukee, WI. 2–5 March. Available at http://www.schoolchoiceinfo.org.

Fuller, Howard L., and George A. Mitchell. 1999. "The Impact of School Choice on Racial and Ethnic Enrollment in Milwaukee Private Schools." Milwaukee, WI: Institute for the Transformation of Learning, Marquette University. Available at http://www.schoolchoiceinfo.org.

Fuller, Howard L., and George A. Mitchell. 2000. "The Impact of School Choice on Integration in Milwaukee Private Schools." Milwaukee, WI: Institute for the Transformation of Learning, Marquette University. Available at http://www.schoolchoiceinfo.org/servlets/SendArticle/4/integ1299.pdf.

Funkhouser, J.E., and K.W. Colopy. 1994. *Minnesota's Open Enrollment Option: Impacts on School Districts*. Washington DC: U.S. Department of Education/Policy Studies Associates.

Gallup Organization. 2000. *The 2000 Presidential Election—A Mid-Year Gallup Report*. 22 June. Available at http://www.gallup.com/poll/releases/pr000622q12.asp.

Gamoran, Adam. 1987. "The Stratification of High School Learning Opportunities." *Sociology of Education* 60:135–155.

Gamoran, Adam. 1996. "Student Achievement in Public Magnet, Public Comprehensive, and Private City High Schools." *Educational Evaluation and Policy Analysis* 18:1–18.

Gauri, V. 1998. *School Choice in Chile: Two Decades of Educational Reform*. Pittsburgh, PA: University of Pittsburgh Press.

Gaviria, A., and S. Raphael. 1997. "School-Based Peer Effects and Juvenile Behavior." University of California at San Diego.

Gilreath, James (ed.). 1999. *Thomas Jefferson and the Education of a Citizen*. Washington DC: Library of Congress.

Glazerman, Steven. 1997. "A Conditional Logit Model of Elementary School Choice: What Do Parents Value?" Chicago, IL: University of Chicago, Harris School of Public Policy.

Glenn, Charles, K. McLaughlin, and Laura Salganik. 1993. *Parent Information for School Choice*. Boston, MA: Center on Families, Communities, Schools and Children's Learning.

Glenn, Charles L. 1989. *Choice of Schools in Six Nations: France, Netherlands, Belgium, Britain, Canada, West Germany*. Washington DC: Office of Educational Research and Improvement.

Glenn, Charles L. 2001a. "Public Education Changes Partners." *Journal of Policy History* 13:133–156.

Glenn, David. 2001b. "The Voucher Vortex." *Lingua Franca* (May/June).

Glewwe, P., and H.A. Patrinos. 1999. "The Role of the Private Sector in Education in Vietnam: Evidence from the Vietnam Living Standards Survey." *World Development* 27:887–902.

Goldhaber, Dan D. 1996. "Public and Private High Schools: Is School Choice an Answer to the Productivity Problem?" *Economics of Education Review* 15:93–109.

Goldhaber, Dan D. 1997. "School Choice as Education Reform." *Phi Delta Kappan* (October):143–147.

Goldhaber, Dan D. 1999. "School Choice: An Examination of the Empirical Evidence on Achievement, Parental Decision Making, and Equity." *Educational Researcher* 28:16–25.

Grant, Gerald. 1988. *The World We Created at Hamilton High*. Cambridge, MA: Harvard University Press.

Greene, Jay P. 1998. "Civic Values in Public and Private Schools." In *Learning from School Choice*, edited by Paul E. Peterson and Bryan C. Hassel. Washington DC: Brookings Institution Press.

Greene, Jay P. 1999a. *Choice and Community: The Racial, Economic, and Religious Context of Parental Choice in Cleveland.* Columbus, OH: The Buckeye Institute.

Greene, Jay P. 1999b. "The Racial, Economic, and Religious Context of Parental Choice in Cleveland." Paper given at annual meeting of the Association for Public Policy Analysis and Management. Washington DC.

Greene, Jay P. 2000a. *The Education Freedom Index.* New York: Center for Civic Innovation at the Manhattan Institute.

Greene, Jay P. 2000b. *The Effect of School Choice: An Evaluation of the Charlotte Children's Scholarship Fund.* New York: Center for Civic Innovation at the Manhattan Institute.

Greene, Jay P. 2001. *An Evaluation of the Florida A-Plus Accountability and School Choice Program.* New York: Center for Civic Innovation at the Manhattan Institute.

Greene, Jay P., William G. Howell, and Paul E. Peterson. 1997. "Lessons from the Cleveland Scholarship Program." Paper given at annual meeting of the Association for Public Policy Analysis and Management.

Greene, Jay P., William G. Howell, and Paul E. Peterson. 1998. "Lessons from the Cleveland Scholarship Program." In *Learning from School Choice*, edited by Paul E. Peterson and Bryan C. Hassel. Washington DC: Brookings Institution.

Greene, Jay P., Paul E. Peterson, and Jiangtao Du. 1997. *Effectiveness of School Choice: The Milwaukee Experiment.* Cambridge, MA: Harvard University Program in Education Policy and Governance.

Greene, Jay P., Paul E. Peterson, and Jiangtao Du. 1998. "School Choice in Milwaukee: A Randomized Experiment." In *Learning from School Choice*, edited by Paul E. Peterson and Bryan C. Hassel. Washington DC: Brookings Institution.

Grissmer, David, Ann Flanagan, Jennifer Kawata, and Stephanie Williamson. 2000. *Improving Student Achievement: What NAEP Test Scores Tell Us.* Santa Monica, CA: RAND.

Gronberg, Timothy J., and Dennis W. Jansen. 2001. *Navigating Newly Chartered Waters: An Analysis of Texas Charter School Performance*. San Antonio and Austin, TX: Texas Public Policy Foundation. Available at http://www.tppf.org.

Guerra, Michael J., Michael J. Donahue, and Peter L. Benson. 1990. *The Heart of the Matter: Effects of Catholic High Schools on Student Values, Beliefs and Behaviors*. Washington DC: National Catholic Education Association.

Guthrie, James W. 1979. "Organizational Scale and School Success." *Educational Evaluation and Policy Analysis* 1:17–27.

Guttman, Amy. 1987. *Democratic Education*. Princeton, NJ: Princeton University Press.

Guttman, Amy. 2000. "Why Should Schools Care About Civic Education?" Pp. 73–90 in *Rediscovering the Democratic Purposes of Education*, edited by Lorraine McDonnell, P. Michael Timpane, and Roger Benjamin. Lawrence, KS: University of Kansas Press.

Harris, Joseph Claude. 2000. "The Funding Dilemma Facing Catholic Elementary and Secondary Schools." In *Catholic Schools at the Crossroads: Survival and Transformation*, edited by James Youniss and John J. Convey. New York: Teachers College Press.

Hassel, Bryan C. 1999. *The Charter School Challenge: Avoiding the Pitfalls, Fulfilling the Promise*. Washington DC: Brookings Institution Press.

Heckman, James J., and Jeffrey A. Smith. 1995. "Assessing the Case for Social Experiments." *Journal of Economic Perspectives* 9:85–100.

Hegarty, Stephen. 2000. "Why Are Florida Children Writing So Much Better?" *St. Petersburg Times* (21 June).

Henig, Jeffrey R. 1994. *Rethinking School Choice: Limits of the Market Metaphor*. Princeton, NJ: Princeton University Press.

Henig, Jeffrey R. 1996. "The Local Dynamics of Choice: Ethnic Preferences and Institutional Responses." In *Who Chooses? Who Loses? Culture, Institutions, and the Unequal Effects of School*

Choice, edited by Bruce Fuller, Richard F. Elmore, and Gary Orfield. New York: Teachers College Press.

Henig, Jeffrey R. 1999. "School Choice Outcomes." Pp. 68–107 in *School Choice and Social Controversy: Politics, Policy, and Law*, edited by Stephen D. Sugarman and Frank R. Kemerer. Washington DC: Brookings Institution Press.

Henig, Jeffrey R., and Stephen D. Sugarman. 1999. "The Nature and Extent of School Choice." Pp. 13–35 in *School Choice and Social Controversy: Politics, Policy, and Law*, edited by Stephen D. Sugarman and Frank R. Kemerer. Washington DC: Brookings Institution.

Hess, Frederick M. 1999. *Spinning Wheels: The Politics of Urban School Reform*. Washington DC: Brookings Institution Press.

Hill, Paul, and Mary Beth Celio. 1998. *Fixing Urban Schools*. Washington DC: Brookings Institution Press.

Hill, Paul T. 1999. "The Supply Side of School Choice." Pp. 140–173 in *School Choice and Social Controversy: Politics, Policy, and Law*, edited by Stephen D. Sugarman and Frank R. Kemerer. Washington DC: Brookings Institution.

Hill, Paul T., Christine Campbell, and James Harvey. 2000. *It Takes a City: Getting Serious About Urban School Reform*. Washington DC: Brookings Institution Press.

Hill, Paul T., Gail E. Foster, and Tamar Gendler. 1990. *High Schools with Character*. Santa Monica, CA: RAND.

Hill, Paul T., Lawrence C. Pierce, and James W. Guthrie. 1997. *Reinventing Public Education: How Contracting Can Transform America's Schools*. Chicago, IL: University of Chicago Press.

Horn, Jerry, and Gary Miron. 1999. *Evaluation of the Michigan Public School Academy Initiative*. Kalamazoo, MI: The Evaluation Center, Western Michigan University.

Horn, Jerry, and Gary Miron. 2000. *An Evaluation of the Michigan Charter School Initiative: Performance, Accountability and Impact*.

Kalamazoo, MI: The Evaluation Center, Western Michigan University.

Howell, William G., and Paul E. Peterson. 2000. *School Choice in Dayton, Ohio: An Evaluation After One Year.* Cambridge, MA: Program on Education Policy and Governance, Harvard University.

Howell, William G., Patrick J. Wolf, Paul E. Peterson, and David E. Campbell. 2000a. "The Effect of School Vouchers on Student Achievement: A Response to Critics." Cambridge, MA: Program on Educational Policy and Governance, Harvard University. Available at http://hdc-www.harvard.edu/pepg.

Howell, William G., Patrick J. Wolf, Paul E. Peterson, and David E. Campbell. 2000b. "Test-Score Effects of School Vouchers in Dayton, Ohio, New York City, and Washington DC: Evidence from Randomized Field Trials." Paper given at the American Political Science Association. Washington DC. September.

Hoxby, Caroline Minter. 1994a. *Do Private Schools Provide Competition for Public Schools?* Cambridge, MA: National Bureau of Economic Research. Available at http://papers.nber.org/papers/W4978.

Hoxby, Caroline Minter. 1994b. *Does Competition Among Public Schools Benefit Students and Taxpayers? Evidence from Natural Variation in School Districting.* Cambridge, MA: National Bureau of Economic Research. Available at http://papers.nber.org/papers/W4979.

Hoxby, Caroline Minter. 1996. "The Effects of Private School Vouchers on Schools and Students." Pp. 177–208 in *Holding Schools Accountable: Performance-Based Reform in Education,* edited by Helen F. Ladd. Washington DC: Brookings Institution.

Hoxby, Caroline M. 2000. "The Battle Over School Choice." PBS. Available at http://www.pbs.org/wgbh/pages/frontline/shows/vouchers/interviews/hoxby.html.

Innerst, Carol. 2000. "Competing to Win: How Florida's A+ Plan Has Triggered Public School Reform." Milwaukee, WI: Institute for the

Transformation of Learning, Marquette University. Available at http://www.schoolchoiceinfo.org.

James, E. 1984. "Benefits and Costs of Privatized Public Services: Lessons from the Dutch Educational System." *Comparative Education Review* 28:605–624.

James, Thomas, and Henry M. Levin (eds.). 1983. *Public Dollars for Private Schools: The Case of Tuition Tax Credits.* Philadelphia, PA: Temple University Press.

Jencks, Christopher. 1966. "Is the Public School Obsolete?" *The Public Interest* (Winter):1827.

Jencks, Christopher, and S.E. Mayer. 1990. "The Social Consequences of Growing up in a Poor Neighborhood." In *Inner-City Poverty in the United States,* edited by L.E. Lynn and M.G.H. McGeary. Washington DC: National Academy Press.

Jepsen, Christopher. 1999a. "The Effectiveness of Catholic Primary Schooling." Chicago, IL: Economics Department, Northwestern University.

Jepsen, Christopher. 1999b. "The Effects of Private School Competition on Student Achievement." Chicago, IL: Institute for Policy Research, Northwestern University. WP99-16.

Jiminez, E., M. Lockheed, and N. Wattanawaha. 1988. "The Relative Efficiency of Public and Private Schools: The Case of Thailand." *World Bank Economic Review* 2:139–164.

Jiminez, E., M.E. Lockheed, E. Luna, and V. Paqueo. 1991. "School Effects and Costs for Private and Public Schools in the Dominican Republic." *International Journal of Educational Research* 15:393–410.

Jiminez, E., and Y. Sawada. 1999. "Do Community-Managed Schools Work? An Evaluation of El Salvador's EDUCO Program." *World Bank Economic Review* 13:415–441.

Johnson, Jean, and Steve Farkas. 1997. *Getting By: What American Teenagers Really Feel About Their Schools.* New York: Public Agenda.

Johnson, Jean, and John Immerwahr. 1994. *First Things First*. New York: Public Agenda.

Kim, J., H. Alderman, and P. Orazem. 1999. "Can Private School Subsidies Increase Schooling for the Poor? The Quetta Urban Fellowship Program." *World Bank Economic Review* 13:443–465.

King, E.M., P.F. Orazem, and D. Wohlgemuth. 1999. "Central Mandates and Local Incentives: The Colombia Education Voucher Program." *World Bank Economic Review* 13:467–491.

Kingdon, G. 1996. "The Quality and Efficiency of Private and Public Education: A Case-Study of Urban India." *Oxford Bulletin of Economics and Statistics* 58:57–82.

Knight, J.B., and R.H. Sabot. 1990. *Education, Productivity, and Inequality: The East African Natural Experiment*. London: Oxford University Press.

Kolderie, Ted. 1990. *Beyond Choice to New Public Schools: Withdrawing the Exclusive Franchise in Public Education*. Washington DC: Progressive Policy Institute.

Kolderie, Ted. 1993. *The States Begin to Withdraw the Exclusive*. St. Paul, MN: Center for Policy Studies.

Krueger, Alan. 1999. "Experimental Estimates of Education Production Functions." *Quarterly Journal of Economics* 114:497–533.

Krueger, Alan B., and Diane M. Whitmore. 2001. *Would Smaller Classes Help Close the Black-White Achievement Gap?* Princeton, NJ: Princeton University, Industrial Relations Section.

Kupermintz, Haggai. 2001. "The Effects of Vouchers on School Improvement: Another Look at the Florida Data." *Education Policy Analysis Archives* 9.

Ladd, Helen F., and Edward B. Fiske. 2001. "The Uneven Playing Field of School Choice: Evidence from New Zealand." *Journal of Policy Analysis and Management* 20:43–64.

Ladd, Helen F., and Janet S. Hansen (eds.). 1999. *Making Money Matter: Financing America's Schools*. Washington DC: National Academy Press.

Lamdin, Douglas J., and Michael Mintrom. 1997. "School Choice in Theory and Practice: Taking Stock and Looking Ahead." *Education Economics* 5:211–244.

Lankford, Hamilton, and James Wyckoff. 1992. "Primary and Secondary School Choice Among Public and Religious Alternatives." *Economics of Education Review* 11:317–337.

Lankford, Hamilton, and James Wyckoff. 2000. "Why Are Schools Racially Segregated? Implications for School Choice Policies." Paper given at the School Choice and Racial Diversity Conference. Teachers College, Columbia University. 22 May.

Lassabille, G., J. Tan, and S. Sumra. 2000. "Expansion of Private Secondary Education: Lessons from Tanzania." *Comparative Education Review* 44:1–28.

Lee, Valerie E., Robert G. Croninger, and Julia B. Smith. 1994. "Parental Choice of Schools and Social Stratification in Education: The Paradox of Detroit." *Educational Evaluation and Policy Analysis* 16:434–457.

Levin, Betsy. 1999. "Race and School Choice." Pp. 266–299 in *School Choice and Social Controversy: Politics, Policy, and the Law*, edited by Stephen D. Sugarman and Frank R. Kemerer. Washington DC: Brookings Institution Press.

Levin, Henry M. 1983. *Cost-Effectiveness: A Primer*. Beverly Hills, CA: Sage Publications.

Levin, Henry M. 1998. "Educational Vouchers: Effectiveness, Choice, and Costs." *Journal of Policy Analysis and Management* 17:373–392.

Levin, Henry M. 2000. *A Comprehensive Framework for Evaluating Educational Vouchers*. New York: National Center for the Study of Privatization of Education, Teachers College, Columbia University.

Levin, Henry M., and Cyrus E. Driver. 1997. "Costs of an Educational Voucher System." *Education Economics* 5:265–283.

Levinson, E. 1976. *The Alum Rock Voucher Demonstration: Three Years of Implementation*. Santa Monica, CA: RAND.

Levinson, Meira. 1999. *The Demands of Liberal Education*. London: Oxford University Press.

Louis, K.S., and B.A.M. Van Velzen. 1991. "A Look at Choice in the Netherlands." *Educational Leadership* 48:66–72.

Macedo, Stephen. 2000. *Diversity and Dissent*. Cambridge, MA: Harvard University Press.

Manning, Willard G., Joseph P. Newhouse, Naihua Duan, Emmett B. Keeler, B. Benjamin, Arleen A. Leibowitz, M. Susan Marquis, and Jack Zwanziger. 1988. *Health Insurance and the Demand for Medical Care: Evidence from a Randomized Experiment*. Santa Monica, CA: RAND.

Martinez, Valerie, Kenneth Godwin, and Frank R. Kemerer. 1996. "Public School Choice in San Antonio: Who Chooses and with What Effects?" In *Who Chooses? Who Loses? Culture, Institutions, and the Unequal Effects of School Choice*, edited by Bruce Fuller and Richard F. Elmore. New York: Teachers College Press.

McDonnell, Lorraine, P. Michael Timpane, and Roger Benjamin (eds.). 2000. *Rediscovering the Democratic Purposes of Education*. Lawrence, KS: University of Kansas Press.

McEwan, Patrick J. 2000a. *Comparing the Effectiveness of Public and Private Schools: A Review of Evidence and Interpretations*. New York: National Center for the Study of Privatization of Education, Teachers College, Columbia University.

McEwan, Patrick J. 2000b. "The Effectiveness of Public, Catholic, and Non-Religious Private Schools in Chile's Voucher System." *Education Economics*. Forthcoming.

McEwan, Patrick J. 2000c. "The Potential Impact of Large-Scale Voucher Programs." *Review of Educational Research* 70:103–149.

McEwan, Patrick J., and Martin Carnoy. 1999. "The Impact of Competition on Public School Quality: Longitudinal Evidence from Chile's Voucher System." Stanford, CA: Stanford University.

McEwan, Patrick J., and Martin Carnoy. 2000. "The Effectiveness and Efficiency of Private Schools in Chile's Voucher System." *Educational Evaluation and Policy Analysis* 22:213–239.

McMillan, Robert. 1998. "Parental Pressure and Competition: An Empirical Analysis of the Determinants of Public School Quality." Unpublished.

Meier, Deborah. 1995. *The Power of Their Ideas: Lessons for America from a Small School in Harlem*. Boston, MA: Beacon Press.

Metcalf, Kim K. 1999. *Evaluation of the Cleveland Scholarship and Tutoring Grant Program: 1996–1999*. Bloomington, IN: The Indiana Center for Evaluation.

Mik, M., and M. Flynn. 1996. "School Size and Academic Achievement in the HSC Examination: Is There a Relationship?" *Issues in Educational Research* 6:57–78.

Mill, John Stuart. 1859/1978. *On Liberty*. Indianapolis: Hackett Publishing Company.

Miron, G. 1993. *Choice and the Use of Market Forces in Schooling: Swedish Education Reforms for the 1990s*. Stockholm: Institute of International Education, Stockholm University.

Miron, G. 1996. "Choice and the Quasi-Market in Swedish Education." *Oxford Studies in Comparative Education* 6:33–47.

Miron, Gary. 2000. *The Initial Study of Pennsylvania Charter Schools: First Year Report*. Kalamazoo, MI: The Evaluation Center, Western Michigan University.

Miron, Gary, and Brooks Applegate. 2000. *An Evaluation of Student Achievement of Edison Schools Opened in 1995 and 1996*. Kalamazoo, MI: The Evaluation Center, Western Michigan University.

Mizala, A., and P. Romoaguera. 2000. "School Performance and Choice: The Chilean Experience." *Journal of Human Resources* 35:392–417.

Moe, Terry M. (ed.). 1995. *Private Vouchers*. Stanford, CA: Hoover Institution Press, Stanford University.

Moe, Terry M. 2001. *Schools, Vouchers, and the American Public.* Washington DC: Brookings Institution Press.

Moore, Donald R., and Suzanne Davenport. 1990. "School Choice: The New Improved Sorting Machine." Pp. 187–223 in *Choice in Education: Potential and Problems*, edited by William Lowe Boyd and Herbert J. Walberg. Berkeley, CA: McCutchan Publishing Corporation.

Moore, M.T., E.W. Strang, M. Schwartz, and M. Braddock. 1988. *Patterns in Special Education Service Delivery and Cost.* Washington DC: Decision Resources Corporation.

Mulholland, Lori A. 1999. *Arizona Charter School Progress Evaluation.* Phoenix, AZ: Morrison Institute for Public Policy.

Murphy, Dan, F. Howard Nelson, and Bella Rosenberg. 1997. *The Cleveland Voucher Program: Who Chooses? Who Gets Chosen? Who Pays?* Washington DC: American Federation of Teachers.

Myers, David, Paul Peterson, Daniel Mayer, Julia Chou, and William G. Howell. 2000. *School Choice in New York City After Two Years: An Evaluation of the School Choice Scholarship Program.* Washington DC: Mathematica Policy Research, Inc.

Nathan, Joe. 1998. "Controversy: Charters and Choice." *The American Prospect* 9 (November–December). Available at http://www.prospect.org.

Nathan, Joe. 1999. *Charter Schools.* San Francisco, CA: Jossey-Bass Publishers.

National Commission on Excellence in Education. 1983. *A Nation at Risk.* Washington DC: National Commission on Excellence in Education.

National Commission on Governing America's Schools. 1999. *Governing America's Schools: Changing the Rules.* Denver, CO: Education Commission of the States.

National Education Association and American Federation of Teachers. 1999. "School Vouchers: The Emerging Track Record."

National Education Association. Available at http://www.nea.org/issues/vouchers/voutrak_.html.

Neal, D. 1997. "The Effects of Catholic Secondary Schooling on Educational Achievement." *Journal of Labor Economics* 15:98–123.

Nechyba, Thomas J. 1996. *Public School Finance in a General Equilibrium Tiebout World: Equalization Programs, Peer Effects and Private School Vouchers.* Cambridge, MA: National Bureau of Economic Research. Available at http://papers.nber.org/papers/W5642.

Nelson, F. Howard. 2000. *Trends in Student Achievement for Edison Schools, Inc.: The Emerging Track Record.* Washington DC: American Federation of Teachers.

Nelson, F. Howard, Edward Muir, and Rachel Drown. 2000. *Venturesome Capital: State Charter School Finance Systems.* Washington DC: U.S. Department of Education, Office of Educational Research and Improvement.

Niemi, Richard G., and Chris Chapman. 1998. *The Civic Development of 9th- Through 12th-Grade Students in the United States: 1996.* Washington DC: U.S. Department of Education, National Center for Education Statistics.

North Carolina Department of Public Instruction. 1998. *Selected Characteristics of Charter Schools, Programs, Students, and Teachers 1997–98.* Durham, NC: North Carolina Department of Public Instruction, Division of Accountability Services.

Oakes, Jeannie. 1985. *Keeping Track: How Schools Structure Inequality.* New Haven, CT: Yale University Press.

Oakes, Jeannie. 1990. *Multiplying Inequalities: The Effects of Race, Social Class, and Tracking on Opportunities to Learn.* Santa Monica, CA: RAND.

Oakes, Jeannie, Adam Gamoran, and Reba Page. 1992. "Curriculum Differentiation: Opportunities, Outcomes, and Meanings." Pp. 570–608 in *Handbook of Research on Curriculum: A Project of the American Research Association,* edited by Philip W. Jackson. New York: Macmillan.

Olsen, Darcy Ann, and Mathew J. Brouillette. 2000. *Reclaiming Our Schools: Increasing Parental Control of Education Through the Universal Tax Credit.* Washington DC: Cato Institute. Policy Analysis Report 388, December 6.

Orfield, Gary. 2001. *Schools More Separate: Consequences of a Decade of Resegregation.* Cambridge, MA: The Civil Rights Project, Harvard University. Available at http://www.law.harvard. edu/civilrights.

Orfield, Gary A. 1990. "Do We Know Anything Worth Knowing About Educational Effects of Magnet Schools?" Pp. 119–123 in *Choice and Control in American Education,* edited by William Clune and John Witte. New York: The Falmer Press.

Orfield, Gary A., and Susan E. Eaton. 1996. *Dismantling Desegregation: The Quiet Reversal of Brown v. Board of Education.* New York: The New York Press.

Orfield, Gary A., and John T. Yun. 1999. *Resegregation in American Schools.* Cambridge, MA: The Civil Rights Project, Harvard University. Available at http://www.law.harvard.edu/civilrights.

Orr, Larry L. 1999. *Social Experiments: Evaluating Public Programs with Experimental Methods.* Thousand Oaks, CA: Sage Publications.

Pangle, Lorraine Smith, and Thomas L. Pangle. 2000. "What the American Founders Have to Teach Us About Schooling for Democratic Citizenship." In *Rediscovering the Democratic Purposes of Education,* edited by Lorraine McDonnell, P. Michael Timpane, and Roger Benjamin. Lawrence, KS: University of Kansas Press.

Peshkin, Alan. 1986. *God's Choice: The Total World of a Fundamentalist Christian School.* Chicago, IL: University of Chicago Press.

Peterson, Paul E. 1998. *An Evaluation of the New York City School Choice Scholarships Program: The First Year.* Cambridge, MA: Program on Education Policy and Governance, Harvard University.

Peterson, Paul E., and David E. Campbell. 2001. *An Evaluation of the Children's Scholarship Fund.* Cambridge, MA: Program on Education Policy and Governance, Harvard University.

Peterson, Paul E., David E. Campbell, and Martin R. West. 2001. *An Evaluation of the BASIC Fund Scholarship Program in the San Francisco Bay Area, California.* Cambridge, MA: Program on Education Policy and Governance, Harvard University.

Peterson, Paul E., Jay P. Greene, and William Howell. 1998. *New Findings from the Cleveland Scholarship Program: A Reanalysis of Data from the Indiana University School of Education Evaluation.* Cambridge, MA: Program on Education Policy and Governance, Kennedy School of Government and the Center for American Political Studies, Harvard University. Available at http://www.ksg.harvard.edu/pepg/nwclvrpt.htm.

Peterson, Paul E., and William G. Howell. 2001. "Exploring Explanations for Ethnic Differences in Voucher Impacts on Student Test Scores." Paper given at the Conference on Closing the Gap: Promising Approaches to Reducing the Achievement Gap. Washington DC. 1–2 February.

Peterson, Paul E., William G. Howell, and Jay P. Greene. 1999. *An Evaluation of the Cleveland Voucher Program After Two Years.* Cambridge, MA: Program on Education Policy and Governance, Harvard University.

Peterson, Paul E., David Myers, and William G. Howell. 1999. *An Evaluation of the Horizon Scholarship Program in the Edgewood Independent School District, San Antonio, Texas: The First Year.* Cambridge, MA: Mathematica Policy Research and Program on Education Policy and Governance, Harvard University.

Petro, Jim. 1998. *Cleveland Scholarship and Tutoring Program.* Cleveland, OH: State of Ohio, Office of the Auditor.

Pioneer Institute. 1998. "Poll Finds Higher Satisfaction Rate Among Charter School Parents." Boston, MA: Pioneer Institute. Available at http://www.pioneerinstitute.org.

Pioneer Institute for Public Policy. 1999. *Massachusetts Charter School Profiles: 1998–99 School Year.* Boston, MA: Massachusetts Charter School Resource Center.

Pool, Bob. 1999. "Catholic Schools Also Big Winners in Tuition Grants." *Los Angeles Times* (30 August).

Potts, Jonathan. 2001. "Education Measure Passes, Easing Way for Vouchers." *Pittsburgh Tribune-Review* (9 May).

Powell, Arthur G., Eleanor Farrar, and David K. Cohen. 1985. *The Shopping Mall High School: Winners and Losers in the Educational Marketplace.* Boston, MA: Houghton Mifflin Company.

Pribesh, Shana, and Douglas B. Downey. 1999. "Why Are Residential and School Moves Associated with Poor School Performance?" *Demography* 36:521–534.

Price, Hugh B. 1999. "The Aim of Education Standards: Victors, Not Victims." Paper given at the National Press Club Newsmakers Luncheon. Washington DC. 10 December.

Psacharopoulos, G. 1987. "Public Versus Private Schools in Developing Countries: Evidence from Colombia and Tanzania." *International Journal of Educational Development* 7:59–67.

Public Sector Consultants and MAXIMUS. 1999. *Michigan's Charter School Initiative: From Theory to Practice.* Lansing, MI: Michigan Department of Education.

Rees, Nina. 1999. "School Choice: What's Happening in the States." *The Heritage Foundation.* Available at http://www.heritage.org/schools.

Riddell, A.R. 1993. "The Evidence on Public/Private Educational Trade-offs in Developing Countries." *International Journal of Educational Development* 13:373–386.

Rose, Lowell C., and Alec M. Gallup. 1999. "The 31st Annual Phi Delta Kappa/Gallup Poll of the Public's Attitudes Toward the Public Schools." *Phi Delta Kappan* 81:41–58.

Rose, Lowell C., and Alec M. Gallup. 2000. "The 32nd Annual Phi Delta Kappa/Gallup Poll of the Public's Attitudes Toward the Public Schools." *Phi Delta Kappan* 82:41–57.

Rothstein, Laura F. 1999. "School Choice and Students with Disabilities." Pp. 332–364 in *School Choice and Social Controversy: Politics, Policy, and Law,* edited by Stephen D. Sugarman and Frank R. Kemerer. Washington DC: Brookings Institution.

Rothstein, Richard. 1998. "Charter Conundrum." *The American Prospect* 9 (July–August).

Rothstein, Richard. 2001. "Lessons: Vouchers Dead, Alternatives Weak." *The New York Times* (20 June).

Rouse, Cecilia Elena. 1998. "Private School Vouchers and Student Achievement: An Evaluation of the Milwaukee Parental Choice Program." *The Quarterly Journal of Economics* 113:553–602.

Rouse, Cecilia E. 2000. "School Reform in the 21st Century: A Look at the Effects of Class Size and School Vouchers on the Academic Achievement of Minority Students." Princeton, NJ: Princeton University, Industrial Relations Section. Available at http://www.irs.princeton.edu.

RPP International. 1999. *A Comparison of Charter School Legislation: Thirty-three States and the District of Columbia.* Washington DC: U.S. Department of Education.

RPP International. 2000. *The State of Charter Schools: Fourth-Year Report.* Washington DC: U.S. Department of Education.

Sander, William. 1996. "Catholic Grade Schools and Academic Achievement." *The Journal of Human Resources* 31:540–548.

Schneider, Mark, Paul Teske, and Melissa Marschall. 2000. *Choosing Schools: Parents, School Choice, and the Quality of American Schools.* Princeton, NJ: Princeton University Press.

Schneider, Mark, Paul Teske, Melissa Marschall, and Christine Roch. 1998. "Shopping for Schools: In the Land of the Blind, The One-Eyed Parent May Be Enough." *American Journal of Political Science* 42:769–793.

Schneider, Mark, Paul Teske, Christine Roch, and Melissa Marschall. 1997. "Networks to Nowhere: Segregation and Stratification in Networks of Information About Schools." *American Journal of Political Science* 41:1201–1223.

Sikkink, David. 1999. "The Social Sources of Alienation from Public Schools." *Social Forces* 78:51–86.

Smith, Christian, and David Sikkink. 1999. "Is Private Schooling Privatizing?" *First Things* 92 (April):1620.

Solmon, Lewis, Kern Paark, and David Garcia. 2001. *Does Charter School Attendance Improve Test Scores? The Arizona Results.* Phoenix, AZ: Goldwater Institute Center for Market-Based Education.

Spring, Joel H. 1976. *The Sorting Machine: National Educational Policy Since 1945.* New York: McKay.

SRI International. 1997. *Evaluation of Charter School Effectiveness.* Sacramento, CA: SRI International.

Stecher, Brian M., and George W. Bohrnstedt (eds.). 2000. *Class Size Reduction in California: The 1998–99 Evaluation Findings.* Sacramento, CA: California Department of Education.

Stevens, N., and G. Peltier. 1994. "A Review of Research on Small-School Participation in Extracurricular Activities." *Journal of Research in Rural Education* 10:116–120.

Swanson, Christopher B., and Barbara Schneider. 1999. "Students on the Move: Residential and Educational Mobility in America's Schools." *Sociology of Education* 72:54–67.

Tenbusch, James P. 1993. "Parent Choice Behavior Under Minnesota's Open Enrollment Program." Paper given at annual meeting of the American Educational Research Association. Atlanta, GA. April 12–16.

Teske, Paul, Mark Schneider, Jack Buckley, and Sara Clark. 2000. *Does Charter School Competition Improve Traditional Public Schools?* New York: Center for Civic Innovation at the Manhattan Institute.

Teske, Paul, Mark Schneider, Melissa Marschall, and Christine Roch. 1998. "Evaluating the Effects of Public School Choice in District 4." SUNY-Stony Brook. Unpublished.

Texas Education Agency. 2000. "Texas Open-Enrollment Charter Schools: Third Year Evaluation, March 2000." Division of Charter Schools, Texas Education Agency. Available at http://www.tea.state.tx.us/charter/eval99/index.html.

Toma, Eugenia Froedge. 1996. "Public Funding and Private Schooling Across Countries." *Journal of Law and Economics* 39:121–148.

Tyack, David. 1974. *The One Best System.* Cambridge, MA: Harvard University Press.

Tyack, David, and Elisabeth Hansot. 1982. *Managers of Virtue: Public School Leadership in America, 1820–1980.* New York: Basic Books.

UCLA Charter School Study. 1998. *Beyond the Rhetoric of Charter School Reform: A Study of Ten California School Districts.* University of California, Los Angeles.

Urban Institute, Brookings Institution, and Committee for Economic Development. 1998. Conference proceedings: *Vouchers and Related Delivery Mechanisms: Consumer Choice in the Provision of Public Service.* October.

Vandenberghe, V. 1998. "Educational Quasi-Markets: The Belgian Experience." Pp. 79–94 in *A Revolution in Social Policy: Quasi-Market Reforms in the 1990s,* edited by W. Barlett, J. A. Roberts, and J. Le Grand. Bristol: The Policy Press.

Walberg, H., and H. Walberg. 1994. "Losing Local Control of Schools." *Educational Researcher* 23:19–26.

Walford, G. 2000. "School Choice and Educational Change in England and Wales." Paper given at the School Choice and Educational Change Conference. Michigan State University. 15–17 March.

Walford, G. in press. "Privatization in Industrialized Countries." In *Privatizing Education,* edited by H.M. Levin. Boulder, CO: Westview Press.

Weinschrott, David J., and Sally B. Kilgore. 1998. "Evidence from the Indianapolis Voucher Program." On *Learning from School Choice*, edited by Paul E. Peterson and Bryan C. Hassel. Washington DC: Brookings Institution.

Wells, Amy Stuart. 1993a. "The Sociology of School Choice: Why Some Win and Others Lose in the Educational Marketplace." In *School Choice: Examining the Evidence*, edited by Edith Rassell and Richard Rothstein. Washington DC: Economic Policy Institute.

Wells, Amy Stuart. 1993b. *Time to Choose: America at the Crossroads of School Choice Policy*. New York: Hill and Wang.

Wells, Amy Stuart. 1999. "California's Charter Schools: Promises vs. Performance." *American Educator* 23:18.

Wells, Amy Stuart, and Robert L. Crain. 2000. "Where School Desegregation and School Choice Policies Collide: Voluntary Transfer Plans and Controlled Choice." Paper given at the School Choice and Racial Diversity Conference. Teachers College, Columbia University. 22 May.

Wells, Amy Stuart, Jennifer Jellison Holme, Alejandra Lopez, and Camille Wilson Cooper. 2000a. "Charter Schools and Racial and Social Class Segregation: Yet Another Sorting Machine?" In *A Notion at Risk: Preserving Public Education as an Engine for Social Mobility*, edited by Richard D. Kahlenberg. New York: The Century Foundation Press.

Wells, Amy Stuart, Ash Vasudeva, Jennifer Jellison Holme, and Camille Wilson Cooper. 2000b. "The Politics of Accountability: California School Districts and Charter School Reform." *Stanford Law and Policy Review*. Forthcoming.

West, Anne, and Hazel Pennell. 1997. "Educational Reform and School Choice in England and Wales." *Educational Economics* 5:285–305.

Wilgoren, Jodi. 2000a. "Two Schools in Florida Adjust as Vouchers Change Classrooms." *New York Times* (14 March).

Wilgoren, Jodi. 2000b. "With Ideas and Hope, a School Goes to Work." *New York Times* (23 August).

Williams, T., and P. Carpenter. 1991. "Private Schooling and Public Achievement in Australia." *International Journal of Educational Research* 15:411–431.

Willms, J. Douglas. 1996. "School Choice and Community Segregation: Findings from Scotland." In *Generating School Stratification: Toward a New Research Agenda,* edited by Alan C. Kerckhoff. Boulder, CO: Westview Press.

Willms, J. Douglas, and Frank Echols. 1992. "Alert and Inert Clients: The Scottish Experience of Parental Choice of Schools." *Economics of Education Review* 11:339–350.

Wilson, Glen Y. 2000. "Effects of Funding Equity of the Arizona Tax Credit Law." *Education Policy Analysis Archives* 8.

Wisconsin Legislative Audit Bureau. 2000. *Milwaukee Parental Choice Program: An Evaluation.* Madison, WI: Legislative Audit Bureau.

Witte, John F. 1998. "The Milwaukee Voucher Experiment." *Educational Evaluation and Policy Analysis* 20:229–251.

Witte, John F. 2000. *The Market Approach to Education.* Princeton, NJ: Princeton University Press.

Witte, John F., Andrea B. Bailey, and Christopher A. Thorn. 1993. *Third-Year Report: Milwaukee Parental Choice Program.* Madison, WI: Department of Political Science and The Robert La Follette Institute of Public Affairs.

Wolf, Patrick, William Howell, and Paul Peterson. 2000. *School Choice in Washington D.C.: An Evaluation After One Year.* Cambridge, MA: Program on Education Policy and Governance, Harvard University.

Wylie, C. 1998. *Can Vouchers Deliver Better Education? A Review of the Literature, with Special Reference to New Zealand.* Wellington: New Zealand Council for Educational Research.

Young, Beth Aronstamm. 2000. *Characteristics of the 100 Largest Public Elementary and Secondary School Districts in the United States: 1998–1999.* Washington DC: National Center for Education Statistics, U.S. Department of Education.

Youniss, James, and Jeffrey A. McLellan. 1999. "Catholic Schools in Perspective: Religious Identity, Achievement, and Citizenship." *Phi Delta Kappan* 81:104–113.